Rogers Cadenhead ✍ **W9-BZU-843**

Radio UserLand™

KICK START

SAMS

800 East 96th Street, Indianapolis, Indiana 46240

Radio UserLand Kick Start

Copyright © 2004 by Sams Publishing

International Standard Book Number: 0-672-32563-2

Library of Congress Catalog Card Number: 2003100475

Printed in the United States of America

First Printing: October 2003

06   05   04   03   4   3   2   1

Trademarks

Warning and Disclaimer

Bulk Sales

Sams Publishing offers excellent discounts on this book when ordered in quantity for bulk purchases or special sales. For more information, please contact

U.S. Corporate and Government Sales
1-800-382-3419
corpsales@pearsontechgroup.com

For sales outside of the U.S., please contact

International Sales
1-317-428-3341
international@pearsontechgroup.com

Acquisitions Editor
Katie Mohr

Development Editor
Scott Meyers

Managing Editor
Charlotte Clapp

Project Editor
Andy Beaster

Copy Editor
Kezia Endsley

Indexer
Ken Johnson

Proofreader
Tracy Donhardt

Technical Editor
Brent Simmons

Team Coordinator
Vanessa Evans

Interior Designer
Gary Adair

Cover Designer
Aren Howell

Page Layout
Eric S. Miller

Contents at a Glance

Table of Contents

About the Author

Rogers Cadenhead is a Web developer and *Linux Magazine* columnist. He has written 17 books on Internet-related topics, including *Sams Teach Yourself Java 2 in 21 Days* and *How to Use the Internet, Eighth Edition.* He is also a Web publisher whose sites receive more than seven million visits a year. He maintains this book's official Web site using Radio UserLand at `www.cadenhead.org/workbench`.

Dedication

To my wife, Mary Christine Moewe, for the first 16 years of forever. We'll always have Arlington, Denton, Fort Worth, Denver, Peoria, Dallas, Jacksonville, Palm Coast, and St. Augustine.

Acknowledgments

I'd like to thank each of the following people:

- The team at Sams Publishing, including Mark Taber, Scott Meyers, Kathryn Mohr, Andrew Beaster, and Kezia Endsley. I have worked with Sams and many of its staff for six years, and this collaboration is both professionally and personally gratifying.

- The developers at UserLand Software—specifically Dave Winer, Jake Savin, and Lawrence Lee—for their assistance during the preparation of this book and for Radio UserLand itself. It's an amazing product that has quickly become an everyday part of my work and a goldmine of inspiration to me as a programmer.

- Brent Simmons, a former UserLand employee and long-time UserTalk programmer whose work as technical editor on this book contributed to it significantly.

- My agent at Studio B, Laura Lewin.

- The webloggers who keep my news aggregator well-fed: Mark Alexander, Danny Ayers, Andrew Bayer, David Bayly, Greg Beato, Rebecca Blood, Steve Bogart, Julian Bond, Jeremy Bowers, Brian Carnell, Heather Champ, Matt Croydon, Christian Crumlish, Derek Dahlsad, Anil Dash, Jeff Diaz, Kat Donohue, Scott Erickson, Richard Eriksson, Rafe Colburn, Gael Fashingbauer Cooper, Wes Felter, Michael Fioritto, Alison Fish, Jim Flowers, Jimi Gooding, Brian Graf, N. David Griffin, Andrew Grumet, Matt Haughey, Elliotte Rusty Harold, J.H. Haviland, Rob Henerey, Matt Hinrichs, Meg Hourihan, Tim Jarrett, Joe Jennett, Scott Johnson, Roger Jones, Jason Kottke, Ehud Lamm, Paul Leclerc, Jason Levine, Richard MacManus, Mikel Maron, Joshua Marshall, Lindsay Marshall, Mike Masnick, Edward Miller, Dave Mitchell, Bruce O'Leary, Les Orchard, Mark Paschal, Phillip Pearson, Steve Pilgrim, Annessa Rink, Jim Roepcke, Dave Rogers, Anita Rowland, Luke Seemann, Dwight Shih, Todd Smith, Kevin Story, Erik Thauvin, Sandor Weisz, and Jeffrey Zeldman.

- My wife, Mary, and sons, Max, Eli, and Sam. I wonder sometimes what my children must think of a father who sits in front of a glowing box muttering to himself all day, but I'm grateful for the love and support I get during the times I manage to tear myself away from its pernicious influence.

—Rogers Cadenhead

We Want to Hear from You!

As the reader of this book, *you* are our most important critic and commentator. We value your opinion and want to know what we're doing right, what we could do better, what areas you'd like to see us publish in, and any other words of wisdom you're willing to pass our way.

You can email or write me directly to let me know what you did or didn't like about this book—as well as what we can do to make our books stronger.

Please note that I cannot help you with technical problems related to the topic of this book, and that due to the high volume of mail I receive, I might not be able to reply to every message.

When you write, please be sure to include this book's title and author as well as your name and phone or email address. I will carefully review your comments and share them with the author and editors who worked on the book.

Email: webdev@samspublishing.com

Mail: Mark Taber
           Associate Publisher
           Sams Publishing
           800 East 96th Street
           Indianapolis, IN 46240 USA

Reader Services

For more information about this book or others from Sams Publishing, visit our Web site at www.samspublishing.com. Type the ISBN (excluding hyphens) or the title of the book in the Search box to find the book you're looking for.

Introduction

This book covers Radio UserLand, one of the most remarkable and unusual software programs to come out for use with Windows and Mac OS in recent years.

Since its first commercial release in 2002, Radio UserLand has been adopted by thousands of people, most of whom appear to be using it for two purposes:

- To publish *weblogs*, diary-style Web sites that have become a huge phenomenon on the Internet

- To read weblogs and other Web content quickly and conveniently without using a browser, a process made possible by an innovative XML format called RSS

Although many of Radio's users might not know it, this $39 product does a whole lot more— Web site publishing, content management, Internet programming, database storage, and Web services with a wide variety of popular Internet protocols: HTTP, HTML, XML, FTP, XML-RPC, SOAP, and RSS.

Thousands of people have tried Radio UserLand for weblogging because of its ease of use— UserLand Software makes the boastful but accurate claim that anyone who installs the product can post an entry on a new weblog within five minutes. The software also offers a popular RSS aggregator for reading news headlines, weblog content, and other information from thousands of potential sources.

Radio UserLand Kick Start focuses on the two most important features that can't be mastered in five minutes:

- The UserTalk programming language, a powerful scripting language created by UserLand for all of its products

- The object database, another UserLand creation, is a persistent data storage and retrieval system that makes working with a database as easy as working with local variables in a program

After covering the weblog publishing and news aggregation capabilities in full, the book demonstrates how to call UserTalk scripts to enhance your own weblogs, store and retrieve data in the database, and write your own UserTalk programs. The focus is on Web services and other Internet programming—two areas of development for which the software is especially well-suited.

The book also answers the following question: Why did they name it Radio UserLand when it has nothing to do with radio or music?

Who Should Read This Book?

Radio UserLand Kick Start is intended for Radio UserLand users who have tried the software's basic features and are ready to take advantage of its database and programming capabilities.

Whether you're an experienced programmer and Web publisher or someone who found Radio simply to publish a weblog, you should be able to benefit from the subjects covered in this book.

How This Book Is Organized

Part I of this book, "Exploring Radio UserLand," covers the core capabilities of the software: the capability to publish a weblog and author articles, read RSS newsfeeds to which you subscribe, publish a site, design its appearance, and call UserTalk scripts written by others to create dynamic content. The last chapter of this section introduces the outliner, a sophisticated writing and programming environment.

Part II of this book, "Using the Object Database," describes how to store and retrieve more than 30 types of data, including simple types, such as strings and integers, and complex types, such as outlines, word-processing text, and scripts. It begins with the first task any Radio user needs to do before making use of the database: backing up data.

Part III of this book, "Writing Scripts with UserTalk," details UserTalk, an extremely flexible programming language that makes it easy to work with data in any form that you need. You learn how to make use of UserLand's scripts—thousands of which can be viewed as source code in the main object database—and write your own to extend Radio's functionality and develop Internet applications.

Rounding it out, four appendixes document protocols used by Radio: RSS, OPML, XML, and XML-RPC.

The Companion Web Site

As you might expect from a book about a Web publishing tool, *Radio UserLand Kick Start* has an official Web site created and maintained with the software: Workbench, the weblog written by author Rogers Cadenhead at http://www.cadenhead.org/workbench. Choose the site's Kick Start link to find source code files, corrections, and updates to the book.

Conventions Used in This Book

This book makes use of the following typographic conventions and terminology:

- Code lines, commands, statements, variables, and any text you see onscreen appear in a mono typeface.

- Placeholders in syntax descriptions appear in an *italic mono* typeface. Replace the placeholder with the actual filename, parameter, or whatever element it represents.

- *Italics* highlight technical terms when they're being defined.

- The ➥ icon is used before a line of code that is really a continuation of the preceding line. Sometimes a line of code is too long to fit as a single line on the page. If you see ➥ before a line of code, remember that it's part of the line immediately above it.

- The book also makes use of Notes, Cautions, and Tips. These special elements appear separately from the text and provide additional information about relevant topics.

NOTE

Notes are used to indicate that you might need additional information to understand the concept being discussed in the text.

CAUTION

Cautions are used to make you aware of a potential pitfall associated with the subject being explained.

TIP

Tips are used to give you extra information that is not generally available. Often this information is something that the author has learned from experience.

PART I

Exploring Radio UserLand

Tuning in to Radio UserLand

"Our product is designed for users; they create the pull, they have the applications. As with personal computers, two generations ago, our application is not on the radar of many IT managers in corporations. It's starting to show up, and we will have an offer for them. But first we want the hearts and minds of users, and propose to win them by giving them power they can use today, not someday in the future."

—UserLand Software founder *Dave Winer*

Radio UserLand is a highly touted Internet content-management system and information-gathering tool for Windows and Mac users.

The software is also, without a doubt, one of the most deceptive programs you will ever own.

Since it was launched on Jan. 12, 2002 by UserLand Software, the program has been adopted by thousands of writers and information junkies, becoming one of the biggest success stories in Silicon Valley during the "dot-com bust," a time when most of the news coming from the region's technological innovators has been cover-your-eyes and break-the-piggy-bank bad.

One of the reasons for this exemplary success is the product's $39 price tag—most content-management software has two, three, or four zeroes in its price and is intended for corporations and other deep-pocket enterprises. UserLand offers a product for this audience, a Web server-based program called Frontier that sells for $899.

Radio UserLand, though, breaks with tradition entirely and offers professional content-management capabilities to penny-pinching personal publishers—a group that includes you, me, the digital-camera-mad cousin, the family genealogist, and anyone else who wants to share something with a global audience on the Web.

The software is best known for three features:

- An editor that can be used to create and publish a *weblog*, a revolutionary new form of personal journalism that has become a phenomenon on the World Wide Web, turning thousands of news consumers into news producers

- A news aggregator, a tool that scours your favorite Web sites and other sources once an hour looking for their latest content, structured as XML data in a format called RSS that has been adopted by thousands of providers

- A service that includes free Web hosting for a year, enabling a new user to begin publishing text, pictures, and other material on the Web within five minutes of installation

These features have become so popular that many of Radio UserLand's users might believe that it's just a weblog publishing and news-reading tool.

However, the truth is far more complicated than that. Radio UserLand isn't just a weblog publisher, information gathering tool, or Web hosting service.

It's also an Internet client/server, Web site editor, Web services platform, outliner, text editor, file server, email gateway, and scripting platform that supports an entire alphabet worth of networking acronyms: HTTP, HTML, XML, FTP, SMTP, POP3, XML-RPC, SOAP, RSS, and TCP.

Radio UserLand is even an MP3 song file playlist manager, a bit of no-longer-promoted functionality that gave the software its name and provided inspiration to its developers.

The program manages to be all of these things (among others) because it's really an integrated development environment and object database that's designed for the rapid development of Internet software (such as a weblog editor, or a news aggregator, or...)

Jon Udell, an *InfoWorld* editor and day-one Radio UserLand user, described it this way in *Byte Magazine*:

> "Like other script- and template-driven Web programming environments, Radio is extensible in a million different ways. Since it does not function primarily as a server, but rather as a client-based tool for writing and Web site management, it may not be immediately obvious why, never mind how, to extend it. Here's why: because optimization and customization of our writing and communication tools is one of the great challenges of the decade. None of the Web's amazing programmability does us a lick of good when it comes to improving how we communicate, since we still communicate mainly in fixed-function email clients that we can't layer interesting applications on top of."

Radio UserLand Kick Start describes this amazing example of stealth technology in full, covering the best-known features, such as the weblog editor and news aggregator, showing how they work under the hood, documenting the object database and programming language, and explaining how to fine-tune these features and take the program into new areas, Internet protocols, and functionality.

Using Radio UserLand

The best way to learn about Radio's main features is to take the software for a test drive. If you aren't already using the program, you can download and install a free 30-day trial from UserLand's Web site at `http://radio.userland.com`.

The remainder of Part I, "Exploring Radio UserLand," describes how to use Radio's weblog editor and news aggregator.

Before you take the wheel, though, a ride as a passenger will be a worthwhile demonstration of the information-routing capabilities through which experienced Radio users can take themselves.

Naturally, I'll be driving.

Starting the Application

As I sit down to work, I fire up the Radio application—on my Windows XP system, the command is Start, All Programs, UserLand, Radio UserLand.

Radio starts in two places at once, a dual interface that took some getting used to at first.

One interface belongs to the Radio application, the software that does most of the work. On Windows, it runs in the background and doesn't open a graphical user interface when the program is started. The only reminder that it's running at all is a small Radio UserLand icon in the System tray.

This icon has a context menu to open the application and undertake other common tasks. To see the menu and choose a command in Windows, right-click the icon, as shown in Figure 1.1. On Macs, hold down the Ctrl key and click Radio's icon in the Dock (OS X) or choose Radio with the Finder (Mac Classic). The Open Radio command opens the application's user interface.

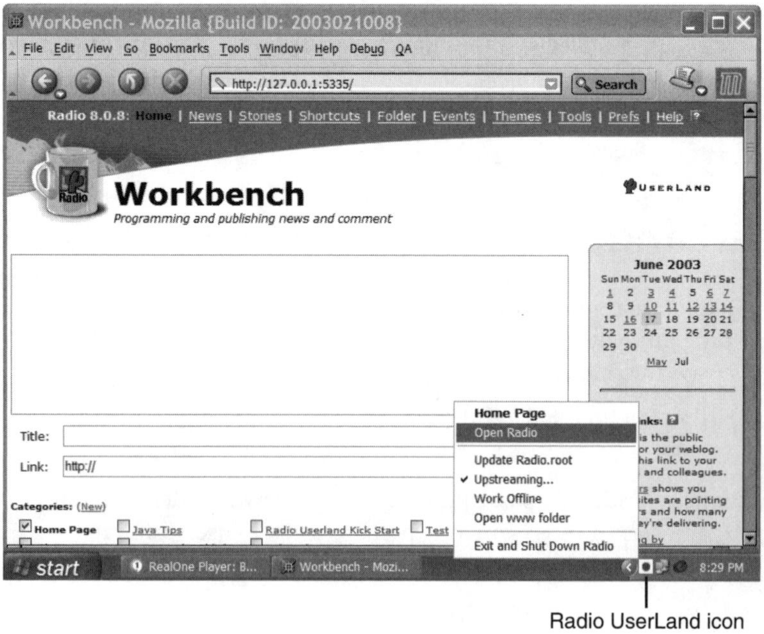

Radio UserLand icon

FIGURE 1.1   Viewing both of Radio's user interfaces.

Figure 1.1 also shows the second interface, a Web page that appears in my default browser. This page and the other Web pages offered by Radio make up the *desktop Web site*, and they are delivered by the application's Web server.

My version of the desktop Web site might be different than yours; the appearance is defined by a template called #desktopWebsiteTemplate.txt in Radio's www subfolder.

Radio is both an Internet client and a server, which makes some unusual interaction possible. You can run Radio remotely over the Internet or a local area network—as a testing installation for this book, I have a second copy running on my laptop, which I can view by opening the URL http://Apollo:5355 (Apollo is the name of that computer on my Windows network). Radio doesn't care where it's delivering Web pages and receiving form input, as long as the correct username and password are provided.

Reading XML Information Sources

The first thing I do after running Radio is catch up on the news. Once an hour, Radio looks for new items from around 200 sources that I follow regularly—a diverse selection of professional media such as the *New York Times* and *CNET*; useful technology weblogs such as *Scripting News*, *RC3.org*, and *Techdirt*; and personal must-reads such as *Sharkbitten*, an

interesting weblog authored by Todd Smith, a neighbor in St. Augustine, Florida, at
`http://www.sharkbitten.com`.

Radio saves me from the tedious task of going to each of these Web sites with my browser on
the chance they contain new information. The news aggregator checks for new items by
reading each source's RSS newsfeed, an XML document that contains headlines, links, and
other content from the site.

To see new items from my subscribed newsfeeds, I click the News link atop any desktop Web
page. A page displays the current hour's news, as shown in Figure 1.2.

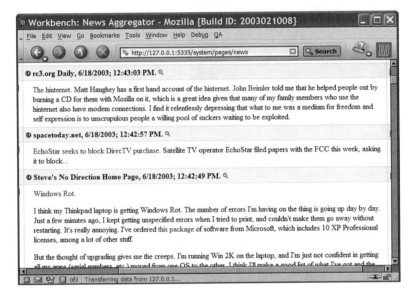

FIGURE 1.2   Reading recent items in RSS newsfeeds.

Although the news aggregator is designed to read RSS, you can extend Radio to collect and
present new items from any kind of XML data.

For example, the U.S. space agency NASA offers content from its *Liftoff News* publication in
an XML format of its own devising.

To keep up with this XML source with the news aggregator, I wrote a short script that translates the data into a form Radio can handle. The script was written with UserTalk, a programming language created by UserLand for use in its products, and stored in the application's
main database, a file called `Radio.root`.

Extending Radio's Capabilities

Radio.root is an object database stored in the main Radio UserLand folder that holds data and scripts that comprise the software's functionality. The source code for thousands of these scripts can be viewed by users, which helped my efforts considerably when I was learning to write my own UserTalk scripts.

Figure 1.3 shows the Radio application open with the object database in one window and the NASA format script in another.

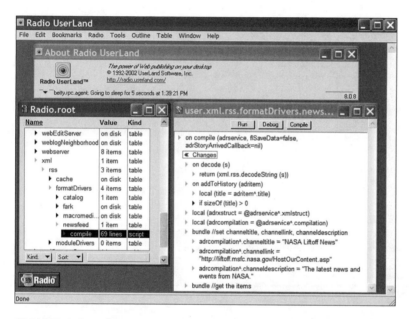

FIGURE 1.3   Writing UserTalk scripts in Radio UserLand.

To open the Radio application's graphical user interface on Windows, right-click the Radio icon in the System tray and choose Open Radio from the menu that appears.

On Macs, it automatically opens when the program is run.

To close it on Windows, close the application window. This doesn't shut down Radio; it just hides the interface.

To shut down Radio while using the application:

- Windows: Choose File, Exit.

- Mac OS Classic: Choose File, Quit.

- Mac OS X: Choose Radio, Quit Radio.

To shut it down anywhere else:

- Windows: Right-click the Radio icon in the System tray and choose Exit and Shut Down Radio.
- Mac OS X: Hold Ctrl, click Radio's Dock icon, and choose Quit.

The script I wrote to read the *LiftOff News* XML file is called a *format driver* by UserLand, and it's one way among many that users can customize or extend the software.

When you know your way around the database, UserTalk language, and UserLand's Web sites, you can make Radio an even more powerful tool for collecting or presenting information.

Finding Documentation

Because there's no official manual for the product, the first question most technical-minded Radio users are likely to ask is where to find documentation for the software's features.

The best answer, I hope, is this book.

However, UserLand continues to offer new features for Radio, which can be upgraded automatically each night as the application runs.

Also, one of the truisms of computer book publishing applies here: There's no better way to spur revolutionary changes in technology than to document the current version extensively in print.

There are several sources for information I check regularly for news about UserTalk programming and new Radio functionality:

- DocServer, http://docserver.userland.com, online documentation for hundreds of *verbs*, scripts in the object database that you can call in your own programs.

  Although the site says the documentation is for Frontier, it covers many features of Radio as well because the same scripts are available in both products.

  Here's an example of a short script that makes use of the clock.now() verb and several date verbs to display the current date in *month/day/year* format:

  ```
  local (w = clock.now());
  local (mdy = date.month (w) + "/" + date.day (w) + "/" + date.year (w));
  dialog.notify ("Date: " + mdy)
  ```

This script opens a small dialog box with a message such as "Date: 7/30/2003".

- UserLand weblogs:

  - Scripting News, http://www.scripting.com, by UserLand Software founder Dave Winer

  - UserLand Product News, http://productnews.userland.com

  - Jake's Brainpan, http://jake.userland.com, by developer Jake Savin

  - Lawrence's Notebook, http://radio.weblogs.com/0001013, by developer Lawrence Lee

  - BackEnd.UserLand.Com, http://backend.userland.com

  Because each of these offers an RSS newsfeed, you can read them using Radio's aggregator.

- UserLand discussion sites and mailing lists:

  - The Radio technical support discussion board, http://radio.userland.com/discuss

  - The Radio user mailing list, http://groups.yahoo.com/group/radio-userland, which contains a copy of each message posted to the aforementioned discussion board

  - Radio-dev, http://groups.yahoo.com/group/radio-dev, a mailing list for programmers developing new scripts and tools for Radio

- Radio.root Updates, http://static.userland.com/updatelogs/Radio.xml, an RSS newsfeed documenting bug fixes and additions to the object database, which occur as often as several times a week. This URL can be read only with the news aggregator.

- *Frontier: The Definitive Guide* (ISBN 1-56592-383-9), a 1998 book by Matt Neuberg that covers Frontier. You can read it online at http://pages.sbcglobal.net/mattneub/frontierDef/ch00.html.

  Although the book doesn't cover Radio and is out-of-date in some areas, it offers coverage of the UserTalk scripting language and the object database that is extremely useful.

- Workbench, http://www.cadenhead.org/workbench.

  Last but not least, my own weblog extensively covers new developments in Radio.

The biggest source for documentation about Radio is the Google search engine. UserLand's Web site at http://userland.com contains more than 199,000 pages, and by limiting a search using the term site:userland.com along with the keywords you are seeking, you can often find pages by UserLand developers or users describing a particular feature of Radio or Frontier.

Extending Radio with Tools

As I work, I add entries frequently to Workbench, a weblog that is devoted to programming and publishing news.

Since the site was launched in February 2002, Workbench has grown into a considerable amount of content managed by Radio: 750 weblog entries organized into eight categories, 30 stories, and around 6,100 files in 650 folders.

Because Radio has become my software of choice for publishing most Web content, it's the most convenient place to maintain my diary for Advogato, an open-source advocacy Web community at http://www.advogato.org. My diary is at http://www.advogato.org/rcaden.

Advogato diaries, which typically serve as work journals for open source developers, can be updated using the site's Web interface or an XML-RPC Web service. Radio is both a Web services client, making use of services on other computers, and a server, providing a way to call its own scripts over the Internet.

XML-RPC, devised by UserLand Software and Microsoft, is a simple protocol that enables XML data to be exchanged using the standard Web protocol HTTP. A program on one computer can call a procedure on another using XML-RPC and receive a return value, which works whether they're on two Internet-connected computers or exist on the same machine.

Radio supports two popular protocols that use the Internet to provide Web services: XML-RPC and SOAP.

The capability to post weblog entries to Advogato is provided by Footbridge, a Radio tool developed by Mark Paschal and released as shareware from http://markpasc.org/code.

Tools are object databases that can be stored in Radio's Data Files folder to extend the software's functionality. Footbridge, which is deployed as a single file called Footbridge.root, contains scripts and data that can be used to route Radio content to Advogato, LiveJournal, and weblog hosting services that use the original Blogger API (such as BlogSpot and Moveable Type).

Tools can have their own pages on Radio's desktop Web site and use them to configure user preferences and make use of its scripts. A Footbridge setup page is shown in Figure 1.4.

You can use such tools to change, replace, or enhance Radio's functionality. There are programs that can turn the software into a knowledge-management publishing tool (such as LiveTopics, offered by Novissio at http://www.novissio.com), a Python development environment (such as Python.root from http://radio.namshub.org), or enhance the news aggregator (MyRadio, offered by Mikel Maron at http://radio.weblogs.com/0100875).

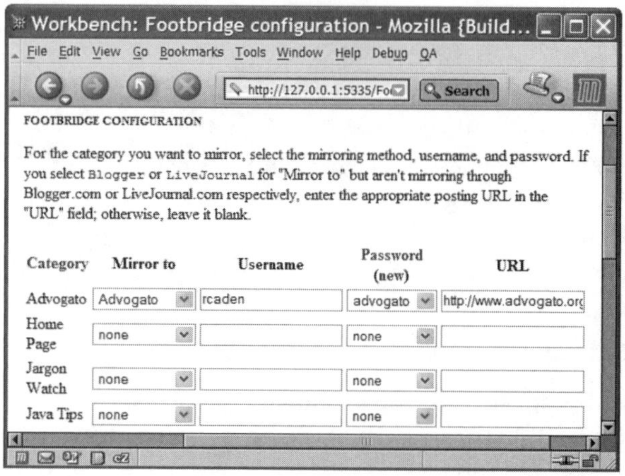

FIGURE 1.4   Configuring a Radio add-on tool.

Publishing Files Automatically

Another reason that I keep Radio running during the workday is to let it handle one of the more burdensome chores of Web development: transferring files to the Web when they are ready for publication.

Radio is designed to publish content automatically to a Radio Community Server, an XML-RPC Web hosting service that's free for a year with the purchase of the software.

Most Radio webloggers are using UserLand's server, http://rcs.userland.com, or the one offered by the online magazine *Salon* at http://blogs.salon.com. There's also a Python Community Server, an open-source project suitable for Radio hosting, at http://www.pycs.net.

As an alternative to community servers, Radio can publish Web sites to any server with File Transfer Protocol (FTP). Because I run my own Linux server, I publish Workbench there with FTP.

Radio uses a method of Web site publishing that may be unique, a process that UserLand calls *upstreaming*:

1. If you are working on a Web page, you save it on your computer in Radio's www folder or one of its subfolders. Your file is either a text file or an XML outline, not an HTML document.

2. Radio finds the file, recognizes that it has been added or changed recently, and uses it as the source material for a Web page.

3. The finished product, a Web page, is uploaded to the server hosting the site.

The result is two versions of your Web content: source files on your computer in text or XML format, and rendered output files on the server in HTML format.

This is illustrated by Figure 1.5, which uses an FTP program to show the source folder on my computer (left pane) and the destination folder on the Web server (right pane).

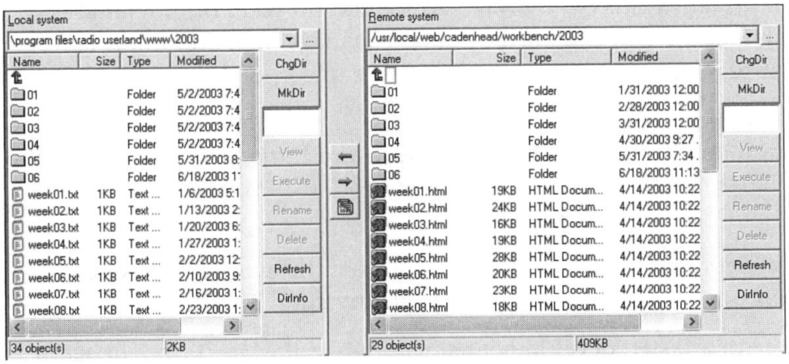

FIGURE 1.5 Viewing local and remote folders managed by Radio.

Upstreaming also can be used for more traditional publishing, uploading a file without modification from your computer to a server. This is what happens when a text file or XML outline is saved in Radio's www\gems folder, a convenient place to store files that should be transferred verbatim.

As Radio runs, it monitors the www folder and its subfolders. If a file is deleted in one of these folders, Radio will detect this and remove the server's version of the file. Radio also looks for new files to upstream and files to upload without modification.

What makes this an essential part of my daily workflow is Radio's capability to designate different folders to publish in different ways and different places.

Right now, I'm using Radio to handle each of these tasks automatically:

- Weblog entries on Workbench and its categories are upstreamed automatically to the /web/workbench folder and its subfolders.

- Files saved to Radio's www\cadenhead folder are uploaded without modification to the /web/cadenhead folder and its subfolders.

- Graphics files saved to Radio's www\client folder are uploaded as is to a different Web server, where they are used as banner ads for another site that I maintain.

Summary

As you have learned from this chapter's ride-along tour, I'm not just a Radio UserLand author. I'm also a client.

Radio UserLand was offered on Jan. 12, 2002, by Dave Winer and his team of programmers under the premise that individuals could exploit the content-management and information-aggregation capabilities that previously had been available only to corporations and other large enterprises.

With the right tools, common data formats such as XML, RSS, and XML-RPC, and the collaborative environment of weblogs, individuals can create new relationships, services, and software.

InfoWorld guru Jon Udell believes that Radio UserLand is a step in the evolution towards a World Wide Web that fulfills one of the original visions of its inventor, Tim Berners-Lee.

"The Web has been in a state of arrested development since shortly after its birth," he wrote for *Byte*. "It was meant, from the start, to be a two-way collaborative writing environment, not a one-way publisher-to-reader environment."

When you move beyond the deceptively simple weblog publishing and news reading capabilities of Radio UserLand and master the application's object database and UserTalk scripting language, you're likely to find that it opens up new avenues for the digital information you consume and the information you produce.

Publishing a Weblog

As you will discover, Radio UserLand is a sophisticated publishing and programming tool suitable for a variety of computing tasks.

First and foremost among these—Radio's capability to serve as a printing press for writing on the Internet.

The software was designed to publish weblogs, an innovative form of online writing that's turning the mass media on its head, transforming thousands of everyday people from news consumers into news makers.

A few minutes after installing the software, you can start a weblog and see your work on the World Wide Web. This chapter covers the process of creating and editing a weblog.

Starting Your Own Weblog

Most people who use Radio are putting it to work as a weblog editor. Weblogs, also called *blogs*, are an addictive way to reach an Internet audience with your writing and keep them coming back.

Weblogs are structured like a diary you read backwards, beginning with the entry most recently written and organized by date. There's considerable variety in weblog content, but they generally lean toward the same basic approach: short items published frequently with links to other places on the Web, accompanied by commentary that's informed by the author's interests, opinions, and personality.

Several hundred thousand blogs are being published today for an audience numbering in the millions, a phenomenon that hasn't escaped the notice of professional journalists.

In the July 3, 2002 *Wall Street Journal*, Peggy Noonan called weblogs "free speech at its straightest, truest, wildest, most uncensored, most thoughtful, most strange. Thousands of independent information entrepreneurs are informing, arguing, adding information…Blogs may one hard day become clearinghouses for civil support and information when other lines, under new pressure, break down."

Whether your goal is to speak truly, wildly, thoughtfully, or strangely, Radio's weblog editor makes it easy to get started.

After the software has been installed, Radio opens a weblog editing page in your Web browser every time you run the program (see Figure 2.1).

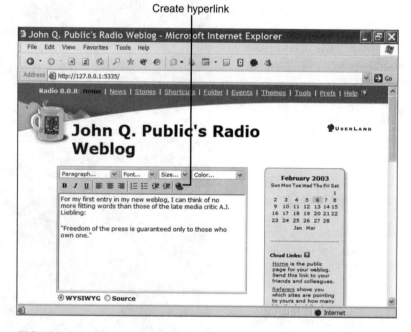

FIGURE 2.1   Radio's weblog editing page on Windows Internet Explorer.

This page, which is part of what UserLand calls the *desktop Web site*, looks like it's on the World Wide Web and can be used like any other Web page.

The page is actually being delivered by Radio's built-in Web server. All of Radio's weblog publishing features are available from this desktop site.

The URL, http://127.0.0.1:5335/, can be bookmarked to return to the desktop Web site at any time while Radio is running.

Writing a Weblog Entry

Weblog entries are written in an editing box on the main page of the desktop Web site. The appearance of the box varies depending on the Web browser that you're using.

On Windows, Internet Explorer users have a text-editing box that's topped with controls like those you see in Microsoft Word. These can be used to work with different fonts, sizes, colors, and formatting as an entry is written. There's also a Create Hyperlink button (see Figure 2.1). To associate a hyperlink with text, select the text and click the button. A dialog box opens asking for the link's URL.

The Internet Explorer editing box has two modes: WYSIWYG, which stands for "What You See is What You Get," and source.

There are two advantages to WYSIWYG mode: You see the entry as it will appear on the weblog and don't need to know any HTML, the markup language that tells a Web browser how to display a page. Writing a weblog in this mode is comparable to creating a document in a word processor like Microsoft Word.

Source mode displays an entry with the HTML markup visible. The advantage of this mode, for writers who are familiar with HTML, is the capability to control exactly how the entry is formatted.

On any browser other than Internet Explorer for Windows, the editing box is much simpler—it offers neither editing controls nor WYSIWYG mode. Entries are only created using source mode (see Figure 2.2).

Once an entry has been written, it can be published on your weblog by clicking the Post to Weblog button below the editing box.

Publishing an entry causes several things to happen:

- On your computer, the entry is saved in a database called `WeblogData.root`, along with information such as the time and date it was posted.

- On the Web, the weblog's home page is updated so that it contains the new entry at the top. Also, a Web page associated with the date is updated to include the entry.

- On the Web, an XML file is created that contains the entry and 9 of the other most-recent entries (assuming you have written that many). This file, the site's RSS feed, enables people to keep up with your weblog without loading it in a Web browser.

- New events show up in Radio's log, available from the Events link.

The events log contains information on what Radio is doing behind the scenes. Every time Radio publishes a document on the Web, a link to the document is displayed in the log.

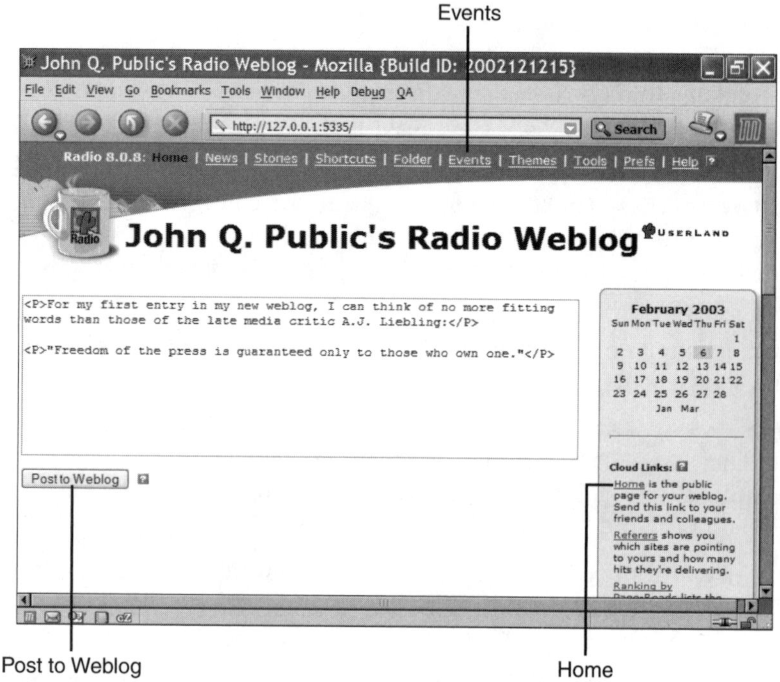

Events

Post to Weblog   Home

FIGURE 2.2   Editing a weblog entry in source mode.

The most important thing to note about Radio's publishing process is that your weblog data is kept on your computer, not on the Web server where it is published.

The most common mistake a new Radio user can make is to deal with a problem by deleting and reinstalling the software. This wipes out all of the existing weblog entries unless they were backed up. Saving your weblog data and other files maintained by Radio is covered in Chapter 9, "Backing Up Data."

Radio publishes files from your computer to the Web through a process called *upstreaming*.

To visit your weblog and see what you've published, click the name of the weblog or the Home link (see Figure 2.2). Your weblog has been published with a standard design and graphics, which can easily be changed.

The RSS file is formatted as XML data. To see the file, find a small orange XML box on your weblog's home page and click it.

You must, of course, be connected to the Internet for your weblog to be updated. If you want to work on your site while not connected to the Internet, you can temporarily suspend Radio's publishing activities.

To turn publishing on or off:

- Windows: Right-click the Radio icon in the system tray and choose Upstreaming from the pop-up menu that appears (see Figure 2.3). A check appears next to Upstreaming when publishing is on.

- Mac OS X: Click and hold the Radio icon in the dock, then choose Upstreaming.

- Mac classic: Switch to the Radio application with the Finder, and then choose the menu command Radio, Web Server, Upstreaming.

While upstreaming is off, new weblog entries will be saved to your weblog's database but not published. When you connect to the Internet later and turn it back on, Radio will catch things up on your site.

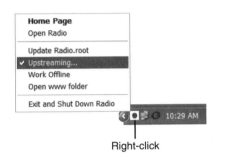

Right-click

FIGURE 2.3   Radio's system tray menu.

Editing an Entry

Radio's weblog editor publishes everything you write on the Web, putting your words in front of the world within a matter of seconds.

If you decide afterward to change something, whether for reasons of grammar, style, or a newfound sense of decorum, an entry can be edited from the home page of the desktop Web site.

Below the editing box, Radio displays the 10 most recent weblog posts alongside a check box and an Edit link (see Figure 2.4).

Click an entry's Edit link to load it in the editing box and make changes, then use the Post Changes button to republish it.

To delete an entry, check the box to the left of the entry, scroll to the bottom of the page, and then click the Delete button. There's no undo function to restore a deleted entry, which is removed from the weblog database. Radio republishes the two pages that contained the entry.

If the entry to be edited isn't one of the last 10 entries, use the calendar atop the desktop home page to find it, as shown in Figure 2.4.

The calendar contains links for every day and month that contains weblog entries. Choose a day's link to reload the desktop Web site with a list of all entries written on that date.

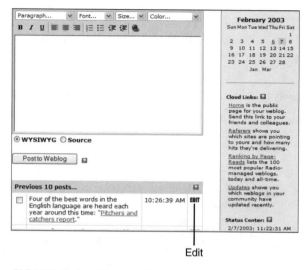

Edit

FIGURE 2.4   Editing weblog entries.

Writing a Story

Radio does not limit the length of a weblog entry, but there may be a limit to the patience of your readers.

Most webloggers compose short one- to five-paragraph entries and publish longer text elsewhere. This can be done in Radio by using the Stories section of your weblog, which is reached by clicking the Stories link atop any page of the desktop Web site (see Figure 2.5).

Stories are saved as text files on your computer in a subfolder of the Radio UserLand\www\stories folder that corresponds to the story's creation date. For example, a story written on August 5, 2003 is saved in the stories\2003\08\05 folder.

Click the Create link to write a new story.

A larger version of the entry-editing box is used to draft stories. Windows Internet Explorer users get the choice of WYSIWYG and source modes; others use a simpler, source-only box.

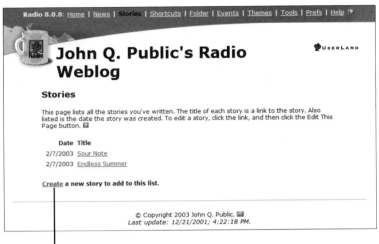

Create

FIGURE 2.5   Editing stories.

Every story must be given a title, which serves as its headline and the basis for its filename—a story titled "Goto Considered Harmful" would be saved on your computer as gotoConsideredHarmful.txt.

You publish a story by clicking the Create New Story button below the editing box. Radio publishes the story as a Web page with a design matching the rest of your weblog. This Web page is upstreamed to the weblog, which you can check by viewing Radio's events log.

To make changes to a story, return to the Stories section of the desktop Web site, click the story's title to load the text, and then click the Edit This Page button at the bottom of the story (see Figure 2.6). The text is loaded into the story-editing box. The Post Changes button at the bottom of the page republishes it.

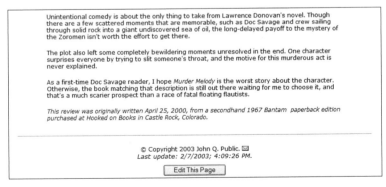

FIGURE 2.6   Making changes to a story.

TIP

Radio will use the entire text of a title, sans spaces, in the filename. This can create some extremely cumbersome URLs for stories. To get around this problem, give the story a short name when creating it, save the story once under that name, and then edit the story later to make the title longer.

To see all of the stories on a Radio weblog, add /stories to the end of its home page URL. The location of a story on the weblog corresponds to its location on the desktop site, with the exception that it's an .html file instead of a .txt file.

Radio's browser-based text editor is much better suited to succinct weblog entries than it is to longer articles. Fortunately, any word processor or text editor can be used to write stories if it can save them as unformatted text.

To use an external text editor to create a story, you must know how to give a story a title and where to save the file.

Radio stories are simple text files that contain the full text of the story with HTML formatting. At the top of the file, before the beginning of the story, a #title directive should be inserted using the following form:

```
#title "title of the story"
```

Replace the text between the quotes with the actual title. For example:

```
#title "Harbottle Dorr"
```

Directives are commands that tell Radio what to do when rendering a file from one format to another. In this case, the text file will be rendered as an HTML document that's upstreamed to the Web.

Another useful directive for stories is #postTime, which has a timestamp for the last time it was updated:

```
#postTime "2/7/2003; 4:15:54 PM"
```

Listing 2.1 contains the text of a story.

LISTING 2.1   The Full Text of harbottleDorr.txt

```
1: #title "Harbottle Dorr"
2: #postTime "2/7/2003; 4:15:54 PM"
3:
4: <p>HARBOTTLE DORR COLLECTION OF ANNOTATED MASSACHUSETTS NEWSPAPERS,
```

LISTING 2.1 Continued

```
 5: 1765-1776</p>
 6:
 7: <p>On January 7, 1765, in the middle of the Stamp Act controversy, Boston
 8: shopkeeper Harbottle Dorr took the current issue of the Boston Evening-Post
 9: and commented on its contents in the margins. Every week thereafter, he
10: collected one or both of the Evening-Post or the Boston Gazette, (sometimes
11: adding a Boston Post-Boy &amp; Advertiser) and continued expressing himself
12: in the margins on the events, referring backward and forward in a maze of
13: cross-references to other documents and stories relevant to the events
14: reported in the news.<br>
15:
16: <p>The final result 12 years later was an astonishing archive—3,280 pages
17: of annotated newspapers, plus the appended documents and Dorr's own indexes
18: to the four volumes he compiled. This entire unbroken run of annotated
19: Boston newspapers will not only allow students of American history a unique
20: look at the pre-Revolutionary era in New England, but will also provide
21: insight into the thinking of citizen Dorr on the controversies and topics
22: of the times.</p>
23:
24: <p>FORMAT: 4 reels of 35mm microfilm</p>
```

Directives must be placed at the top of a story with no blank lines above or between them. If an empty line were inserted between Lines 1–2 of Listing 2.1, Radio would include the literal text #postTime "2/7/2003; 4:15:54 PM" as the first line of the story.

A story will be published on your weblog if it is saved anywhere in the www\stories folder or one of its subfolders. However, it only shows up in the desktop Web site's stories section if you save the file in a subfolder of www\stories that corresponds to a year, month, or date.

NOTE

This example Web page describes the collection of Harbottle Dorr, an American from the Revolutionary War era who marked up newspapers with his own commentary and context-providing notes. He would have been a natural weblogger.

Figure 2.7 shows how the Harbottle Dorr page has been rendered on the Web. The graphics, formatting, and overall look of the page are not handled within the story's file—all of that is accomplished through a collection of Web templates called a *theme*.

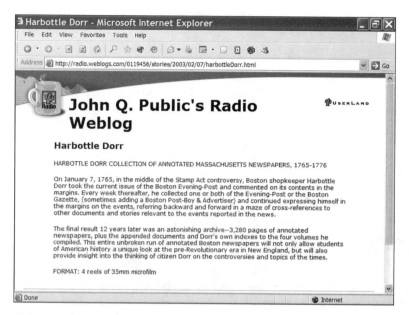

FIGURE 2.7   Reading a story on the Web.

Editing Your Preferences

Radio's weblog editor, like the rest of the software, is highly configurable. You can change the number of previous posts shown on the desktop home page, opt out of Weblogs.Com notification, and tailor it several dozen other ways.

To see what you can change, click the Prefs link atop any desktop Web page. Several preferences affect the weblog editor.

- The Previous Posts preference determines how many recent entries to display below the editing box on the desktop home page.

- The Participate in the Weblogs.Com community? preference determines whether your weblog will show up on that site each time you update.

Weblogs.Com is one of the most popular sites in the weblogging community; it comes up first in a Google search for the term "weblogs" and receives thousands of visits each day.

Using Weblogs.Com attracts two kinds of visitors: people who scan the site's update list for sites to read and software robots looking for sites to add to Google, weblog directories, and other services.

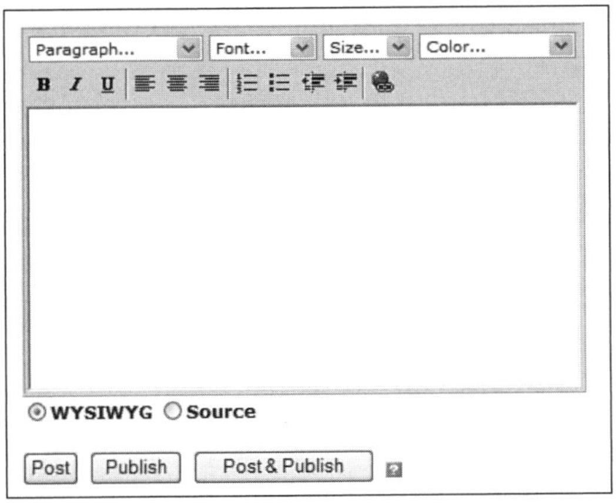

FIGURE 2.8 Submitting weblog entries.

The Three buttons or one? preference makes the publication of weblog entries a two-step process, replacing the Post to Weblog button with three buttons: Post, Publish, and Post & Publish (see Figure 2.8).

The Post button stores an entry in the WeblogData.root database but does not publish it on the Web. This enables an entry to be saved while it's still being worked on, links and formatting to be double-checked, and other fastidious behavior.

The Publish button publishes all unpublished entries, updating the Web pages and XML files on your weblog that contain them.

The Post & Publish button combines both of these steps.

Summary

Radio UserLand's weblog editor is built atop a sophisticated content-management system that can be used on any kind of Web content, not just weblogs.

Writing a story outside of Radio is a good way to begin looking at the inner workings of this "printing press." Web pages created with Radio can pull content from its database files, convert XML data and other forms into HTML, and contain the output of scripts that run each time a page needs to be published.

The end result is a considerable amount of Web content that's easy to produce and maintain. In less than a year, my technology weblog, Workbench, has taken on 550 pages, 750 weblog entries, and a life of its own.

Enhancing a Weblog

3

One of the reasons for Radio UserLand's popularity is the simplicity it brings to weblog publishing. Within minutes of installation, the software can be used to start a new weblog and publish a first entry on the World Wide Web.

Weblogs are often works in progress, improved incrementally by their authors as they learn more about the format and see ideas they'd like to adopt on other Web sites.

This kind of tinkering is standard operating procedure for Radio users. As you move beyond the beginner-friendly publishing features and learn more about its capabilities, you can enhance your weblog with support for categories, descriptive titles on entries, link lists, and other improvements.

Radio's content-management system makes it easy to putter around with a site, because you can publish changes quickly, whether a weblog consists of 10 pages or 1,000.

Adding Titles and Links to Entries

A weblog is often compared to a diary because of its chronological order of publication and the informal style of writing that typifies the form.

Many weblogs are comparable to emails, presenting entries dashed off with little forethought by their authors. Others are more like professional publications, with titles and hyperlinks for each entry.

When Radio is first installed, weblog entries are published without titles, which lends itself to a more loose approach.

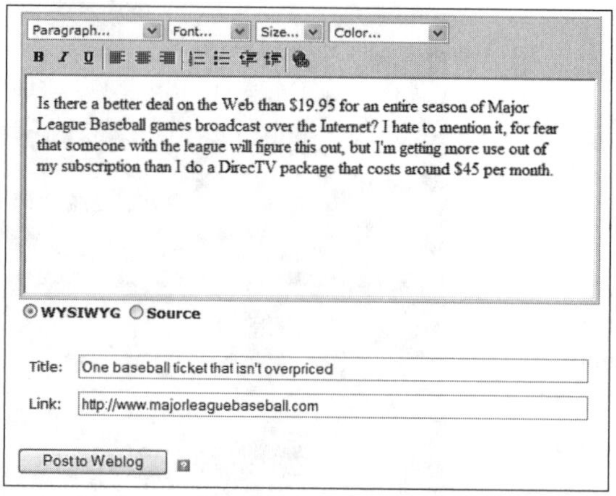

FIGURE 3.1 Creating weblog entries with optional titles and links.

However, that's easily changed; a Radio-created weblog can be as informal as a teenager's daily journal or as formal as *The New York Times*.

Figure 3.1 shows Radio's weblog editor with two new fields: Title and Link.

These fields, which are missing when Radio is installed, are turned on using the software's Prefs page, a long list of preferences that customize the appearance of a weblog and many other aspects of its performance.

To see the current preferences and make changes, click the Prefs link at the top of any desktop Web page.

In the Weblog section, the Item-Level Title & Link preference page determines whether each weblog entry has a title or hyperlink.

The title functions as a headline, describing or summarizing an entry.

The hyperlink, which is different than the links that are part of a weblog entry, can be used for several purposes. For example:

- On a weblog that selects the best sports stories from daily newspapers, a story's headline could serve as the title and a story's URL as the link.

- On a weblog that describes a cross-country bicycling trip, the headline could be each destination and the link could go to the entry describing that stop on the trip.

To turn on titles and links, open the Item-Level Title & Link page and select the option to add Title and Link text fields to the weblog editor.

While you're doing that, UserLand recommends that a related option be selected to generate links whenever the Link field is left blank. If you select it, Radio uses each weblog entry's link as its default value.

After titles are turned on, whenever you pen a weblog entry, Radio publishes the title and accompanying link as the first line of each entry and saves them in the WeblogData.root file with the rest of the entry's information. Titles and links are not added to older entries, although you can load each one in the editor and add them manually.

Figure 3.2 shows part of a weblog page with a baseball-related item that contains a title and link, and two other items that lack them.

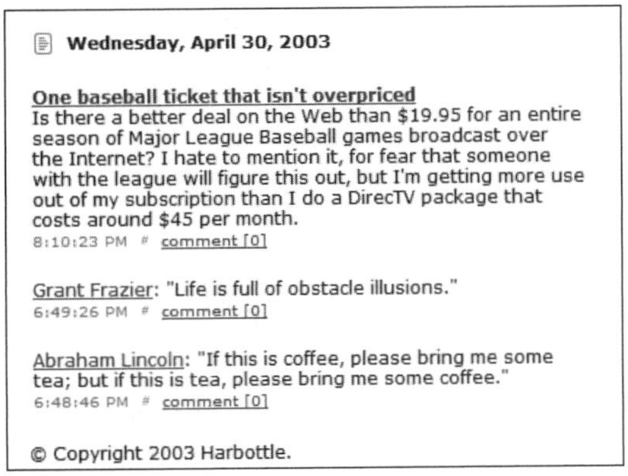
Wednesday, April 30, 2003
One baseball ticket that isn't overpriced
Is there a better deal on the Web than $19.95 for an entire season of Major League Baseball games broadcast over the Internet? I hate to mention it, for fear that someone with the league will figure this out, but I'm getting more use out of my subscription than I do a DirecTV package that costs around $45 per month.
8:10:23 PM # comment [0]
Grant Frazier: "Life is full of obstacle illusions."
6:49:26 PM # comment [0]
Abraham Lincoln: "If this is coffee, please bring me some tea; but if this is tea, please bring me some coffee."
6:48:46 PM # comment [0]
© Copyright 2003 Harbottle.

FIGURE 3.2 Displaying weblog entries with and without titles.

If titles are turned off later, they won't be published on the weblog, even for older entries that included them.

Titles and links make each entry more useful to anyone who reads your weblog with an *RSS news aggregator,* a program that periodically checks Web sites that share their headlines and other information using a standard XML format. There's also a benefit if you want to encourage other Web sites to use this XML format to republish material from your weblog.

Radio's news aggregator is covered in the next chapter, "Reading RSS Newsfeeds with the News Aggregator."

> **CAUTION**
>
> The display of titles and links is dictated by the weblog's theme, a set of templates that establish the appearance of a Web site maintained with Radio. The default weblog theme displays titles and their links above the text of an entry, but this might not be true if you're using another theme. There's a lot more on this subject in Chapter 6, "Designing a Weblog Theme."

> **NOTE**
>
> On my Workbench weblog, I recently began using titles and links after months of doing without them. The title provides a headline for the entry and the link is left blank, causing Radio to link the title to that entry.
>
> Writing headlines takes time, but I think it enhances the readability of the weblog. As someone who reads more than 150 weblogs and other sites with Radio's news aggregator, I've become a big fan of titles—they stand out as I'm skimming through new entries from all of those different sources.

Categorizing a Weblog

Although Radio's weblog editor is designed primarily for the creation of a single weblog, this constraint can be overcome by organizing entries into categories.

Categories, which are disabled when Radio is installed, make it possible to file each weblog entry in one or more topic areas of your own creation. They're off when Radio is installed but can be turned on using the Categories preference.

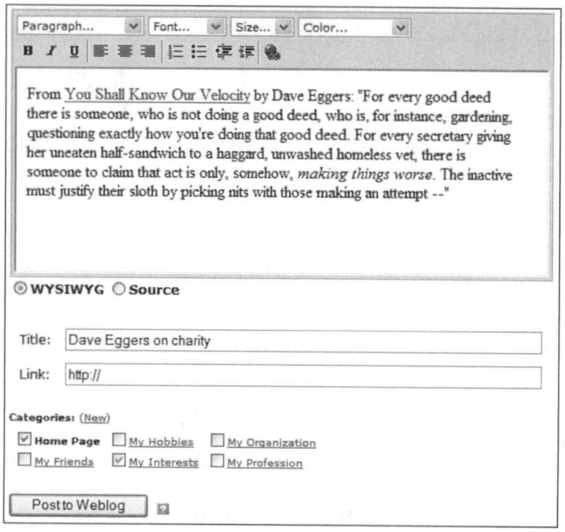

FIGURE 3.3   Filing a weblog entry in two categories.

There are six categories set up when Radio is installed: the home page (the main category) and five others: My Friends, My Hobbies, My Interests, My Organization, and My Profession. You can add other categories and delete all the existing categories (aside from the home page).

Figure 3.3 shows the weblog editor with categories turned on.

A weblog entry is filed in one or more categories by marking their check boxes (as in Figure 3.3). The Home Page box is selected by default; remove this mark to keep an entry out of the main weblog.

To enable categories, click the Prefs link on any page of the desktop Web site and look for the Categories link in the Weblog section.

There are several ways to present the weblog entries that are filed in a category:

- Entries can be displayed on Web pages and in an RSS file specific to that category.

- The Web pages for a category take the same form as the main weblog and have a design based on a theme. If you don't choose a theme, the weblog's theme is used.

- A category's home page is the weblog URL followed by /categories/categoryNameHere. (Spaces are stripped from the category name and the first letter is always lowercase, so *My Interests* becomes /categories/myInterests and *Politics* becomes /categories/politics.)

- New entries to a category can be publicized on Weblogs.Com, the service listing newly updated weblogs, or omitted from that site.

- The category's RSS file has the URL of the category's home page followed by /rss.xml, such as /categories/politics/rss.xml.

- Entries can be offered only as RSS files.

- Entries can be routed somewhere else using Web services that support XML-RPC or SOAP, two protocols for exchanging information between Internet-connected computers.

TIP

If you are ever in doubt about where Radio is publishing something—such as a weblog entry sent to a new category—view the Events log. It contains a link to each file upstreamed by Radio to a Web server.

Each category is given its own folder inside Radio's www\categories folder. The name corresponds to the category's URL.

When you publish a category as a Web page, it can function as its own weblog with a name, description, and appearance completely different than the main weblog.

As an alternative, a category can serve as a section of the main weblog. My own weblog has categories for each of the subjects I cover most often: Radio UserLand, Salon Blogs, Java, and technical jargon. Each category uses the same design as the main weblog.

The most unusual way to use a category is as a holding place for information that is routed elsewhere.

For example, the Advogato Web site at http://www.advogato.org is a popular community for open-source computer programmers and other developers. Each site member can offer a diary describing current programming projects, bug fixes, current technology news, and other chatter.

As described in Chapter 1, "Tuning in to Radio UserLand," diary entries can be submitted to Advogato using an XML-RPC Web service.

This can be accomplished with Footbridge, a Radio add-on program offered as shareware by Mark Paschal. The software forwards a category to Advogato interface using XML-RPC. Once you set up a category to use this, all entries posted to that category show up on your Advogato diary.

By combining categories with Web services, Radio becomes an authoring tool for anything that offers a public XML-RPC or SOAP interface.

> **NOTE**
>
> Footbridge also can be used to send weblog entries to LiveJournal diaries and weblogs published using Moveable Type or Blogger software. The program is distributed as a .root file that should be placed in Radio Userland's Tools folder. To find out more and download the file, visit http://markpasc.org/code/radio/footbridge.

Configuring a Category

You can edit an existing category to change its name, description, and the way it is presented on the Web by following these steps:

1. Click its name on the desktop home page in the Categories list below the weblog editor.

    An Edit Category page is displayed (Figure 3.4).

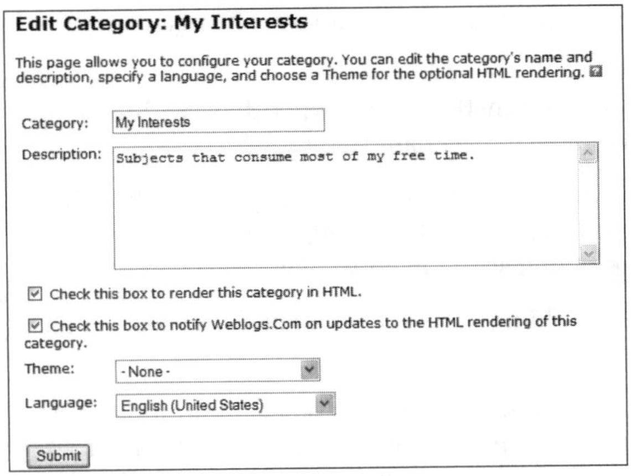

FIGURE 3.4   Tinkering with a weblog category.

2. Use the Category field and Description text area field to adjust these settings.

3. The name and description are used on Web pages and RSS files for the category (assuming that it has a theme design which makes use of this information, as most do).

   A change to a category's name is reflected in Web pages and RSS files, but its URL remains unchanged.

4. To present the category as Web pages, check the Render This Category in HTML check box.

5. To make the category show up on Weblogs.Com, check the relevant check box.

6. If the category is published as Web pages, you can choose a design with the Theme drop-down menu.

   Once you're familiar with themes, you can assign one to the category. To use the main weblog's theme instead, choose None.

7. Click Submit to make your changes official.

The changes you have made to a category won't be reflected in the site until you publish a weblog entry that belongs to it. (A way to speed this process up is discussed in Chapter 5, "Upstreaming Files to a Web Server.")

Creating a New Category

There's no restriction on the number of categories a Radio weblog can offer.

To add a category, follow these steps:

1. On the desktop home page, click the New link at the top of the Categories list (below the weblog editor).

   The New Category page is displayed, containing the same fields as the Edit Category page described in the preceding section.

2. Fill out the fields as desired.

   The name you choose for a category is used to create its URL, so a shorter name creates a less cumbersome address.

   One way to get around this issue is to create the category with a short name that would make a good URL, save the category, and then edit it later to lengthen the name.

Deleting a Category

You can delete categories as well, which removes them from the list below the weblog editor. Follow these steps:

1. Click the Prefs link on any desktop Web page to see the preferences page, and then click the Categories link in the Weblog section.

2. Click the Categories page link.

   The Categories page is displayed, listing all of your categories.

3. Check the check box of the category (or categories) to delete and click the Delete button.

Deleting a category does not remove any of the category's weblog entries, files, or folders.

If you want to remove a category's Web pages or RSS file from the Web, open the www\categories folder and delete the category's folder. Within minutes, Radio will automatically detect the change and delete the files.

Adding and Removing Links

Radio takes care of most of the navigational links required on a weblog; links to the home page and the archive page created for each day's entries are created automatically.

On sites that use the default theme or another built-in theme, a calendar linking to daily archive pages is displayed.

Links to stories, categories, and other pages can be set up with the navigator links feature.

Navigator links can be used for site navigation and a *blogroll*, a list of links to weblogs and other sites that you frequent.

A weblog's navigator links are stored in a file called #navigatorLinks.xml in Radio's www folder.

Listing 3.1 contains an example of this file.

LISTING 3.1 The Full Text of #navigatorLinks.txt.

```
 1: <navigator>
 2:    <item name="Home" pagename="/"/>
 3:    <item name="Stories" pagename="/stories"/>
 4:    <item name=" "/>
 5:    <item name="Favorites"/>
 6:    <item name="Blog. Bonanza" pagename="http://radio.weblogs.com/0111413/"/>
 7:    <item name="FuzzyBlog" pagename="http://radio.weblogs.com/0103807/"/>
 8:    <item name="Jim Flowers" pagename="http://radio.weblogs.com/0113212/"/>
 9:    <item name="Second P0st" pagename="http://blogs.salon.com/0000002/"/>
10:    <item name="Sticky String" pagename="http://radio.weblogs.com/0101433/"/>
11:    <item name=" "/>
12:    <item name="Reference"/>
13:    <item name="Frontier" pagename="http://frontier.userland.com/"/>
14:    <item name="Radio Userland" pagename="http://radio.userland.com/"/>
15:    <item name="Weblogs.Com" pagename="http://www.weblogs.com"/>
16:    <item name="&lt;br&gt;"/>
17: </navigator>
```

You can edit this file directly with any text editor or use the Navigator links preference page on the desktop Web site (click Prefs, look in the Weblog section, and then click Navigator links).

This file is formatted like an XML dialect (although it isn't officially XML—it lacks an ?xml processing instruction as the first line).

Even if you don't know anything about XML, the format is pretty simple.

The navigator links file must have a single root element named navigator that contains one or more item elements representing each link.

Each item element has a name attribute that contains text and an optional pagename attribute that contains the URL that should be linked to the text.

Items can be of three types:

- Relative links to local pages on the same site as the weblog:

```
<item name="Stories" pagename="/stories"/>
```

- External links to Web pages:

```
<item name="Blog. Bonanza" pagename="http://radio.weblogs.com/0111413/"/>
```

- Unlinked text, such as blank links, headings, and entity-encoded HTML:

```
<item name=" "/>
<item name="Reference"/>
<item name="&lt;br&gt;"/>
```

Each weblog category can use the navigator links of the main weblog or offer its own. To create links for a category, follow these steps:

1. Open Radio's \www\categories folder.

2. Open the category's folder.

3. Create a new #navigatorLinks.xml file there.

If there is no #navigatorLinks.xml file in a folder, Radio finds and uses the one in the main \www folder.

This occurs because the software employs an inheritance system for preferences and settings based on the hierarchy of file folders within the main Radio folder.

If a specific folder does not contain a configuration file, Radio climbs up the hierarchy of folders looking for that file. When it finds one, that file is used.

For example, if you have a \www\categories\politics folder, here's where Radio looks for the navigator links file when entries are published to that category:

1. www\categories\politics

2. www\categories

3. www

Radio quits when it finds the file. If all else fails, there should be a #navigatorLinks.xml file in Radio's www folder, because that's where the main weblog's navigator links are defined.

Summary

Radio UserLand encourages publishers to poke around with its features and try new things with a site. It can republish an entire weblog with ease, regardless of how many pages it contains.

When you add link lists, categories, item titles, and other features to a weblog, these changes can be reflected immediately.

This is a marked difference from the experience of creating a site as a set of static files that must be edited by hand. You'll see many other examples of how to reap the benefits of Radio's content management system in subsequent chapters.

Reading RSS Newsfeeds with the News Aggregator

Radio UserLand publishes weblog entries in two formats: HTML Web pages that can be viewed with a browser and text files structured as *RSS files*, an XML format created so that software can make use of Web content.

Radio is a voracious consumer and producer of RSS, the most popular format used by Web sites to share headlines, hyperlinks, and other content for non-browser use.

In turn, many Radio users become voracious consumers of RSS because it's a great way to keep up with weblogs, newspapers, and other sources that provide RSS files.

RSS files, which are called *newsfeeds*, can be read with the Radio news aggregator, which downloads them as frequently as once an hour from selected sites and presents new items on a Web page for quick browsing.

Exchanging Information with RSS

Most World Wide Web users stay informed by checking the same sites regularly, a process that can be extremely tedious and frustrating when those sites aren't updated on a regular schedule.

The popularity of weblogs exacerbates this problem, because many of these sites are labors of love that are updated when inspiration strikes and real-world responsibilities permit.

If a weblog or another site offers an RSS newsfeed, there's no longer a need to load the site in a Web browser just to see if it has been updated. You can subscribe to that newsfeed with an RSS news aggregator and let it check the site regularly for updates.

When an update is found on one of your subscribed sites, the aggregator presents that new content, a portion of it, or just a hyperlink to it, depending on how the site's publisher has decided to make use of RSS.

There are currently more than 31,000 RSS feeds you can read with a news aggregator, according to Syndic8, an RSS directory and how-to resource published at http://www.syndic8.com.

These feeds employ one of several popular versions of RSS. Radio produces feeds in RSS 2.0, a format created by Netscape and UserLand Software, and can read feeds in all RSS formats.

An RSS newsfeed contains one rss element, which surrounds a channel element describing the file and one or more item elements for each item in the feed.

Like many XML dialects, the RSS format is pretty easy to understand simply by looking at it. Listing 4.1 contains a pared-down example borrowed from Scott Johnson's FuzzyBlog!, a weblog on programming that's published using Radio.

LISTING 4.1 The rss.xml File from the FuzzyBlog! Weblog

```
 1: <?xml version="1.0"?>
 2: <rss>
 3:   <channel>
 4:     <title>The FuzzyBlog!</title>
 5:     <link>http://radio.weblogs.com/0103807/</link>
 6:     <description>Marketing 101. Consulting 101. PHP Consulting. Random
geeky stuff. I Blog Therefore I Am.</description>
 7:   </channel>
 8:   <item>
 9:     <title>PHPCON 2003 Presentations Online!</title>
10:     <link>http://radio.weblogs.com/0103807/2003/05/06.html#a1635</link>
11:     <description>I know it took too long. I'm sorry. Still here's a
&lt;a href="http://www.fuzzygroup.net/phpcon2003"&gt;dose of frothy, exciting
php goodness&lt;/a&gt;. And that's not all! I even threw in Dirk Elmendorf's
PHP Database Design BOF slides (with his approval).</description>
12:   </item>
13:   <item>
14:     <title>Recommended: Registry Mechanic</title>
15:     <link>http://radio.weblogs.com/0103807/2003/05/06.html#a1632</link>
16:     <description>Found via the Gnome folks newsletter. Well worth
```

LISTING 4.1 Continued

```
➡&lt;A href="http://windows.fileoftheday.com/archives/000008.html"&gt;
➡downloading&lt;/A&gt; and running on your box. I'm not going to report how
➡many issues it found save to say that the number was odd, the number was
➡not prime and the number was large. Thanks
➡&lt;A href="http://chris.pirillo.com/"&gt; Chris&lt;/A&gt;!</description>
17:  </item>
18: </rss>
```

The `channel` element in lines 3–7 offers information about the feed and its provider. There's a title, a link to FuzzyBlog! at the URL `http://radio.weblogs.com/0103807`, and a description of the site.

Items in an RSS file are organized in reverse chronological order with the most recently published item first. An RSS newsfeed can contain as many or as few items as desired, but most contain around 10–15.

In Listing 4.1, the first item in the feed is in lines 8–12. It has the headline `"PHP 2003 Presentations Online!"` and a link to that weblog entry on FuzzyBlog! The full entry is offered in the `description` element; some weblogs are provided in full using RSS and others offer only headlines or truncated text. Radio publishes the entire text of each weblog entry in the RSS feed.

There's a lot more that you can define in an RSS file, but these elements represent the core features of the format. A full description of the different versions of RSS and the particulars of RSS 2.0 are covered in Appendix A, "RSS."

Using the News Aggregator

You can read RSS newsfeeds using Radio's news aggregator. The aggregator checks the feeds to which you've subscribed once an hour, skipping some hours when the feed is unlikely to be updated.

The aggregator is set up with subscriptions to more than a dozen newsfeeds from media outlets such as *BBC News*, the *New York Times*, and *InfoWorld*; personal weblogs by UserLand Software founder Dave Winer, programmer Wes Felter, and others; and the `Dictionary.Com` *Word of the Day*.

As the *Word of the Day* newsfeed demonstrates, there's no reason an RSS file must contain news or weblog entries. Anything that's presented over the Web can be offered using RSS.

You can view the Radio news aggregator by clicking the `News` link at the top of any page of the desktop Web site. New items from subscribed RSS newsfeeds are presented on a single page in reverse chronological order (see Figure 4.1).

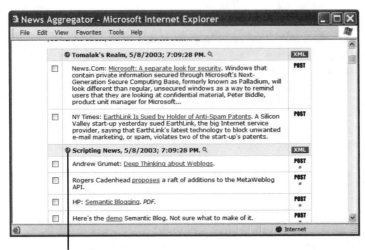

Globe

FIGURE 4.1 Reading RSS newsfeeds with the news aggregator.

This page presents headlines, headline links, and descriptive text from each new item found in subscribed RSS files. Some are presented with a headline that links to a story, followed by its lead paragraph or a summary. Others are more free-form, containing text, linked text, and even graphics.

The source of the RSS file is presented at the top of all new items from that file. Click the globe alongside its name to visit that site.

The RSS file itself is linked to an orange XML box to the right of its name. This graphic has become one of the most popular ways to signify the presence of an RSS feed on a Web site; you'll see them often on weblogs produced by Radio, another UserLand product called Manila, and other sites.

You can delete or publish each new item presented by the news aggregator on your weblog.

To delete one or more items, check the box to the left of each one, scroll to the top or bottom of the page, and then click Delete.

The items are deleted from AggregatorData.root, the database file that's used as a temporary storage place for new RSS data.

However, there's no need to delete items after they've been viewed. Radio will do this automatically when an item is more than 24 hours old.

TIP

You can increase or decrease the deletion time with the Archiving Options preference. Click Prefs, scroll to the News Aggregator heading, and then click Archiving Options.

Items that should be published are routed from the news aggregator to the weblog editor. To select an item for presentation on your weblog, click the Post link to the right of that item.

The item appears in the editor with its links intact and an extra link tacked on the end that credits the source (see Figure 4.2).

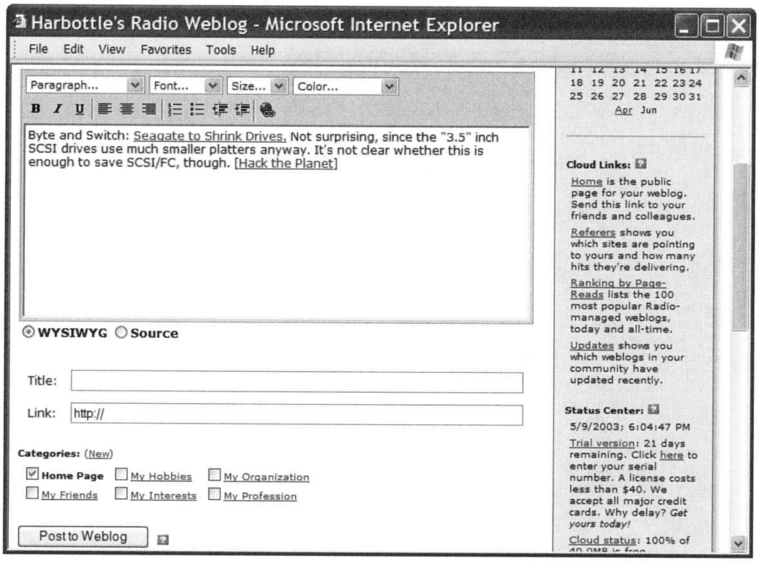

FIGURE 4.2   Publishing an item from someone else's newsfeed.

You can edit the text copied from the news aggregator or submit it as-is.

If you post items often from the news aggregator to your weblog, Radio can return to the aggregator after an item is published. Click Prefs on any desktop page, scroll to the News Aggregator section, and then click Where to go after posting? A check box turns this feature on and off.

CAUTION

It's common practice among weblog publishers, especially within the Radio community, to use the verbatim text of someone else's item accompanied by a link to the originating site. Some publishers may object to the practice or consider it a violation of their copyright, so keep that in mind as you post items from the aggregator.

Subscribing to RSS Newsfeeds

Radio's news aggregator keeps track of the RSS newsfeeds to which you've subscribed. The software installs with more than a dozen subscribed feeds.

To see your subscriptions, click the News link on any desktop Web page to view the news aggregator, and then click the subscribed link in the paragraph at the top of the page. The Subscriptions page is displayed.

On a Web site, the presence of RSS feeds is usually indicated by an orange XML box, an orange RSS box, an RSS link, or something similar (as shown in Figure 4.3).

Subscribe using
Radio Userland   XML box

FIGURE 4.3   Viewing a weblog that offers RSS feeds.

Figure 4.3 shows the home page of jenett.radio, a weblog published by Joe Jenett that offers an RSS newsfeed. The site's published at http://www.coolstop.com/radio.

You can use an XML box to subscribe to that site's RSS feed. Copy the box's link to the clipboard, reopen the Subscriptions page, paste the link in the URL text field, and click Add.

If the file is in one of the formats that Radio recognizes, it will be added to your list of subscriptions. At this time Radio can handle RSS 2.0 and all of its predecessors (RSS 0.91 through RSS 0.94); RSS 1.0; and an early syndication format called *scriptingNews*.

Items from the new feed will begin showing up in the aggregator within an hour.

Some weblogs offer an easier way for Radio users to read an RSS newsfeed: the orange cactus coffee mug icon in Figure 4.3. Click one of these mugs to open the Subscriptions page with that link already pasted in the URL text field. All you have to do is click Add to subscribe.

RSS subscriptions are saved in aggregatorData.root, the same database file that holds recent items from each feed.

Radio also saves your list of subscribed feeds in a file called mySubscriptions.opml in the www\gems folder, sharing this information with UserLand and publishing it on your weblog.

UserLand collects this information and other data on RSS usage to present several reports on the most popular RSS feeds read by Radio users.

> **CAUTION**
>
> Even when this feature is turned off, the old mySubscriptions.opml file will still be available on your weblog. To remove it, delete the file from the www\gems folder on your computer. Within a few minutes, Radio will notice the change and delete the file from the server hosting your site.

To see one of these reports, open the desktop home page, look in the Cloud links sidebar, and click the Ranking by Page-Reads link. You also can load the page by visiting the URL http://www.weblogs.com/rankingsByPageReads.html.

You can opt out of this feature, which stops Radio from updating mySubscriptions.opml or sharing it with UserLand. Click Prefs on the desktop Web site, scroll to the News Aggregator section, and click the mySubscriptions.opml link. A check box turns this preference on and off.

Keeping a mySubscriptions.opml file around makes it easier to use other news aggregator programs. Several programs can import RSS subscriptions from this file, including AmphetaDesk, NetNewsWire, and NewsGator.

UserLand also collects information each time you find new items in an RSS feed, using this information to compile a report for each weblog that lists Radio users who are actively reading its newsfeed.

This information is a great way to find new Radio weblogs of interest, but you can opt out if desired and keep your RSS usage private. Click Prefs, and then on the Preferences page, click the Web Bug Simulator link. A check box turns this feature—which UserLand calls a *Web bug*—on and off.

Changing News Aggregator Preferences

You can adjust (or even turn off) Radio's news aggregator by editing the software's preferences. To see what customizations are possible, click the Prefs link at the top of any desktop Web page and scroll to the News Aggregator section of the Preferences page.

The Enable the aggregator? preference turns the aggregator on and off. The Scan on startup? preference causes Radio to immediately look for new items when it begins running, rather than waiting for the next hourly check.

The How many items? preference, which is initially set to 100, determines the maximum number of items shown on the News Aggregator page.

The When and how the aggregator runs preference controls the minute at which each hourly newsfeed check takes place. You can also use it to read multiple newsfeeds at the same time by devoting additional threads to the process. The more threads you use, the faster the hourly check occurs. Using a large number of threads can tax your system's resources and make all programs run slower during a check, so some experimentation is required to find the right setting.

The How the aggregator handles channel errors preference tells Radio what to do when an RSS feed stops working. After 48 errors have taken place during hourly checks of a particular newsfeed, the software cancels the subscription to that newsfeed. You can change this setting to make it more or less likely to give up on an erroneous feed.

Filing RSS Items to Read Later

Radio's support for categories is typically employed to organize weblog entries into topic areas or publish more than one weblog with the software.

You can use categories also as a filing place for items of interest that turn up in the news aggregator.

Because Radio integrates a news aggregator and weblog editor, it's easy to publish items to a category that you want to read later or archive for some other purpose.

To file items in their own category, follow these steps:

1. If categories have not been turned on, click the Prefs link on any page of the desktop Web site, click the Categories link in the Weblog section, and then check the box that enables the feature.

   Category check boxes appear on the weblog editor, enabling a post to be assigned to one or more categories.

2. On the desktop home page, click the New link next to the Categories heading.

   The New Category page opens.

3. Fill out the fields of the page, selecting a name, description, and theme (choosing None causes the weblog's theme to be used).

4. Check the check box to render this category in HTML.

5. If the category is intended primarily for your own use, keep the notify Weblogs.Com check box empty.

6. Click Submit.

7. To make it easier to file items, change the Where to go after posting? preference if you haven't already. Click Prefs, click that preference's link, and then select the return to the News Aggregator page after posting check box.

A new category for filed RSS items appears on the weblog editor, which can be offered to readers of the site or used personally.

This is just one of the ways that you can use categories for purposes other than weblog publishing. You can incorporate Radio's categorization feature in many kinds of information and workflow routing, thus making use of Web services and Internet protocols to exchange information with other servers and programs.

Summary

Radio UserLand's news aggregator is a popular feature even among users who don't publish a weblog. It takes a lot of the tedium out of the process of checking your favorite sources of information on the Web.

The news aggregator checks RSS newsfeeds up to once per hour, presenting items you have not seen before on a single Web page for easy reading.

RSS, a simple XML format, can deliver headlines, links, weblog entries, and other kinds of content. It's at the center of an innovative content management flow that can go in multiple directions, handling information you want to share, information you want to receive, and even a combination of both.

Upstreaming Files to a Web Server

The content-management system employed by Radio UserLand removes one of the biggest hassles associated with Web publishing: the requirement to manually transfer documents to a Web server when they're ready to be shared with the world.

Radio makes use of an innovative multi-protocol publishing system called *upstreaming*, a process that can transfer exact copies of files or transform them from one format to another when they are published.

Upstreaming is configured on a folder-by-folder basis, making use of the same file system-based inheritance hierarchy as navigator links and other features of the software.

Once upstreaming is set up, files are published automatically to the chosen destination whenever they are saved for the first time or are modified.

Publishing Web Pages and Other Files

Upstreaming, a Web publishing technique devised by UserLand Software, is like uploading on steroids.

Radio can use upstreaming to upload files, transferring them without modification from your computer to a destination on an Internet server or local network.

It also can take a file saved on your computer in one format and render it in another, transferring the rendered output to the destination instead of the original file.

This transformation occurs for two kinds of files (although Radio can be extended to support others): text files, which have the MIME type text/plain, and OPML outline files, which have the type text/x-opml.

As Radio renders a text file, it produces different kinds of output based upon the contents of the file:

- Directives at the top of the file, which begin with the # character, set up preferences that affect how Radio renders the file.

- HTML formatted text in the file is rendered without modification.

- *Macros*, special non-HTML tags that cause Radio to execute a UserTalk script or display text, are replaced with their output.

- Programming statements written in the UserTalk scripting language are executed, causing any output they produce to be rendered.

Macros and UserTalk code are surrounded by <% and %> characters in the file.

Because the upstreamed file is a Web page, it is stored under the .HTML file extension instead of .TXT or .OPML.

Listing 5.1 contains a simple example of a text file that Radio can render as a Web document.

LISTING 5.1   The Full Text of countdown.txt

```
1: #title "Christmas Countdown"
2:
3: <p>Only <%secsToChristmas()%> shopping seconds until Christmas <%year%>.
```

The countdown.txt file makes use of all four kinds of content.

The #title directive defines "Christmas Countdown" as the title of the page. A macro, <%title%>, can be placed anywhere on the page where the title should appear (such as an HTML title tag).

The year macro, which is surrounded by <% and %> characters, is replaced with the current year.

The UserTalk script secsToChristmas() is called, producing a comma-formatted number that indicates the number of seconds until the next Christmas Day. This output replaces the script call and its enclosing <% and %> tags.

The rest of the file is HTML text, which is placed on the page without modification.

When Radio is installed, its www folder is set up to render text files and OPML files as Web documents.

If the file in Listing 5.1 was saved in Radio's www folder, Radio upstreams it under the name countdown.html in the same folder as the weblog home page, placing a link to the new page in the Events log (click Events at the top of any page of the desktop Web site to see the log).

Figure 5.1 shows the resulting Web page.

FIGURE 5.1   A Web page upstreamed by Radio.

Although this example has a bug that will surface from December 26 through 31 of every year, it should demonstrate the dynamic nature of Radio's upstreaming feature.

Radio also can upload files without modification, which occurs when:

- The file is not a text or OPML file.

- The upstreaming folder has been set up to publish text and OPML files without rendering them in HTML.

Upstreaming is set up for a folder by creating an upstream file in that folder.

An upstream file has the name #upstream.xml and contains XML data in a simple format that designates where files will be published, how they will be published, and the username and password required to access that server or network location.

Like other file-based configuration in Radio, this feature uses the file system for an inheritance hierarchy. If a folder contains an upstream file, its settings apply to all subfolders (and their subfolders, and so on) unless they have an upstream file of their own.

NOTE

The Christmas countdown example also illustrates another aspect of upstreaming that's worth noting: The number of seconds is determined when the page is created and published. Radio doesn't produce a page that keeps counting down as Christmas draws closer.

Radio evaluates UserTalk code and expands macros when a text file or OPML file is being upstreamed, producing output associated with that moment in time. The scripts won't be run again until the file is edited in some way or upstreamed again, such as when a command in the Radio application's Radio, Publish menu is used.

For example, consider the following hypothetical folder hierarchy:

- `Radio UserLand\www` contains an upstream file that publishes to UserLand's Radio Community Server (http://radio.weblogs.com)

- `Radio UserLand\www\categories` does not contain an upstream file

- `Radio UserLand\www\categories\salon` contains an upstream file that publishes to the Salon Blogs server (http://blogs.salon.com)

> **NOTE**
>
> When looking for files to upstream, Radio only monitors the `Radio UserLand\www` folder and its subfolders. The other folders contained within the `Radio UserLand` folder will not be upstreamed, even if an `#upstream.xml` file was placed in any of them.

Files saved in the www and www\categories folder are upstreamed to the UserLand server. Files saved in www\categories\salon are upstreamed to Salon Blogs.

The contents of an upstream file dictate where files in the same folder are published, if at all. Listing 5.2 contains the simplest upstream file, which specifies that nothing in a folder should be published.

LISTING 5.2   A Non-Publishing #upstream.xml File

```
1: <?xml version="1.0"?>
2: <upstream type="none" version="1.0"/>
```

This file is used to declare folders off limits to Radio's upstreaming feature.

If a folder will be upstreamed through one of the `#upstream.xml` configurations described in the next three sections, all text and OPML files contained in that folder are rendered as HTML when published.

To turn off rendering and cause the files to be upstreamed without modification, you need to add a directive to the preferences file in that folder, which has the name #prefs.txt:

`#flRender false`

The flRender directive is a Boolean value that equals false to turn file rendering off or true to turn it on. The default is true.

As you might expect, preferences files use inheritance; if there is no file, Radio climbs up the folders until it finds one. You can create a #prefs.txt file in any folder contained within www.

Directives such as flRender must be placed at the top of a file, one to a line, with no blank lines between them.

The www\gems folder created by Radio during installation includes a preferences file that turns off rendering. You can save text files and outlines in this folder to publish them on the Web in their existing format.

A directive in the preferences file applies to all files in that folder. You can place directives in individual files as well, as illustrated in the Christmas countdown example in Listing 5.1.

Another useful directive for rendering purposes is renderedFileExtension, which you can place in a file to give the rendered file a different extension than .HTML.

For example, if you are rendering a file that should have the PHP extension, place the following directive on its own line at the top of the file, along with other directives:

```
#renderedFileExtension "php"
```

Publishing to a Community Server

The most popular way to publish a Radio weblog is to use the *Radio Community Server,* Web server software offered by UserLand that hosts files received through upstreaming rather than through FTP or another transfer protocol.

The Radio Community Server, which also is called the *cloud*, offers other features for weblogs, including referral reports, site popularity reports, and hosting for visitor comments made in response to weblog entries.

UserLand and Salon Blogs both offer Radio Community Server hosting, as do a few other Internet services. There's also an open-source clone called the Python Community Server that supports most of the official community server's features, along with some additional ones, including user-selectable URLs such as http://www.pycs.net/zia (as compared to the numeric ones assigned by Radio servers such as http://radio.weblogs.com/0123698).

All community servers implement XmlStorageSystem, a Web service protocol created by UserLand to support upstreaming and other features available in Radio.

At present, the following community servers offer hosting to Radio weblogs:

- UserLand's Radio Community Server: http://radio.xmlstoragesystem.com/rcsPublic/help
- AIESEC: http://radio.aiesec.ws/rcsPublic/help
- Le Weblog: http://rcs.leweblog.com/rcsPublic/help
- Salon Blogs: http://rcs.salon.com/rcsPublic/help
- Python Community Server: http://www.pycs.net

Listing 5.3 contains an #upstream.xml file used to publish to the Radio Community Server.

LISTING 5.3   A Community Server #upstream.xml File

```
 1: <?xml version="1.0"?>
 2: <upstream type="xmlStorageSystem" version="1.0">
 3:     <usernum>123698</usernum>
 4:     <name>Harbottle</name>
 5:     <passwordName>default</passwordName>
 6:     <server>radio.xmlstoragesystem.com</server>
 7:     <port>80</port>
 8:     <protocol>xml-rpc</protocol>
 9:     <rpcPath>/RPC2</rpcPath>
10:     <soapAction>/xmlStorageSystem</soapAction>
11: </upstream>
```

The #upstream.xml file in Listing 5.3 uses a simple XML dialect to define and access a community server.

The root element is upstream, which contains all other elements in the file. The upstream element must have the type attribute "xmlStorageSystem" and the version attribute "1.0", and it contains the following elements:

- The usernum element contains the user ID number assigned by the community server to your weblog.

- The name element contains your username on that server.

- The passwordName element contains the name under which your password is saved in the Radio.root database.

- The server and port elements identify the server and port where the community server receives files and other requests.

- The protocol, rpcPath, and soapAction elements indicate how the server will make use of XML-RPC or SOAP, the two Web services protocols supported by the community server.

Out of all these elements, the only ones you might need to edit in some circumstances are the usernum, name, and passwordName elements. The rest are set up for you when Radio is installed or when you move from one community server to another.

For security reasons, passwords are not specified in an upstream file. Instead, the value of passwordName is used to retrieve the password in Radio's main database.

The names of passwords stored in the database are displayed on the Passwords preference page (click Prefs on any desktop Web page, scroll down to Advanced, and then click Passwords). You can use this page also to change a password.

To add a new password to `Radio.root`, use the New Password preference (click Prefs, and then click New Password).

The Status Center section of the desktop home page offers a report that describes the community server to which a site is being published. Click the Cloud status link to view it.

One of the things it reveals is the type of files that can be upstreamed to the server. Community servers only accept files with permitted file extensions.

> **TIP**
>
> You can move from one community server to another with the Change Community Server form on the desktop Web site at `http://127.0.0.1:5335/system/pages/changeCommunityServer`.
>
> On the page, fill out the Server field with the URL required on the destination server, and then type the password you want to use in the Password and Repeat Password fields.
>
> When you use this feature, Radio replaces the existing `#upstream.xml` file in the `www` folder with one set up to use the new community server instead. Pages and other files are no longer upstreamed to the original server.

At this time, the Radio Community Server accepts the following extensions: CLASS, CSS, DOC, FTDS, FTMB, FTOP, FTSC, FTTB, GIF, GZ, HQX, HTM, HTML, ICO, JPEG, JPG, JS, OPML, PDF, PNG, PPT, ROOT, RSS, SIT, SVG, SWF, TEXT, TXT, WAV, WML, XLS, XML, XSL, XTM, and ZIP.

Publishing to an FTP Server

Radio also can upstream to a Web host that receives uploads using File Transfer Protocol (FTP), the most commonly available method for transferring files to a Web server.

Publishing to an FTP server instead of a community server does not reduce Radio's upstreaming functionality; text and outline files can be rendered during the transfer and other files and folders can be uploaded without modification.

Functionality related to the cloud will be unavailable—none of the links in the Cloud status section of the desktop home page will describe the Web server on which the site is published.

Listing 5.4 contains an upstream file that's being used to publish a Web site using FTP.

LISTING 5.4   An FTP Server #upstream.xml

```
1: <?xml version="1.0"?>
2: <upstream type="ftp" version="1.0">
3:     <username>rcade</username>
4:     <passwordName>ftp</passwordName>
5:     <server>cadenhead.org</server>
6:     <path>/usr/local/web/cadenhead/workbench</path>
7:     <url>http://www.cadenhead.org/workbench/</url>
8:     <mode>passive</mode>
9: </upstream>
```

CAUTION

If the messages on Radio's customer support discussion board are any indication, many new users run into two problem areas when configuring an upstream file to use FTP: They leave the final slash character (/) off the end of the url value or specify a path element without beginning it with either a slash or a tilde character (~), depending on what's required on their Web host to use FTP.

The elements in the file are identical to those in a community server upstream file, with these exceptions:

- The upstream element must have the type attribute "ftp" and the version attribute "1.0".

- The server element identifies the FTP server.

- The path element contains the folder where the weblog home page should be stored.

- The url element contains the base URL of files published to that folder.

- The mode element, which is optional, can be active or passive, specifying an FTP transfer mode.

There's no restriction on the extension of files upstreamed to an FTP server, although some hosting servers impose their own or block their Web server from some file types.

Publishing to a Network Folder

The final way to set up an upstream file is to specify a file folder as the destination, as demonstrated in Listing 5.5.

LISTING 5.5   A File System #upstream.xml

```
1: <upstream type="fileSystem" version="1.0">
2:     <folder>\\Outside\SharedDocs\weblog</folder>
3:     <url>http://www.example.com/weblog/</url>
4:     <server>Outside Server</server>
5: </upstream>
```

Your computer must have read-write access to the destination folder; Radio doesn't take care of this.

This kind of upstream file would presumably be used to publish files over a local network to an Internet or intranet server that hosts Web files, but that's not a requirement. Radio can upstream to another folder on the same computer.

The following elements are employed:

- The upstream element must have the type attribute "fileSystem" and the version attribute "1.0".

- The folder element identifies the server and path of the destination folder (or just the path when upstreaming to the same computer).

- The url element contains the base URL of files published to that folder.

- The server element provides a descriptive name of the destination server.

The url and server elements don't affect upstreaming. They are used to make the Events log more useful when publishing events are reported, as shown in Figure 5.2.

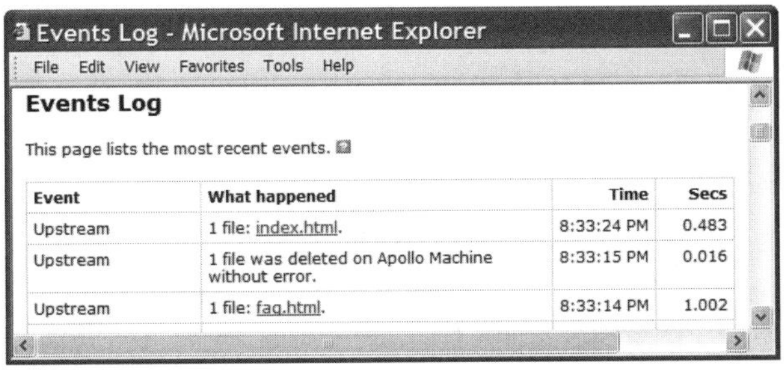

FIGURE 5.2   Upstreaming events in the Events log.

Publishing Two Weblogs at the Same Time

Although it might appear that Radio is limited to the publication of a single weblog, the software's categorization and upstreaming features make it possible to publish more than one weblog simultaneously.

Each category of a Radio weblog is given its own subfolder in the `www\categories` folder, as described in Chapter 3, "Enhancing a Weblog."

<table>
<tr><td>

NOTE

The only thing that links the two weblogs appears to be a single line of the category's RSS file. Radio prefaces the category name with the name of the main weblog—so a category of the Workbench weblog named JargonWatch has the name "Workbench: JargonWatch" in its RSS newsfeed.

The reason this is important? `Weblogs.Com` and most news aggregators consider this part of the RSS newsfeed to be the title of the weblog.

</td><td>

When a category's entries are published as Web pages, it has most of the features of the main weblog, including daily archive pages, a calendar of links to the archive, and its own RSS file. You can add other features, such as navigator links specific to that category.

If an upstream file is placed in a category's folder, all of its files will be published to the destination specified by that folder. It could be a Web host that receives files by FTP, another Radio Community Server, or another location.

</td></tr>
</table>

If the destination is on a different server or domain name than the main weblog, visitors to the site will have almost no way to know that the two weblogs are connected to each other.

One feature of the main weblog that isn't easily offered in a secondary weblog is support for *stories*, longer articles that are published separately from weblog entries.

You can create stories in the category's folder or any of its subfolders (you could recreate the same year and month folders found in the `www\stories` folder and put story files in those folders).

They will be upstreamed to the same server as the rest of the category's files and can be viewed using links in the Events log.

However, there won't be an index of stories like the one offered in the main weblog. You can overcome this limitation by creating your own UserTalk script that generates a story list for a category. Extending Radio with your own programming is the focus of Part III, "Writing Scripts with UserTalk."

Summary

File transfer is accomplished in Radio UserLand through the use of upstream files, simple XML files that indicate where Web pages, graphics, and other files should end up when they are published by the software.

Upstream files, which are named #upstream.xml and stored in the folder they control, enable publishing to take place whenever a file is created or modified in a folder within Radio's www folder and its subfolders.

Upstreaming, a process devised by UserLand Software for use in Radio, makes it easy to automate one of the more tedious tasks required of a Web publisher: uploading files to the server that publicly hosts them.

Through this process, files can be transferred without modification or transformed from one format to another as they are published.

Designing a Weblog Theme

6

The appearance of a Radio UserLand-produced weblog is dictated primarily by a set of five template files. These templates establish the HTML-formatted text that appears above, beside, and below the body content of each page of the Web site.

Templates can contain HTML text and programming statements written in the UserTalk scripting language.

A site's templates are collected to form a *theme*, a set of files that you can save together and use on any Radio weblog.

Creating Dynamic Web Pages

Web pages are produced by Radio when they are upstreamed from your computer to the Web server that hosts the site. A page published with Radio UserLand combines material from three sources:

- An HTML formatted text file that represents the body of the page

- One or more templates that will be combined with the body

- UserTalk code, which can be placed on the body page or templates, producing HTML output

This last ingredient is what makes Radio-produced pages dynamic. UserTalk, the programming language developed by UserLand for use in Radio and its other products, can produce HTML text that's based on a variety of interactive sources, including the Radio object database, Web services, and data over such Internet protocols as FTP and POP3.

Defining a Theme's Template Files

A Radio theme consists of three templates that define an entire page and two templates that define a section of a page:

- `#itemTemplate.txt`, a section template formatting an individual weblog entry

- `#dayTemplate.txt`, a section template formatting a day of weblog entries

- `#homeTemplate.txt`, a template for the weblog home page and weblog archive pages

- `#desktopWebsiteTemplate.txt`, a template for the desktop home page

- `#template.txt`, a template for every other page, including stories, the story index page, and every page in the desktop Web site except for the home page

---

TIP

The easiest way to back up your weblog's existing design is to turn it into a theme.

On the Themes page, click the this page link in the paragraph at the top of the page. The Create Theme page is displayed. Choose a name for the theme—I use today's date as part of the name so I know when it was saved—and click Create Theme. The theme is saved as a single file with the .FTTB extension in the Themes folder, becoming one of the choices on the Themes page.

You can get rid of old theme backups by deleting them from the Themes folder.

The templates for a weblog are saved in Radio's www folder, the root folder of the Web site. Each is prefaced by a # character so that Radio will not upstream these files to the server hosting the site. (You can make use of this yourself; any file you preface with # will not be published.)

You create a theme by packaging together these five templates, graphics that are used by the templates, and some additional files.

To choose a theme, click the Themes link at the top of any desktop Web page. The Themes page displays the built-in themes and any others that have been stored in Radio's Themes folder.

When you choose a theme, Radio replaces the existing template files with those of the theme. You can't get the original files back, so it's worthwhile to back up your existing files before making any changes to a template or choosing a new theme.

After choosing a new theme or making changes to any of the five template files, the weblog should be republished (in whole or in part). Follow these steps:

1. Open the Radio application.

2. Choose one of the commands on the Radio, Publish menu, such as All Weblog and Category Pages to republish all weblog pages or Entire Website to republish stories and everything else.

Republishing these files can be time-consuming—a weblog with several hundred entries can take several hours, even using a high-speed DSL or cable modem connection.

Formatting Weblog Entries

The item template determines the appearance of each entry in a weblog. Listing 6.1 contains the default theme's item template.

LISTING 6.1   The Full Text of #itemTemplate.txt

```
 1: <table width="100%" cellpadding="1">
 2:   <tr>
 3:     <td valign="top">
 4:       <br><div class="itemTitle"><b><%itemTitle%></b></div><%itemText%><br>
 5:       <font class="small" size="-1" color="gray"><%when%>  
➥<%permalink%>  <%commentLink%></font>
 6:     </td>
 7:     <td valign="top" align="right" nowrap>
 8:       <%enclosure%>
 9:     </td>
10:   </tr>
11: </table>
```

As you can see from Listing 6.1, a template consists of HTML formatted text that should be familiar to Web designers and something that's unfamiliar: tags surrounded by <% and %> characters.

These are *macros*, special non-HTML tags that cause Radio to execute a UserTalk script or display text.

When a weblog entry is published, Radio expands all of the macros in the item template, adding any HTML they produce. The end result is incorporated into weblog pages that include the entry.

Figure 6.1 shows the weblog editor being used to create a new entry.

When this entry is published, Radio expands the macros in the item template, producing the HTML shown in Listing 6.2. The output of macros is shaded gray; HTML text from the template is white.

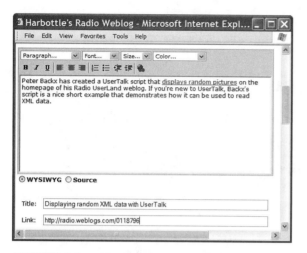

FIGURE 6.1 Creating a new weblog entry.

LISTING 6.2 A Weblog Entry Using the Default Template

```
1: <table width="100%" cellpadding="1">
2:    <tr>
3:      <td valign="top">
4:        <br><div class="itemTitle"><b><a href="http://radio.weblogs.com/
   0118796" class="weblogItemTitle">Displaying random XML data with UserTalk</a>
   </b></div>Peter Backx has created a UserTalk script that <A href="http://
   radio.weblogs.com/0118796/stories/2003/02/19/randomLinkForRadioUserland
   .html">displays random pictures</A> on the homepage of his Radio UserLand
   weblog. If you're new to UserTalk, Backx's script is a nice short example
   that demonstrates how it can be used to read XML data.<br>
5:        <font class="small" size="-1" color="gray">12:36:03 PM  
   <a href="http://radio.weblogs.com/0123698/2003/05/12.html#a10"><img src=
   "http://radio.weblogs.com/0123698/images/woodsItemLink.gif" border="0" width="7"
   height="9" alt="" /></a>  <a href="http://radiocomments2.userland.com/
   comments?u=123698&amp;p=10&amp;link=http%3A%2F%2Fradio.weblogs.com%2F
   0123698%2F2003%2F05%2F12.html%23a10" onclick="window.open (this.href,
   'comments', 'width=515, height=480, location=0, resizable=1, scrollbars=1,
   status=0, toolbar=0, directories=0'); return(false);" title="Click here to
   comment on this post." class="commentLink">comment [<script type=
   "text/javascript" language="JavaScript">commentCounter (10)</script>]</a></font>
```

LISTING 6.2   Continued

```
 6:          </td>
 7:          <td valign="top" align="right" nowrap>
 8:
 9:          </td>
10:        </tr>
11:      </table>
```

The end result is shown in Figure 6.2, a portion of a weblog home page.

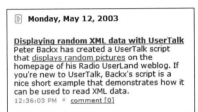

Monday, May 12, 2003

Displaying random XML data with UserTalk
Peter Backx has created a UserTalk script
that displays random pictures on the
homepage of his Radio UserLand weblog. If
you're new to UserTalk, Backx's script is a
nice short example that demonstrates how it
can be used to read XML data.
12:36:03 PM   #   comment [0]

FIGURE 6.2   A weblog entry formatted with the
default item template.

The default item template includes six macros:

- `itemTitle`: the title of the weblog entry (if it includes one)

- `itemText`: the text of the entry

- `when`: a timestamp indicating the date and time it was published

- `permalink`: the URL of the entry

- `commentLink`: a link that can be used to comment on the entry

- `enclosure`: the link to a file associated with the entry (if enclosures are enabled and the entry includes a file)

You can edit the existing item template, moving macros around and making changes to the HTML, or replace it entirely.

The item template also can include these macros:

- `editButton`: an Edit link, which appears only when the entry is displayed on the desktop Web site

- `itemNum`: the ID number of the entry, which is used as part of the link to the entry (and stored internally in `weblogData.root`, the database that holds weblog entries)

TIP

In my experience, it's easier to learn what the macros do and start templates from scratch, plugging the macros in where they should be displayed.

By doing this, you can design your weblog using Web design software, such as Microsoft FrontPage, Macromedia Dreamweaver, or an HTML editor. Put dummy text where macros should go, and then use this test page to create each of the templates.

- paddedItemNum: the ID number of the entry padded with one or more prefixed "0" digits so that the number is eight digits long (for example, if the ID is 245, the padded version is 00000245)

- source: the source of the weblog entry, if it was routed from the news aggregator to the weblog editor before publication

When Radio publishes a weblog page, an entire day's entries are formatted according to the day template file, #dayTemplate.txt.

The default theme's day template is shown in Listing 6.2.

LISTING 6.2   The Full Text of #dayTemplate.txt

```
1: <table cellpadding="5" cellspacing="0" border="0">
2:    <tr>
3:       <td valign="middle"><%archiveLink%></td>
4:       <td><b><%longDate%></b></td>
5:       </tr>
6:    </table>
7: <%items%>
8: <br>
```

This template makes use of the following macros:

- archiveLink: a graphical link to that day's weblog archive page

- dayOfWeek: the name of the weekday (such as Monday)

- items: all of the weblog entries for that day, beginning with the most recent, using the item template for the formatting of each entry

- longDate: the date in this format: Monday, May 12, 2003

- shortDate: the date in a shorter format: 5/12/2003

The template must contain an items macro in order to present entries for that day. The other macros are optional.

Formatting Weblog Pages

The appearance of a Radio weblog is determined by two page templates: the home page template, #homeTemplate.txt, which is used on the weblog home page and all weblog archive pages; and the main template, `#template.txt`, that's used for articles and any other page of the site.

A third template is used for the desktop home page, `#desktopWebsiteTemplate.txt`. Every other page of the desktop site uses the main template.

The page templates in the default theme and the other built-in themes contain a lot of macros, calls to UserTalk scripts, and even some UserTalk code that's executed when the page is published, producing HTML output.

Macros, UserTalk scripts, and code are all surrounded by `<%` and `%>` characters. Macros and UserTalk scripts look alike and function similarly, but scripts can contain one or more parameters that are surrounded by parentheses.

For example, `radio.macros.mailto()` and `radio.macros.imageref("icon.gif")` call scripts that produce HTML output.

The following macros and UserTalk scripts are useful in the three page templates:

- `authorMailAddress`: the email address of the weblog's author, which is set with the User Identity preference (click `Prefs`, and then click `User Identity` to change)

- `authorName`: the author of the weblog (also part of the User Identity preference)

- `bodytext`: the main contents of the Web page

- `description`: the description of the weblog, as set with the Title and Description preference (`Prefs, Title and Description`)

- `navigatorLinks`: the navigator links for the weblog, which are determined by the `#navigatorLinks.txt` file in the same folder as the weblog's template files

- `now`: a timestamp for the last time the page was published, using this format: `5/12/2003; 3:33:48 PM`

- `radioBadge`: a small Radio logo graphic that links to the software's home page at `http://radio.userland.com`

- `radio.macros.getLastUpdate()`: a timestamp for the time the page was last edited in the format `5/12/2003; 3:33:48 PM`

- `radio.macros.mailto()`: an envelope icon that links to an email form on UserLand's servers—mail is delivered to the address associated with your weblog (from the User Identity preference)

- `radio.macros.staticSiteStatsImage()`: an invisible graphic that UserLand employs to track visits to your weblog and present reports on the most popular weblogs published with the software

- `radio.macros.weblogUrl()`: the URL of the weblog's home page, which includes a trailing slash character (`/`), as in `http://blogs.salon.com/0001068/`, the URL of Kat Donohue's Salon weblog

- `radio.macros.xmlCoffeeMug()`: an orange Radio coffee mug graphic that links to the RSS feed of the weblog or a weblog category

- `radio.weblog.drawcalendar()`: the calendar of links to daily weblog archive pages

- `rssLink`: a small orange XML graphic that links to the RSS feed of the weblog or a weblog's category

- `siteName`: the title of the weblog, set by the Title and Description preference

- `title`: the title of the page

- `year`: the year the page was last edited

TIP

To see how this works, open Radio's www folder and create a new text file that contains two lines:

```
#title "Sample page"
<h1>Free the bound periodicals!</h1>
```

Save the file with a name such as sample.txt, wait a minute or two and check the Events log. Radio publishes a Web page that uses the main template, #template.txt, and displays the contents of sample.txt in place of bodyText.

TIP

Radio's built-in themes were developed by Bryan Bell, a Web designer who specializes in theme designs for UserLand Web publishing programs. He's frequently coming up with new themes, which you can use easily by saving their packaged file in Radio's Themes folder. To see what's available, visit his weblog at http://www.bryanbell.com.

The bodyText macro is the only one that must be included in the templates for them to function correctly. It displays different things on different pages.

On the weblog home page, the macro will be expanded to display one or more days worth of weblog entries, formatted using the day and item templates.

On daily weblog archive pages, the macro displays one day's entries.

Everywhere else, the macro displays the body content of those pages.

The macro and script that display links to RSS newsfeeds, `radio.macros.xmlCoffeeMug()` and `rssLink`, do different things depending on the page that contains them. If the page is part of a category, they link to the category's RSS newsfeed. Otherwise, they link to the weblog's newsfeed.

Radio templates also call two UserTalk scripts that are used to incorporate graphics into pages: `radio.macros.imageref()` and `radio.macros.imageUrl()`.

The `radio.macros.imageref()` script takes one required parameter: the path and name of a graphics file that should be displayed on a page, as in this example:

```
<%radio.macros.imageref("/system/images/weblogDefault/header1.gif")%>
```

This script inserts HTML that will display the graphic on the page at its actual size. The reason to use this script rather than an img tag is because it works on pages published to the Web and on the pages viewed as part of the desktop Web site.

It also can be called with several optional parameters:

- align: the value to use as the image's align attribute, which can be "left," "right," or "center"

- alt: the text of the image's alt attribute, which is used to provide a description or cutline of the image

- hspace: the value of the image's hspace attribute, which represents the empty horizontal border around the image in pixels

- vspace: the value of the image's vspace attribute, which sets its vertical border in pixels

Parameters are separated with commas in a UserTalk macro. Optional parameters can be identified with their names followed by a colon, as in this example:

```
<%radio.macros.imageref("/system/images/weblogDefault/header1.gif",
➥alt: "My Weblog", hspace: 5, vspace: 5)%>
```
The radio.macros.imageUrl() script also takes a graphic file as a parameter, inserting the URL of the graphic at that position on a page.

```
<%radio.macros.imageUrl("/system/images/weblogDefault/headerBg.gif")%>
```

Formatting the Desktop Web Site

Radio users who make use of themes are likely to alter the appearance of the desktop Web site, because changes to the main template, #template.txt, are reflected on every desktop page other than the home page.

The desktop home page uses its own template, the file #desktopWebsiteTemplate.txt.

Several UserTalk macros are useful on the desktop and main templates:

- radio.macros.cloudLinks(), a list of useful links to the weblog home page and some reports compiled by the server hosting the site

- radio.macros.editThisPageButton(), the Edit this Page button, which appears only when the entry is displayed on the desktop Web site

- radio.macros.editorsOnlyMenu(), the row of links to pages in the desktop Web site

- radio.macros.statusCenter(), a list of links containing information about the weblog, such as the amount of space remaining for new pages and files on the server hosting the site (UserLand offers 40MB to each weblog, which you can expand for a fee)

- `radio.macros.supportCenter()`, links to official and unofficial tech support for Radio

- `radio.macros.weblogEditBox()`, the weblog editor form, which only appears on the desktop Web site

- `radio.macros.weblogRecentPosts()`, the list of recent posts displayed below the weblog editor on the desktop home page

These scripts display HTML only on pages that are part of the desktop Web site. When they are called on pages published to the Web, they display an empty string.

Summary

The design of a Radio UserLand weblog is established by its theme, a set of templates, graphics, and other files packaged together into a single file.

Template files contain HTML text, calls to UserTalk scripts, and other UserTalk code. The contents of a template are displayed around the main contents of each page.

There are five templates in each theme: two section templates that establish the appearance of weblog entries, and three page templates that create the entire page design.

Themes make it easy to select a new design for a Web site, which Radio can republish in its entirety with a single command.

Calling Scripts to Create Weblog Content

Radio UserLand publishes Web content dynamically, combining HTML formatted text with the output of macros and programming statements written with UserTalk, UserLand's scripting language.

All Web content begins as a text file stored in Radio's www folder and its subfolders.

If you look through some of these files, you'll see the extent to which Radio uses UserTalk scripts to produce the contents of Web pages.

Scripts draw information from sources such as Radio's object database, XML files, and Web services, producing HTML format that's incorporated on pages as they are upstreamed. They're an effective way to extend the functionality of a Web site.

Calling UserTalk Scripts

Radio produces Web pages by reading text files that contain HTML formatted text, macros that are expanded into HTML, and UserTalk statements that are executed during the publication process, a process called *rendering*.

UserTalk script calls and other statements are placed within <% and %> characters, as in this example:

```
<p>This page last updated on
<%radio.macros.getLastUpdate()%>
```

When a page containing this HTML is rendered, the output of the `radio.macros.getLastUpdate()` script will be published in place of the script call, like so:

```
<p>This page last updated on 5/16/2003; 3:21:38 PM
```

As you move beyond Radio's standard features, one of the ways to benefit from UserTalk before you know the language is to call scripts written by UserLand Software and other developers. There are hundreds of scripts that might be useful in your own publishing projects.

The scripts offered by UserLand Software as a built-in part of Radio are often called *verbs* or *macros* to describe their purpose. *Verbs* are scripts that constitute the core functionality of UserTalk, whereas *macros* are scripts that are executed to produce content when a file is rendered. Many verbs can be called as macros.

Macros are called as a page is being published, producing static output that does not change until the page is republished. This normally does not occur again until the page is modified or something else causes it to be republished, such as the Radio application's `Radio`, `Publish`, `Entire Website` menu command.

When a macro calls a script, it is followed by parentheses that can be filled with one or more parameters that configure the script. For example:

```
<%file.readWholeFile("C:\\Program Files\\Radio Userland\\www\\foot.htm")%>
```

The `file.readWholeFile()` script displays the contents of the file, which is specified as the only parameter to the script.

The file will be included verbatim, so it should only contain HTML text, not macros or UserTalk statements.

Every script parameter has a name in UserTalk—the same name as the variable that will hold it in the script. This name can be used in the call:

```
<%file.readWholeFile(f:"C:\\Program Files\\Radio Userland\\www\\foot.htm")%>
```

In the `file.readWholeFile()` script, the file parameter is named `f`.

When a script is called with more than one parameter, the parameters should be separated by commas.

UserTalk scripts can have required parameters that must be specified in a call and optional parameters that can be omitted. When an optional parameter is not specified, a default value will be assigned to that parameter.

Parameters are ordered so that required parameters are first, followed by optional ones. The required parameters can be specified with or without names, as long as they are in the proper order. Optional parameters can be specified with their names.

The following sections describe some of the macros that can be used to generate content on Radio weblogs.

FIGURE 7.1 Displaying RSS items on a Web page.

Displaying an RSS Newsfeed on a Web Page

When RSS originated, the main use of the format was to enable one Web site to display headlines and links from another.

A UserTalk script can be employed to incorporate an RSS newsfeed on your weblog, even if the newsfeed is not a part of your site.

The `xml.rss.viewRssBox()` script presents the contents of an RSS newsfeed on a Web page, as demonstrated in Figure 7.1.

The script is called with 11 parameters that affect the contents of the box and how it is displayed. The only required parameter is `url`, which specifies the URL of the RSS newsfeed. All other parameters can be omitted when the script is called.

The parameters, which are listed in order, follow:

1. `url`: the Web address of the RSS newsfeed, which should be a full URL even if it is part of your own Web site

2. `boxTitle`: the text to display in the box's title bar, which links to the Web site of the newsfeed's provider (default: use the title provided by the newsfeed)

3. `width`: the width of the box, in pixels (default: 125)

4. `frameColor`: the color of the box's lines (default: black, hexadecimal #000000)

5. `titleBarTextColor`: the color of the text in the title bar (default: black, hexadecimal #000000)

6. `titleBarColor`: the background color of the title bar (default: light blue, hexadecimal #ADD8E6)

7. `boxFillColor`: the background color of the box where news items are displayed (default: white, hexadecimal #FFFFFF)

8. `timeZone`: the time zone of the time displayed in the title bar (default: PST)

9. `adrStoryArrivedCallback`: a script to call when the newsfeed contains a new item (default: no script should be called)

10. `maxItems`: the number of items from the newsfeed to display, beginning with the most recent item (default: display all items)

11. `timeZoneOffsetHours`: the difference in hours between the time zone to display in the RSS box and the one on the computer running Radio (default: 0)

The following script creates the box shown in Figure 7.1:

```
<%xml.rss.viewRssBox("http://www.csmonitor.com/rss/top.rss",
➥boxTitle:"Christian Science Monitor", timeZone: "EST")%>
```

To make the box invisible, the `frameColor`, `titleBarColor`, and `boxFillColor` parameters should be the same color as the background, as in this example for a white background:

```
<%xml.rss.viewRssBox ("http://www.csmonitor.com/rss/top.rss",
➥boxTitle:"Christian Science Monitor", timeZone: "EST", frameColor: "#FFFFFF",
➥titleBarColor: "#FFFFFF", boxFillColor: "#FFFFFF")%>
```

Because the contents of the RSS box are determined during the rendering of the page, it works best on the weblog home page or another page that's updated often.

Displaying Google Search Results on a Web Page

The search engine Google offers a Web service that can be used by software to request the top search results for any given query.

The `google.macros.box()` script displays the top results for any query on a Web page, as shown in Figure 7.2.

UserLand calls this a *Google box,* and before you can display one, you must sign up for a free account from Google and receive a license key, which is available from the URL `http://www.google.com/apis`.

After you have received your license key in an email from Google, it must be added to Radio's main database, `Radio.root`.

This can be done from Radio's desktop Web site—a dummy article will be created with a few UserTalk statements that add the key to the database:

1. Click the Stories link on top of any desktop Web page.

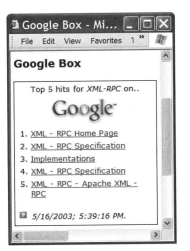

FIGURE 7.2 Displaying search result links on a Web page.

The Stories page is displayed.

2. In the paragraph on top of the page, click the Create link to create a new article.

The New Story page appears.

3. In the Title field, enter **None** or any other text.

4. In the Text box, enter the following two lines, replacing *yourlicensekey* with the text of the key you received from Google:

```
<%google.init()%>
<%user.google.key="yourlicensekey"%>
```

5. Click Create New Story.

The story will be created, which causes the macros to be executed, adding the license key to the database. You can return to the Stories page and delete the dummy article at any time.

Once Google's license key is in the database, you can call the `google.macros.box()` script. It takes a required `searchterm` parameter and eight optional parameters:

1. `searchterm`: the text of the search query to look for on Google

2. `ctResults`: the number of pages to list in the results, which can be no larger than 10 (default: 10)

3. `tableWidth`: the width of the box, in pixels (default: 191)

4. `frameColor`: the color of the box's lines (default: black, hexadecimal #000000)

5. `boxColor`: the background color of the box (default: white, hexadecimal #FFFFFF)

6. `helpLink`: the page linked to the small question mark icon below the box (default: the URL `http://radio.userland.com/googleBox`, a UserLand page describing Google boxes)

7. `textClass`: the name of the class to which text in the box belongs, which can be used with Cascading Style Sheets to apply formatting (default: no class, and text is given the HTML `font size -1`)

8. `align`: the alignment of the text, which can be left, center, or right (default: no alignment is set)

The following script creates the box shown in Figure 7.2:

```
<%google.macros.box("XML-RPC", tableWidth: 240, ctResults: 5)%>
```

Google limits users of its Web service to 1,000 requests per day, a maximum you're extremely unlikely to hit by calling this script on a Web page published with Radio.

Like RSS boxes, the Google results change only when the page containing the box is republished.

Displaying RSS Subscriptions on a Web Page

Many Radio weblogs feature a *blogroll*, a list of links to sites favored by the publisher. This list is created with the navigator links feature, an XML file containing site names, URLs, and headings.

Another way to present a blogroll is to make use of mySubscriptions.opml, a list of subscribed RSS newsfeeds that Radio can maintain automatically.

To set up this preference, click Prefs on any desktop page, and then click mySubscriptions.opml. The file is normally saved in Radio's www\gems folder.

The radio.macros.blogroll() script displays the sites in mySubscriptions.opml or any other outline as a blogroll, using a format shown in the right column of the Web page in Figure 7.3.

FIGURE 7.3   Displaying a subscribed feed outline on a Web page.

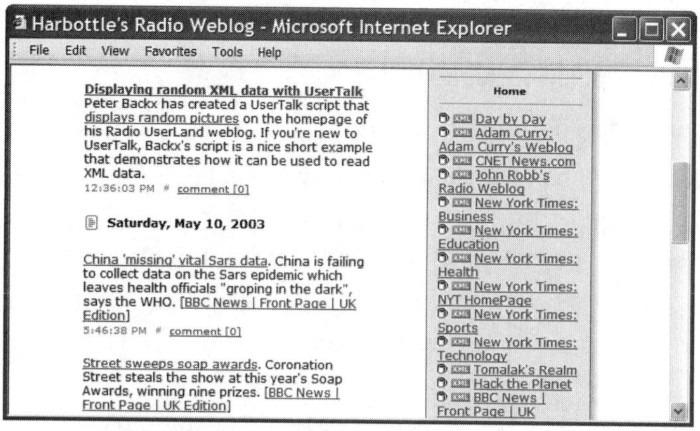

The only required parameter is opmlUrl.

The parameters are as follows:

1. `opmlUrl`: the URL of the outline file that contains RSS subscriptions or any other outline containing site links

2. `flProcessMacros`: a Boolean that determines whether macros will be expanded (true) or not (false) (default: false)

3. `cssPrefix`: text that will be used as the first part of three Cascading Style Sheet class names used to display links (default: *blogroll*, which causes the class names to be `blogrollLink`, `blogrollLinkedText`, and `blogrollText`)

4. `flXmlButton`: a Boolean that determines whether an XML button linking to the OPML file should be displayed (true) or not (false) (default: true)

5. `recentlyUpdatedLinkPrefix`: text that should be displayed before a link that has been recently updated, if the outline file contains this information (default: no text)

6. `recentlyUpdatedLinkSuffix`: text that should be displayed after a link that has been recently updated (default: no text)

The following script creates the blogroll shown in Figure 7.3:

```
<%radio.macros.blogroll(radio.macros.weblogUrl()+"gems/mySubscriptions.opml")%>
```

Cascading Style Sheets can be used to format the text of each item in the blogroll. The `cssPrefix` parameters determine the names of these classes—if the default value of `blogroll` is used, the classes will be `blogrollLink` for the item link, `blogrollLink` for the text of the link, and `blogrollLinkedText` for the entire item.

Displaying Newly Updated Weblogs on a Web Page

Weblogs.Com, a service offered by UserLand Software at `http://www.weblogs.com`, publishes an index of the most recently updated weblogs. This site has become a central hub of the weblogging phenomenon.

CAUTION

Because the `radio.macros.blogroll()` script can be configured to expand macros, there's a security risk involved in displaying an outline published by someone else. If that outline contains macros and UserTalk statements, they will be processed by Radio without restriction. UserLand recommends that macros be expanded only in an outline from a trusted source.

Every day, thousands of weblogs notify Weblogs.Com that a new entry has been published. Radio supports this upon installation, although it also can be turned off (click `Prefs` on any desktop Web page, and then click `Participate in the Weblogs.Com community?`).

Radio offers a way to keep track of when your favorite weblogs show up on Weblogs.Com:

1. If you aren't on the desktop home page, click the Home link on any desktop page.

2. Scroll to the Status Center sidebar, and then click Weblogs.

3. The Weblogs.Com On The Desktop page opens, as shown in Figure 7.4. Weblogs that have updated within the last hour are listed in the left column.

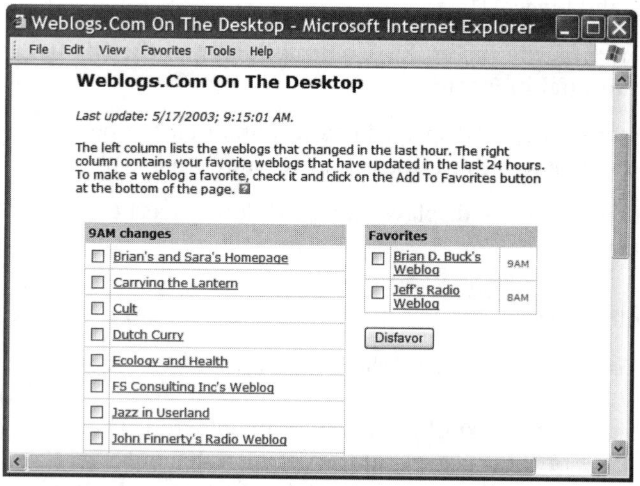

FIGURE 7.4   Monitoring Weblogs.Com from Radio.

4. To monitor one or more of these weblogs, click their check boxes, scroll to the bottom of the page, and click Add to Favorites.

   The weblog will be added to the Favorites column of the page whenever it has been updated within the prior 24 hours.

Radio checks Weblogs.Com once per hour, updating the desktop page.

Your Weblogs.Com favorites can be shared on a Web page with the radio.macros.viewFavoriteWeblogs() script, as shown in the circled portion of the Web page in Figure 7.5.

The list of favorites in Figure 7.5 is created by calling the script with no parameters in the weblog's home page template:

```
<%radio.macros.viewFavoriteWeblogs()%>
```

The list will only be as current as the page on which it is published.

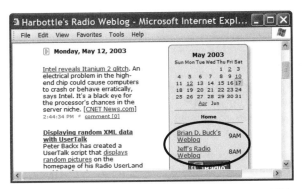

FIGURE 7.5   Sharing Weblogs.Com favorites on a Web page.

Both of the script's parameters are optional:

- preText: HTML text that should be placed before each item (default: none)

- postText: HTML text that should be placed after each item (default: none)

The preText and postText parameters can be used to format list items using the HTML font tag or a div tag and Cascading Style Sheets.

Adding Google Search Links to Weblog Entries

The item template in the file #itemTemplate.txt establishes the formatting of each weblog entry, displaying information such as the text of the item, its title, and a permalink.

The radio.macros.googleIt() script can be called in the item template to add Google search capabilities to any weblog that uses entry titles.

It takes two parameters:

- postnum: the ID number of the weblog entry, which is required and can be specified using the itemNum macro

- linetext: the text of the link (default: Google It!)

Listing 7.1 contains the default item template with a Google search added after the comment link.

LISTING 7.1   The Full Text of #itemTemplate.txt

```
 1: <table width="100%" cellpadding="1">
 2:   <tr>
 3:     <td valign="top">
 4:       <br><div class="itemTitle"><b><%itemTitle%></b></div><%itemText%><br>
 5:       <font class="small" size="-1" color="gray"><%when%>
➥  <%permalink%>  <%commentLink%>  
➥<%radio.macros.googleIt(<%itemNum%>)%></font>
 6:     </td>
 7:     <td valign="top" align="right" nowrap>
 8:       <%enclosure%>
 9:     </td>
10:   </tr>
11: </table>
```

In Listing 7.1, the inserted script call is displayed with a gray background.

When the item template includes this script, every weblog entry with a title will include a Google It! link that searches Google for the text of the title. See Figure 7.6 for an example.

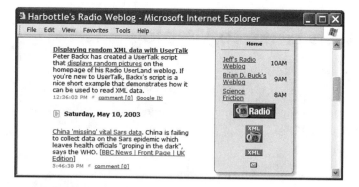

FIGURE 7.6   Offering Google searches with weblog entries.

Summary

Scripts connect Radio UserLand Web pages with the outside world, collecting information from Radio's object database, Web services, XML files, and other sources.

When a Web page containing a script is rendered, the HTML output of the script is incorporated into the page. The rendered page is then upstreamed to a Web server.

Most of the heavy lifting in Radio is handled by scripts, as you can see by examining the text files that make up the desktop Web site and your weblog.

Scripts provide the dynamic capabilities of Radio's content-management system.

TIP

The scripts covered in this chapter are just a selection of more than a hundred scripts included in Radio or provided by other developers.

Visit the following sites to find more scripts:

- Andy Fragen's scripts from the Surgical Diversions weblog: `http://radio.weblogs.com/0001017/publicTools/scripts`
- Mark Pascal's Radio tools: `http://markpasc.org/code/radio`
- Andy Sylvester's Scripts page, part of a directory of Radio and UserLand resources: `http://ruminations.weblogger.com/directory/143/scripts`

Creating Outlines

Radio UserLand includes a robust outliner that can be employed to create, modify, and organize text. Although many kinds of information can be represented by an outline, Radio's outliner is put to work most often on three kinds of content:

- Web documents in HTML or XML

- UserTalk scripts

- Data in Radio's object database

This chapter describes the core features of Radio's outliner, which is one of the most sophisticated tools of its kind in any software. The practice and terminology of outlining are introduced, followed by specific details of Radio's implementation.

Understanding Outlines

It's impossible to make full use of Radio without mastering the program's outliner.

Dave Winer, the principal founder of UserLand Software, is one of the world's biggest advocates for outliners. Over the last quarter century he created several of the most popular commercial outliner products, including ThinkTank, Ready!, and MORE, and continued working on outliners even after the market for stand-alone outlining software dried up. Outliners have been a core part of UserLand's Internet products since the launch of the company in 1988.

Outliners attract a cult following, as demonstrated by the number of people who continue to use products like MORE years after development was abandoned. The

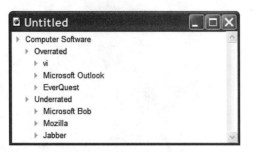

FIGURE 8.1 An outline listing computer software.

discussion board on `Outliners.Com`, a Web site run by UserLand, has more than 1,600 messages from current users of MORE, ThinkTank, and similar products. "Word processors, presentation programs, script editors, project planners, personal information managers, all have outliners built into them now," says Winer. "Perhaps this offers the most likely explanation of what happened to outliners, the idea was good enough that it found its way into every other application category."

An outline is a list of related items that has been structured into a hierarchy to show the relationships between different items. An example is shown in Figure 8.1.

People who have never used outliners might be skeptical of their usefulness. An outline, after all, is just a list of items grouped together with icons and indentation. Microsoft Word and other word processors have offered outlining capabilities for years, but many users probably don't realize the feature is there. Although outliners are an essential component of file navigation, help files, the Windows Registry, and a lot of other software, you might not see much need for them in your own projects.

Outlines are a simple and flexible way to create and view a list of items, displaying different parts of the list as desired.

In an outline, relationships are established between items based on where they are located and how far they are indented to the right. The outline hierarchy represents a family tree of parent-child relationships: Items grouped together with the same indentation are the children of a parent directly above them with lesser indentation. In Figure 8.1, the parent "Underrated" has three children: "Microsoft Bob," "Mozilla," and "Jabber." Parents also can be children themselves—the parent "Computer Software" has two children: "Overrated" and "Underrated." Radio calls child items *subheads*.

In an outline, each horizontal level of indentation represents a level of the outline. Subheads can be at the same level without having the same parent—in Figure 8.1, "EverQuest" and "Mozilla" are at the same level but are not siblings. One has "Overrated" as a parent and the other has "Underrated."

The child items of a parent can be interactively displayed (expanded) or hidden (collapsed), making it possible to view as much or as little of the outline as desired. Collapsing an item collapses everything below it in the hierarchy.

Radio.root			
Name	**Value**	**Kind**	
▶ examples	on disk	table	
▶ scratchpad	13 items	table	
suites	5 items	table	
▶ custody	12 items	table	
▶ people	49 items	table	
▶ states	on disk	table	
▶ webEdit	on disk	table	
▶ webEditServer	on disk	table	
▶ system	13 items	table	
▶ user	32 items	table	
▶ websites	8 items	table	
▶ workspace	19 items	table	
Kind: ▼ Sort: ▼			

FIGURE 8.2   Radio's object database.

Each item in an outline is marked by a small icon, such as a triangle, a plus or minus sign, or a bullet. This icon also can be used to indicate whether a particular item has subheads that are not being displayed. In Radio, each item has a black triangle when it has collapsed subheads and a gray triangle when it has expanded subheads or no subheads at all.

Radio's object database, Radio.root, can be viewed and modified as an outline. Figure 8.2 shows one view of this database.

As depicted in the figure, most items in the outline are collapsed away from view, which is the norm when working with the database. Radio.root contains thousands of items—if every subhead was expanded at the same time, finding a particular item in the outline would be an arduous task. Instead, it's easier to find something by expanding an item to see its subheads, expanding one of the subheads, and so on until the desired item is located. This process is called *drilling down* into the outline.

After drilling down to a group of subheads in an outline, the parent of those heads will be visible, as will its parent, and so on up the hierarchy.

To take a more focused view of a portion of an outline, a parent's subheads can be *hoisted*. Hoisting causes a group of related subheads to be displayed as if those items and their subheads were the only thing in the outline. The parent and all other parts of the outline disappear from view (see Figure 8.3).

CAUTION

Radio.root contains thousands of lines of UserTalk scripting code and data that are required for the proper function of the software. The care and feeding of this database is covered in the chapters of Part II, "Using the Object Database." Making any changes to the database before learning how to work with it (and back it up) could cause Radio to stop functioning correctly.

Untitled	
▷ Microsoft Bob	
▷ Mozilla	
▷ Jabber	

FIGURE 8.3   Hoisted items in an outline.

The outline shown in the figure displays only three items—the subheads of the "Underrated" item shown in Figure 8.1. There's no way to find and expand anything higher up in the hierarchy.

Although hoisting makes it look as if the rest of the outline has been deleted, the items are still present. To return to a less focused view of the outline, the subheads can be dehoisted. *Dehoisting* reverses the last hoisting request, making all the items that it hid visible again.

Items can be moved up or down an outline by being promoted or demoted. These requests move a group of child subheads that share the same parent. *Demoting* moves one or more subheads down one level, indenting them further to the right. *Promoting* moves one or more subheads up one level so they are less indented than before.

Returning to Figure 8.3, if "Jabber" were demoted, it would become the child subhead of "Mozilla." If "Mozilla" and "Jabber" were demoted, both would become children of "Microsoft Bob."

There's more jargon associated with the practice of outlining, but the terms are best learned within the context of Radio's particular implementation. At this point, you should have some familiarity with the concepts of parents and subheads, levels, expanding, collapsing, hoisting, dehoisting, promotion, and demotion.

Writing an Outline

To begin a new outline in Radio, choose the menu command File, New. A window appears with a gray triangle next to a blinking cursor. The text of an outline item can be entered at that cursor.

The outliner functions like a text editor. When you press the keyboard Enter key (Return on the Mac), a new outline item is added and the cursor moves to accept input at that position.

PC users might run into some confusion because there are two Enter keys on most PC keyboards and they accomplish different things in Radio's outliner (see Figure 8.4).

Keyboard Enter key   Keypad Enter key

FIGURE 8.4   Enter keys on a PC.

When entering items in an outline on Windows, use the keyboard Enter key, not the keypad Enter key.

Macs avoid this problem by having a Return key and an Enter key—enter items with the Return key on a Mac.

To move the cursor to a different item in an outline, use the four arrow keys.

As items are being entered, they can be moved using four commands of the Outline, Move menu:

- Outline, Move, Up

- Outline, Move, Down

- Outline, Move, Left

- Outline, Move, Right

An example outline is shown in Figure 8.5.

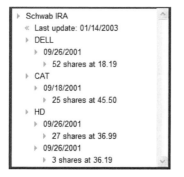

FIGURE 8.5   A stock portfolio outline.

On the Move menu, the Up, Down, Left, and Right commands move the item in that direction if such a move is possible.

Moving an item up or down changes the order of subheads that share a common parent. Moving an item left or right changes the parent of the item.

There are many instances where it isn't possible to move an item in a specified direction, depending on the placement of the item in relation to its parent and other subheads. For example, in Figure 8.5 the item "52 shares at 18.19" can only be moved to the left. It's directly below a parent, making a move to the right impossible, and it has no other subheads, preventing a move up or down. Radio keeps track of this automatically, preserving the structure of an outline by ignoring impossible requests.

When an item is successfully moved, all of its subheads move along with it, even if they are collapsed away from view.

Keyboard shortcuts for each of the move commands are shown in Table 8.1.

TABLE 8.1

Movement Shortcuts

DIRECTION	WINDOWS	MAC
Up	Ctrl+U	Cmd+U
Down	Ctrl+D	Cmd+D
Left	Ctrl+L	Cmd+L
	Shift+Tab	Shift+Tab
Right	Ctrl+R	Cmd+R
	Tab	Tab

The outliner can be used as a programmer's editor for UserTalk, Radio's built-in scripting language, and other programming languages.

To support this purpose, an item in an outline can be designated as a *comment*, a descriptive statement explaining what a script is doing at a particular place in a program. Comments will be ignored when Radio runs a UserTalk script.

The menu command Outline, Toggle Comment turns a normal outline item into a comment and vice versa. There's also a keyboard shortcut for this command: Ctrl+\ (backslash) on Windows and Cmd+\ on Macs.

The icon for a comment is a chevron character ([<<]). The outline in Figure 8.5 includes one comment: `"Last update: 01/14/2003"`.

A comment can have subheads of its own as long as all of them are comments also. Radio handles this automatically when toggling comments—if an item with three subheads is turned into a comment, all four become comments.

Later, if this item is changed from a comment to a normal item, all of its subheads will become normal items unless they were separately turned into comments at some point.

TIP

When modifying a UserTalk script, Radio developers often put a timestamp in a comment along with a description of the changes that were made on that date. To insert a timestamp containing the current date, time, and your initials in an outline, press Ctrl+4 (Windows) or Cmd+4 (Mac OS). Radio's object database includes many comments of this kind to track the development history of scripts.

To save an outline, choose the menu command File, Save. The first time the file is saved, a name can be given to the file or a default name such as `untitled.opml` or `untitled-2.opml` will be used.

Outlines are saved as OPML (Outline Processor Markup Language), a format created by UserLand for the representation of outlines. Files are given the file extension `.opml` and the MIME type `text/x-opml`.

Modifying an Outline

Radio's outliner can be used to open and edit any file in OPML format. Although these files are normally given the .opml filename extension, that's not a requirement—Radio will open any OPML file.

The outliner can open local files and files published on the Internet. Choose the menu command File, Open to load a local outline or File, or Open URL to load an outline using a URL. Outlines opened from a URL can be edited and saved locally, which does not alter the contents of the original outline.

The outliner functions in two editing modes: selection mode and content mode.

Selection mode is used primarily to work with existing items without changing their text. Items can be moved, sorted, deleted, and the like. In selection mode, the currently selected item is displayed with white text in a black box. In Figure 8.6, the outline is in selection mode and "Microsoft Bob" is selected.

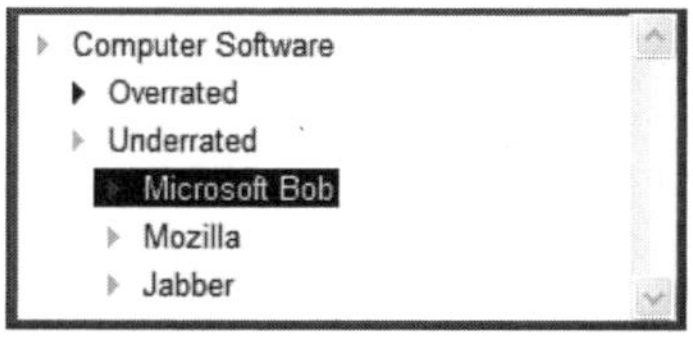

FIGURE 8.6   Outlining in selection mode.

In selection mode, the arrow keys select a different item, moving the black box around. The up and down arrows go up and down within a group of subheads, never leaving them to go to an item at a different level. The left and right arrows go up and down among any visible item regardless of level.

A mouse also can be used to select items. While in selection mode, click an item's triangle icon or click anywhere in the whitespace to the right or left of the item.

Content mode is used to make changes to the text of existing items and add new items using the keyboard. In content mode, a cursor blinks at a position in the outline.

To switch from one mode to the other, press the keypad Enter key. On a Windows laptop or another computer that lacks a keypad, press F2 to switch modes.

When an OPML file is being edited, these two modes are pretty flexible. If text is entered while the outliner is in selection mode, Radio deletes the selected item, switches to content mode, and places the new text at that position.

Many of the commands to move an item will work in both selection mode and content mode. For example, the Up, Down, Left, and Right commands can be used in either mode.

The standard cut, copy, paste, and undo functions work in either mode. They're listed in Table 8.2.

TABLE 8.2

Standard Editing Functions and Shortcuts

MENU COMMAND	WINDOWS	MAC
Edit, Cut	Ctrl+X	Cmd+X
Edit, Copy	Ctrl+C	Cmd+C
Edit, Paste	Ctrl+V	Cmd+V
Edit, Undo	Ctrl+Z	Cmd+Z

To delete the current item, use the cut command in any mode or press the Delete key while in selection mode.

In Radio, the undo command wipes out the last action taken while editing—it can be used to put items back in an outline that were deleted, remove a typo entered with the keyboard, and the like. This feature can correct only the last action.

Several commands on the Outline menu affect one or more subheads of the current item.

- The Outline, Promote command causes all subheads of the item to move up one level, becoming siblings instead.

- The Outline, Demote command causes all siblings below the item to become subheads of that item.

Figure 8.7 contains two outlines with the same items indented differently.

FIGURE 8.7   Promoting and demoting items.

The outline on the left contains a few errors that could be fixed with promotion or demotion. The outline on the right shows the effect of these corrections.

With "Asahi Shimbun" selected, the Promote command moves all of its subheads—"Hokkaido Shimbun" and "Yomiuri Shimbun"—to the left.

With "South Korea" selected, the Demote command moves the two siblings below it—"Dong-a Ilbo" and "Seoul Shimbun"—to the right, making them its subheads.

Both commands have shortcuts: Ctrl+[and Ctrl+] to promote and demote on Windows and Cmd+[and Cmd+] to promote and demote on Macs. They work in both editing modes.

These additional commands manipulate subheads and work in either mode:

- The Outline, Delete All Subheads command deletes all of the subheads of the current item.

- The Outline, Sort command sorts the current item and all of its siblings in alphabetical order.

- The Outline, Make First command moves the current item above all of its siblings.

- The Outline, Make Last command moves the current item below all of its siblings.

CAUTION

There appears to be a bug in the undo command for both the Windows and Mac OS versions of Radio. When Delete All Subheads is used to remove all subheads, undo does not bring them back.

The last two commands on the Outline menu affect two subheads at one time.

- The Outline, Join command merges the current item with the sibling below it. If the item has subheads, these will be unaffected.

- The Outline, Split command splits the current item into two items, making them siblings.

Before splitting an item, go into content mode and place the cursor at the spot where the item should be divided.

Remembering these commands is likely to take some practice; the Radio outliner is one of the most sophisticated of its kind and has a lot of "power user" features for people who have been expressing themselves in outline form for many years.

Radio also supports a more intuitive way to manipulate an outline: by using the mouse to select an item and drag it to a new location.

An item can be dragged anywhere on the outline and released, placing it (and its subheads) at a new location.

Clicking and dragging can be used to change the order of subheads and make an item a subhead of another item.

As an item is dragged around, arrow icons appear in place of the other icons (see Figure 8.8). The direction of the arrow shows what will happen if the item is released at that position. In the figure, the arrow is pointing downward to indicate that "Yomiuri Shimbun" would become a sibling right below "Asahi Shimbun." If the arrow were pointing down and to the right (compass southeast), "Yomiuri Shimbun" would become a subhead of "Asahi Shimbun" instead.

More than one item can be selected at a time before being dragged:

- To select consecutive items, hold down the Shift key while clicking the first and last item to be chosen.

- To select non-consecutive items, hold down the Ctrl key (Windows) or the Cmd key (Mac OS) and click each item.

FIGURE 8.8   Dragging an item around.

Viewing an Outline

Outlines are a versatile means of representing information because they condense a large amount of data into a small space. An outline user can see as much or as little of the data as desired by expanding and collapsing portions of the outline.

Radio outlines can be expanded and collapsed using the mouse, commands of the Outline menu, and the keyboard.

An item that has collapsed subheads is displayed with a black triangle icon in the outliner. To expand these subheads in either selection mode or content mode, press the keypad + (plus) key. To collapse subheads, press keypad - (minus).

The outline must be in selection mode for any of the remaining methods in this section to work.

An item that has collapsed subheads is displayed with a black triangle icon in the outliner. To expand these subheads, double-click the item, or choose Outline, Expand.

All of the item's subheads will become visible. If these subheads have their own subheads, they will remain collapsed. To expand everything under a particular item, choose Outline, Expand All Subheads.

To expand an entire outline at once, choose Outline, Expand Everything.

There are often times when it's useful to simplify an outline by hiding some of its items from view. To collapse the subheads of an item, double-click the item, or choose Outline, Collapse.

To collapse all of the siblings of an item, making only their parent visible, choose Outline, Collapse to Parent.

To collapse an entire outline, choose Outline, Collapse Everything.

The last contextual tricks offered by Radio's outliner are commands to hoist a portion of an outline (and dehoist it later).

Hoisting makes an item and its subheads appear as if they were the only items in the outline. The other portions of the outline still exist, but they are hidden from view and can't be modified. Choose Outline, Hoist to accomplish this.

The Outline, De-Hoist command backs out of the most recent hoisting, showing what the outline looked like beforehand.

An outline can be hoisted to reduce its visible content and then hoisted again to reduce it even further. The Outline, De-Hoist All command fully restores the visibility of an outline no matter how many times it has been successively hoisted.

Using Links in Outlines

Radio outlines can serve as hypertext documents, containing hyperlinks to URL-addressed data, such as HTML pages, XML files, OPML outlines, and RSS files.

Each link is associated with the text of an item. To add a link, select the item and choose the menu command Outline, Add Link (shortcuts: Ctrl+K on Windows and Cmd+K on Macs). A dialog box opens asking for the URL to which the link connects.

Items that have hyperlinks are displayed with a blue up-arrow icon (see Figure 8.9). To see the URL of a linked item, select the item and choose Outline, Get Info.

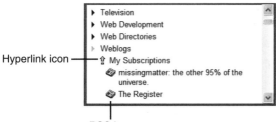

FIGURE 8.9   Creating hyperlinked outlines.

Hyperlinks are live when the outline is in selection mode. To visit an item's link, double-click the hyperlink icon, double-click the whitespace alongside the item, or press keypad + (plus).

If the link connects to a Web page or similar document, that resource will be opened in a browser.

If the link connects to an OPML or RSS file, Radio will open it in the outliner, incorporating the contents of the file seamlessly into the outline. The effect is comparable to expanding an item that has subheads; after the file loads, it expands in place as one or more subheads of the linked item.

RSS feeds have their own icon in the outliner: a small newspaper (also shown in Figure 8.9). Double-clicking the item opens the items in the feed, enabling you to use the outliner as an RSS reader.

OPML files are being employed in varied ways on Radio weblogs and other Radio-created sites.

The link feature of Radio's outliner makes it possible to use the software as a bookmark manager and publish the bookmarks on the Web in a Yahoo-style directory.

FIGURE 8.10   Managing bookmarks in an outline.

To create an outline for this purpose, group linked items together under a common parent. Give the parent a descriptive name but do not associate a link with it. One example: Provide links to several online bookstores under a parent called "Books."

Figure 8.10 shows a portion of an outline used for organizing Web bookmarks.

The bookmarks outline can have as many levels as desired. It should be saved in a folder that will be upstreamed to the Web in OPML format. One place that's suitable for this purpose, under Radio's default configuration, is its www\gems folder.

After saving the outline to an upstreaming folder, check Radio's Events page. When the outline has been published, its URL will show up in an event description.

To publish a directory using this OPML file, you place the `radio.macros.directoryFrame()` macro on a Web page managed by Radio (such as a new story). This macro takes an OPML file on the Web and renders it on a UserLand server, placing it inside an HTML `IFRAME` tag to make it appear as if it were part of a page on your site.

The macro has only one required parameter: the URL of the OPML file. Here's an example:

```
<%radio.macros.directoryFrame ("http://www.cadenhead.org/workbench/gems/
➥bookmarks.opml")%>
```

Once the story has been published, its URL will be shown on Radio's Events page.

The `directoryFrame()` macro can be called with several optional parameters to specify things such as the appearance of the directory frame. The following example specifies a frame that's 1,500 pixels tall, 600 pixels wide, and has links on the text of each item:

```
<%radio.macros.directoryFrame
("http://www.cadenhead.org/workbench/gems/
➥bookmarks.opml", height:"1500",
width:"600", flLinkText:"true")%>
```

UserLand documentation on the directoryFrame() macro can be found at this URL:

http://radio.outliners.com/directoryOutliner

Summary

This chapter introduced the core concepts of outlining and demonstrated how they were embodied by Radio UserLand. The outliner, one of the most complex in any software, supports features such as expanding, collapsing, promotion, demotion, hoisting, dehoisting, click-and-drag editing, and hypertext.

Radio's outliner can be used to represent a wide selection of data. It's employed most often to create Web documents that will be published as HTML or XML, UserTalk scripts, and items in Radio's object database.

Once the outliner has been mastered, it's a powerful way to visualize, create, and maintain textual information.

PART II

Using the Object Database

Backing Up Data

9

Radio UserLand's content-management system and all of its other features are built on top of an object database, a sophisticated data structure that contains most of the code and data that runs the software.

You can find the main object database, Radio.root, in the software's installation folder.

Most of the code that gives the software its functionality is written in the UserTalk scripting language, stored in Radio.root, and exposed to users. You can view this code to learn how Radio is programmed and even modify it yourself, at the risk of introducing bugs and altering the software's performance in other unpleasant ways.

The next three chapters explore Radio.root and the other object databases. Because these files can be an extremely perilous place for a new learner to putter around, the first topic covered is how to back up and restore the software and all of Radio's databases and files.

Running the Radio Application

Up to this point, the only user interface covered with Radio has been the desktop Web site, the set of pages on your computer that are viewed with a Web browser and served by the software.

Radio includes a Web server that delivers pages, logs requests, and errors, and receives form input. It can do all of this within a single computer or over the Internet.

The software's weblog publishing and news aggregation features are supported primarily through the desktop Web site, the interface that can be used with any Web browser.

The object database, scripting, and other expert features of the software require a second interface: the application that works behind-the-scenes as a Web server, content-management system, and news aggregator.

The Radio application, which is running in support of the desktop Web site, is normally hidden from view on Windows and runs without need of user input on any operating system.

To view the application:

- Windows: Right-click the Radio icon in the System tray and choose Open Radio (see Figure 9.1).

- Mac Classic: Choose the application with the Finder.

- Mac OS X: Click the application in the Dock.

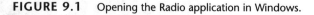

Radio Userland icon

FIGURE 9.1   Opening the Radio application in Windows.

The application's user interface consists of a menu bar and an About Radio UserLand dialog box, as shown in Figure 9.2.

If the dialog box is not visible, choose the menu command Help, About Radio UserLand (Windows), Radio, About Radio UserLand (Mac OS X), or Apple Menu, About Radio UserLand (Mac Classic).

The menu bar contains different menus based on how the software is being used. For example, as an outline is being edited, an Outline menu appears on the bar.

The About Radio UserLand dialog box displays messages about the status of the software, the resources it is using, and operations it is performing.

A useful feature of this dialog box is the status message, which you can use to ensure the software is doing what you expect as it upstreams files, retrieves RSS newsfeeds, and handles other tasks.

TIP

There's an intermittent problem with Radio in which a menu doesn't appear on Radio at times that it should. To cause the application to display missing menus, choose Tools, Developers, Fresh Menus or press Ctrl and the minus key (Windows) or Cmd and the minus key (Mac OS).

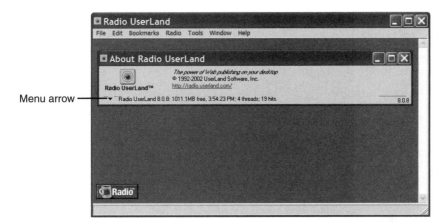

Menu arrow

FIGURE 9.2   Using the Radio application interface.

The status message is usually displayed by default. If it isn't being shown, click the Menu arrow in the About Radio UserLand dialog box and choose StatusMessage from the drop-down menu that appears.

On Windows, you can minimize the Radio application by closing the application's window. This doesn't close the application, so the desktop Web site will continue to work.

To fully shut down Radio:

- Windows: Right-click the Radio icon in the System tray and choose Exit and Shut Down Radio from the contextual menu that appears.

- Mac OS X: Choose Radio, Quit Radio.

- Mac OS Classic: Choose File, Quit.

Backing Up a Weblog

The biggest challenge in backing up Radio is knowing what you need to save. A Radio weblog consists of several kinds of files:

- Text and OPML files that are rendered as Web pages as they are upstreamed to a Web server. These files are stored in the www folder and its subfolders.

- Files that are published without modification when they are upstreamed to a server. These files are in subfolders of the www folder that have been set up for this purpose, such as the www\gems folder.

- Database files, including the main database `Radio.root` and other databases in Radio's `Tools` and `Data Files` folders.

- XML files containing backups of all weblog entries, stories, templates, and preferences. These files are saved in the `www\backups` folder.

- Web pages containing weblog entries, weblog archives, and articles. These files are created on the Web server when text and OPML files are rendered as they are upstreamed to the server.

One of the most common misconceptions about Radio, if help requests on the customer support discussion board are any indication, is that a weblog can be restored using its Web pages. New users often believe those pages are all they need if a hard drive failure or another problem knocks out the `Radio UserLand` folder or an entire hard drive.

Unfortunately, the opposite is true: The only files that aren't useful for backup purposes are the rendered Web pages.

In order to publish a weblog, Radio requires all of the files in the `www` folder, the main database `Radio.root`, and three databases in the `Data Files` folder: `aggregatorData.root`, `weblogData.root`, and `weblogsComData.root`.

The `Radio.root` file is the primary object database and is the software's most important component. It contains all of the scripts and data required to run Radio, scripts added by tools that enhance the software, and configuration data specific to your installation (for instance, the weblog ID number, user passwords, and preferences).

Although you can reinstall Radio to get a new copy of `Radio.root` and bring it up to date, all of your configuration data and tool scripts would be lost.

The `www` folder and its subfolders contain all of the source material for the published Web site aside from weblog entries, categories, and preferences that are stored in database files. The folders hold articles, preferences in `#prefs.txt` files, and upstreaming files called `#upstream.xml`.

Three databases in the `Data Files` folder should always be backed up:

- The `aggregatorData.root` database holds RSS subscriptions, preferences, and archived news items.

- The `weblogData.root` database contains all weblog entries, categories, and preferences.

- The `weblogsComData.root` database stores Weblogs.Com favorites and preferences.

The `Tools` folder contains *tools*, which are databases with scripts and data that enhance Radio's capabilities. The software comes with four tools: `manilaBloggerBridge.root`, `myPictures.root`, `staticSites.root`, and `whois.root`.

If you have installed any tools (simply by saving them in this folder) or used the ones that come with Radio, the files in this folder should be included in a backup.

Tools also use the Data Files folder to store user data and preferences, so any other databases present in that folder should be saved.

NOTE

When Radio is installed, the location of the Radio UserLand folder is stored internally in Radio.root. For this reason, when restoring the software or moving it to a new computer, the same folder location should be used.

A few other folders can contain files that require backup: new themes you have created in the Themes folder and scripts you have saved in the Macros and Web Services folders.

The easiest way to back up all of these files is to save the entire Radio UserLand folder. This can be time-consuming and cumbersome—it could be 100MB or more in size—and includes a lot of files that you can restore simply by reinstalling Radio.

However, if you have enough space on your backup drive or other storage media, reinstalling the entire folder is all that's required to restore the software.

Before backing up Radio, the software must be shut down so that all of its open database files are closed correctly.

Depending on the speed of your computer, it can take 3-5 minutes for the software to shut down completely. Radio needs this time to save recent database changes in all of the open databases.

To restore the site completely from a backup or put it on a new computer, follow these steps:

1. If you still have a Radio UserLand folder on the computer, save a backup copy of it somewhere else and delete the original folder.

2. Download a new copy of Radio from UserLand's Web site at http://radio.userland.com.

3. Install the software in the same location as before (Windows: Program Files\Radio UserLand; on Mac OS X: /Applications/Radio UserLand; on Mac Classic: :Applications (Mac OS 9):Radio UserLand).

   Do not launch it yet.

4. Copy the backup files, saving them in the same locations as before and overwriting the existing files of the same name.

5. Start Radio.

Everything should be restored. When you view the desktop home page, the most recent entries should be listed. Before publishing a new entry, make sure everything is in order. Browse the desktop site for stories, theme templates, navigator links, and other components of your site.

Restoring a Weblog from an XML Backup

If Radio is left running in the evening, the software saves all weblog entries, articles, templates, and preferences as XML files in the www\backups folder once per night between midnight and 1 a.m.

You can also perform backups manually. Visit the desktop page http://127.0.0.1:5335/system/pages/backup and click Backup Now.

These files can be upstreamed to the server hosting the site, making it possible to restore the weblog from the most recent server backup.

Backups are set with the Nightly Backups preference (click Prefs on any desktop Web page, and then click Nightly Backups). When Radio is installed, backups are saved in the backups folder, but are not upstreamed.

You can use these backup files to restore a Radio weblog that has been lost because of database corruption, hard drive failure, or other problems.

If you are hosting your weblog on a Radio Community Server and upstreaming backups to that server, you can view the backup folder. Simply add /backups to the weblog's home page URL, as in http://radio.weblogs.com/0123698/backups.

If you need to restore Radio from a server backup and you can view the backups folder on that folder, save a copy of all files in that folder. They could be overwritten inadvertently as you attempt to restore the site, leaving you without any backup files.

In order to restore a Radio weblog from an XML backup, you must know your Radio user number and password.

To restore the site, follow these steps:

1. If you still have a Radio UserLand folder on your computer, save a backup copy of it somewhere else and delete the original folder.

2. Download a new copy of Radio from UserLand's Web site at http://radio.userland.com.

3. Install the software in the same location as before. Launch it.

   The "It Worked!" page opens in a Web browser to indicate that the software has been installed successfully.

4. If you can't remember your password, try this:

   ■ In the "Forgot your usernum and password?" section, type your email address in the Email address field.

   ■ Click the Submit button below the Email address field.

   UserLand mails the user number and password to your email address.

5. Scroll down to the "Are you re-installing Radio?" section and fill out the Usernum and Password fields. Click the adjacent Submit button.

   Radio will be set up with the correct account information, but none of your old weblog entries or other data will be present yet.

   At this point, Radio still needs to upgrade the main `Radio.root` database with several updates that were released after the installation program.

6. If you're using Windows, open the Radio application (right-click the Radio icon in the System tray). It's already open on the Mac OS.

7. Choose the menu command File, Update Radio.root.

8. A dialog box opens asking whether Radio should connect to `http://radioupdates.userland.com` and download updates to `Radio.root`. Confirm this by clicking OK.

   The About Radio UserLand window displays the progress of the software update and any other activity (see Figure 9.3).

   When an update completes successfully, Radio displays a count of the number of parts that have been installed. If an update fails, Radio might not display anything in response.

FIGURE 9.3   Monitoring an attempt to update `Radio.root`.

> **CAUTION**
>
> Radio displays error messages if it cannot install a part of the upgrade. You can disregard these errors; click Continue installation to dismiss the error dialogs and to continue setting up the database.

9. Repeat steps 7–8 until Radio finishes an update by displaying the message: "0 new parts loaded from 'radioupdates.userland.com'." This indicates that there are no more updates left to install.

   At this point, there will now be a `www\backups` folder on your computer. The files in this folder will prevent the weblog from being restored using the server backup.

10. Delete the `backups` folder.

11. Visit the desktop Web page `http://127.0.0.1:5335/system/pages/backup`.

12. Click the Restore Now button and confirm the choice on the next page.

   A Web page displays the current status of the restore procedure, refreshing as more parts of the weblog are restored on your computer.

   When it's done, you'll see the message: "Your preferences, weblog posts, templates, stories and aggregator subscriptions have been restored."

If the weblog and all of its files were restored successfully, you'll be able to see your most recent entries on the desktop home page. Look around the desktop site for stories, theme templates, and navigator links.

Summary

With proper backups, it's safe to begin exploring `Radio.root` and the other object databases that you can view and edit with Radio UserLand.

Although the desktop Web site and Radio's file system features (such as upstreaming) contain a large number of features, most functionality offered by the software is contained within the main object database and the scripts within it.

Radio's code, which you can view and modify, is written in UserTalk, the scripting language created by UserLand Software for all of its publishing and information aggregation products.

Learning to work with object databases is the first step towards becoming a UserTalk programmer.

Exploring the Object Database

10

The most important component of Radio UserLand is a multiple-megabyte file called Radio.root.

Radio.root, which is located in the same folder as the Radio application, is a persistent hierarchical object database that holds scripts, data, outlines, and other kinds of information.

The scripts in the database, written in the UserTalk language devised by UserLand Software, comprise most of the software's functionality—storing, retrieving, and manipulating the data contained within the file.

Because these scripts can be viewed and modified without restriction, exploring the object database is a good way to begin learning how to write scripts to extend Radio's capabilities.

Viewing the Object Database

UserLand Software considers the object database to be the foundation of all of its software, beginning with the first version of Frontier, a content-management and information publishing product that preceded Radio.

"Because the object database came before anything else, it's very tightly integrated with everything else, with real synergies," explains UserLand founder Dave Winer. "When we started developing Frontier in 1988, the very first feature we built was the object database. It's the storage system for Frontier scripts, but it's very different from the kinds of storage systems usually available in scripting environments."

Name	Value	Kind
▶ examples	55 items	table
▶ scratchpad	on disk	table
▶ suites	5 items	table
▶ system	13 items	table
▶ user	28 items	table
▶ websites	8 items	table
▶ workspace	3 items	table
▹ notepad	on disk	outline
▹ saveCopyOpenDatabases	on disk	script
userlandSamples	17 items	table
▹ blogger	on disk	table
▹ callNewsIsFree	on disk	script
▹ callSoapExamples	on disk	script
▹ clonePublicRadioFiles	on disk	script

Kind ▼   Sort ▼

FIGURE 10.1   Editing the object database
`Radio.root`.

Radio's main object database, often called the ODB, is a loosely organized and extremely flexible means of representing data.

It's a departure from relational databases that consist of highly structured files organized into tables, records, and fields, as typified by Microsoft Access, FileMaker Pro, and many other popular database programs.

Radio's database can be viewed as an outline, which enables it to be browsed and modified with the software's sophisticated outliner. To view and edit the database, with the Radio application open, choose the menu command Windows, Radio.root.

Because the database is represented as a hierarchical outline, the capabilities of Radio's outliner can be employed on the database. Items can be renamed, deleted, and moved; child subheads can be expanded, collapsed, promoted, and demoted; and so on.

NOTE

The general use of Radio's outliner is described extensively in Chapter 8, "Creating Outlines." This chapter focuses on the ways in which a database outline is different from other outlines edited with the software.

As shown in Figure 10.1, a database differs in appearance from other outlines. It is displayed as a table with three columns:

- Name, the name of an item in the database

- Value, the size of the item (in terms of items for tables, lines for scripts, and the like) or on disk, which indicates the item has not been loaded into memory yet, making a more precise size count unavailable

- Kind, the type of information the item represents

Many of the items in the database are *tables*, items whose purpose is to contain their own child items. These children can be tables or any other kind of information the database might hold.

The database can hold a sizeable hierarchy of tables—up to 25 levels deep—and be as large as 2GB.

For performance reasons, Radio only loads parts of the database into memory as they are needed.

When the object database is first opened, it displays seven tables: examples, scratchpad, suites, system, user, websites, and workspace.

Within these tables lie most of the code that runs the Radio application and the features covered during Part I: the content-management system tailor made for the production of weblogs, news aggregator for RSS newsfeed reading, and the rest of its considerable feature set. Even the menus on top of the menu bar are created, customized, and operated using scripts located within these tables. Radio consists of several layers: a core kernel of fast C code that runs the application and database, the UserTalk scripts and data in the database run by that kernel, and the desktop Web site run by some of those scripts.

Although the database is essential to the performance of the software and is regularly updated by UserLand Software, it's also intended as a workspace and storage place for your own use. You're encouraged to make parts of it your own, as long as you know where you can safely work and what you should avoid touching at all. (At this point, you're probably beginning to recognize why the chapter on backing up the database preceded all of the chapters on using it.)

The tables in the object database can be expanded and collapsed as you can any item in an outline (double-click an item, use the numeric keypad's + and - keys, choose Outline, Expand or Outline, Collapse, and so on).

When it is first opened, the object database is displayed as a table because the *root*, the parent of all items in the database, is itself a table.

The seven root tables serve the following purposes:

- The system table provides most of Radio's core functionality. The contents of this table are updated frequently by UserLand Software in automatic nightly upgrades.

  This table is a good place to learn about Radio's capabilities (and UserTalk), but any changes you make could be overwritten at any time by UserLand.

- The user table holds numerous user preferences and data specific to your installation of Radio, such as your serial number, weblog ID number, and passwords.

  Radio can be customized in numerous ways by editing the contents of this table. For example, the user.menus table contains several custom menus for the Radio application: Bookmarks, Radio, and Tools. You can edit this table to modify these menus or add new ones to the program's menu bar.

  Many preferences that customize Radio are in the user.prefs and user.radio.prefs table. Some of these preferences can be set using the Prefs page of the desktop Web site, but others can be changed only by editing the database.

- The `suites` table extends Radio's capabilities in a manner similar to tools, the stand-alone databases stored in Radio's `Tools` folder.

   Many of the tables here are used by WebEdit, a client-server suite for editing Radio and Frontier databases over the Internet in collaboration with other developers.

- The `workspace` table provides a place for projects that are currently in development and experimental projects offered for public testing by UserLand.

   This is a good place for your own personal projects and simple scripts offered by other Radio and Frontier users.

- The `websites` table holds Web sites that are stored in the database and published using the Static Sites tool.

   Radio's weblog features are an extension of a template-based Web site publishing system—any kind of site can be created and maintained with the software.

   Sites can be created as files, as Radio does in the production of weblogs, or saved in tables. The `websites` table offers a place for the latter.

- The `scratchpad` table serves as a holding place for transitory data that doesn't need to be kept around and can be overwritten at any time.

- The `examples` table demonstrates how dozens of different data types can be represented in the object database.

   Radio's `Table` menu can be used to create each of the data types. All of these are contained in `examples`, which is used in some of UserLand's online documentation.

An important thing to note about the main object database is the fact that UserLand Software is busy working there at all times.

UserLand can update the object database automatically each night if Radio is running, a preference that is enabled when the software is installed (using the Periodic updates preference—click Prefs on any desktop Web page, and then click Periodic updates). The database also can be updated manually: click File, Update `Radio.root`.

When the database is updated, specific items and their children will be added or modified while the rest of the database is left alone. If you make changes to a part of the database that is later updated by UserLand, your work will be overwritten and cannot be recovered (aside from restoring a backup file and losing the benefit of the update).

UserLand publishes an RSS newsfeed documenting its database changes, which may happen as frequently as several times a week. To track the "Radio.root updates" feed with the news aggregator, subscribe to the URL `http://static.userland.com/updatelogs/radio.xml`.

Most of the changes are made in the system table, which delivers most of Radio's functionality. UserLand issues bug fixes, rewrites scripts, and offers new features here frequently—it's a good idea to leave this table alone.

Occasionally, UserLand updates something in the user table—most recently to modify a preference that affected a script in the system table.

The best way to avoid collisions with UserLand is to use the scratchpad table for temporary data and the workspace table for personal projects and simple scripts you'd like to call from a Web page or template.

There is one part of the workspace table that might be changed—workspace.userLandSamples—which contains experimental scripts released by UserLand.

In Chapter 20, "Creating and Distributing Tools," you create your own object database and completely avoid the risk of losing work in an update to Radio.root.

Using the Object Database

The object database is edited like any other outline. You can rename items and change their values directly in the outliner.

> **TIP**
>
> In an excellent background tutorial on the object database, Phillip Suh offers a good suggestion for carving out your own space in the database: Create a table in workspace with your initials, putting your own projects there until you give them a more permanent home later.
>
> The tutorial was written in 1999 for an old version of Frontier, but most of it remains applicable to Radio. It's on the Web at http://old.scriptmeridian.org/tutorials/odb.

To add an item to a table, select an item and press the keyboard Enter key (Windows) or Return key (Mac OS). A dummy item of the form Item #x is added with (nil) as the value and (none) as the data type.

An existing item can be duplicated using copy (Ctrl+C or Cmd+C) and paste (Ctrl+V or Cmd+V). A dialog box appears asking whether to duplicate the item, which saves it under the same name with # and a number tacked on.

To change the value of a string, Boolean, or another simple value, click once in the Value column of that item. A cursor appears, enabling the existing text to be edited.

Working with data types is covered in Chapter 11, "Creating New Tables and Other Data."

Because the object database is persistent, any changes made as it is edited will be saved automatically within minutes. The only time this does not occur is when Radio crashes before the most recent changes can be saved, but in my experience, these kinds of problems are rare.

CAUTION

Persistence, an extremely beneficial trait when the object database is being accessed in a UserTalk script, can be nerve-wracking for a first-time user navigating its contents for the first time—any fumble-thumbed mistake can alter or remove something Radio needs to function properly.

One of the root tables, `scratchpad`, is perfect for experimentation and testing. Radio doesn't put anything inside that table it needs to keep around.

In many instances, you can undo the most recent edit by selecting Edit, Undo, Ctrl+Z (Windows), or Cmd+Z (Mac OS).

As you drill down into the database, expanding tables to view their contents, you'll discover quickly how much of the database consists of tables within tables.

The object database holds a giant hierarchy of tables that serves two purposes.

First, the tables enable the database to be organized into increasingly more specific categories. Figure 10.2 shows the object database with part of the `system` table expanded.

As you can see in Figure 10.2, the `system` table contains several tables that represent different functionality in Radio. One of these is the `environment` table, which holds items related to the operating system running the software. This table holds items such as `isWindows`, a Boolean value that's `true` if Radio is running on Windows, and `osFlavor`, a string that provides some information about the version of the operating system in use.

Name	Value	Kind
▸ system	13 items	table
▸ agents	6 items	table
▸ callbacks	22 items	table
▸ compiler	6 items	system..
▸ deskscripts	on disk	table
▸ environment	14 items	system..
▸ browserControlEnabled	true	boolean
▸ isMac	false	boolean
▸ isWindows	true	boolean
▸ osFlavor	NT	string [2]

Kind: ▾   Sort: ▾

FIGURE 10.2   Viewing items in the `system` table.

Even though the object database is organized loosely, the parent-child relationships represented by an outline serve a descriptive function.

The second purpose of the hierarchy of tables is to provide an address for each item in the database, which can be used to refer to that item in a UserTalk script, a macro on a page template, Web service call, and many other ways.

The name of each item in the database must start with a letter and can contain letters, numbers, and underscore characters ("_"). It should be no longer than 32 characters.

Every item in the object database has a unique address. Items follow a simple dot-notation addressing convention: The name of an item is prefixed by the name of its parent table followed by a period. Because this is true of the parent, and its parent, and so on, the result is a series of names separated by periods from the root down to the item.

For example, the expanded outline in Figure 10.2 shows a portion of the `system` table. This table contains the tables `system.agents` and `system.environment`. The latter table contains Boolean values named `system.environment.isMac` and `system.environment.isWindows`, and a string named `system.environment.osFlavor`.

To use or create an item in the database, refer to its address.

You can open the database at an address using the Jump feature:

1. Press Ctrl+J on Windows, Cmd+J on Mac OS, or choose Tools, Developers, Jump.

   A dialog box opens.

2. In the Enter an Address to Jump to field, enter the address.

   If the address is a table, Radio opens a window with the database *hoisted* to that table (in other words, hiding its parent, sibling items, and anything else in the database). An example is shown in Figure 10.3.

   If the address is not a table, Radio opens a window hoisted to its parent.

   There's no way to dehoist the outline shown in this window to see the rest of the database.

3. To bookmark this location in the table, making it easy to return to later, choose Bookmarks, Add Bookmark.

   A dialog box opens to confirm the address.

4. Click OK.

   The address appears as an item in the Bookmarks menu.

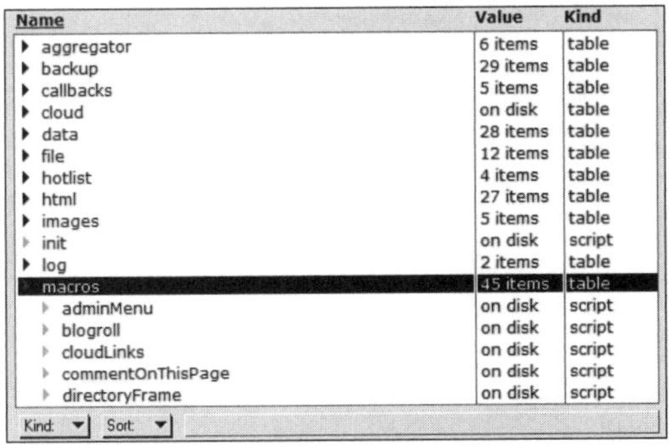

Name	Value	Kind
▶ aggregator	6 items	table
▶ backup	29 items	table
▶ callbacks	5 items	table
▶ cloud	on disk	table
▶ data	28 items	table
▶ file	12 items	table
▶ hotlist	4 items	table
▶ html	27 items	table
▶ images	5 items	table
▶ init	on disk	script
▶ log	2 items	table
macros	45 items	table
▷ adminMenu	on disk	script
▷ blogroll	on disk	script
▷ cloudLinks	on disk	script
▷ commentOnThisPage	on disk	script
▷ directoryFrame	on disk	script

Kind: ▼   Sort: ▼

FIGURE 10.3   Viewing part of the object database.

You also can use an address in the database to call scripts and refer to data in macros.

For example, you could add the following macro to a Web page or template in Radio:

```
<p>OS Flavor:
<%system.environment.osFlavor%>
```

When the page is rendered, the macro will be replaced with the string value of that database item (on Windows NT or XP, it equals "NT").

The same kind of reference can be used to call UserTalk scripts contained within the database. The template files contained in Radio's default theme call several scripts, including this one:

```
<%radio.macros.getLastUpdate()%>
```

This script returns a string containing a timestamp of the page's last update, in the form 5/25/2003; 4:11:45 PM.

This macro calls one of the scripts in the `system.verbs.builtins.radio.macros` table, `getLastUpdate()`.

It could also be called by the full name, as in this example:

```
<%system.verbs.builtins.radio.macros.getLastUpdate()%>
```

The shorter call can be used because the `system.verbs.builtins` table is in Radio's *path*, the list of places it looks for an address.

The path includes each of the following locations:

- The root table
- Any of the following tables:

  `system.verbs.globals`

  `system.macintosh.globals (Mac OS only)`

  `system.verbs.builtins`

  `system.compiler.kernel.lang`

  `system.macintosh (Mac OS only)`

  `system.compiler.kernel`

  `system.verbs.constants`

  `system.macintosh.constants (Mac OS only)`

  `suites`

  `system.verbs.apps`

  `system`

  `system.extensions`

  `system.verbs.colors`

  `system.compiler.files`

- Database files in Radio's `Tools` and `Data Files` folders

Radio keeps looking in this list, from top to bottom, until it finds a valid address. In the example of `radio.macros.getLastUpdate()`, the following prospective addresses are reviewed:

- `radio.macros.getLastUpdate` (invalid, keep looking)
- `system.verbs.globals.radio.macros.getLastUpdate` (invalid, keep looking)
- `system.verbs.builtins.radio.macros.getLastUpdate` (valid)

The path helps to avoid one of the limitations of Radio's object database: No address can be represented as a string more than 255 characters long.

Modifying User Preferences in the Database

The Prefs page of Radio's desktop Web site contains several dozen preferences that affect how the software functions. Although a great deal of customization can be achieved by modifying these preferences, there are other things that you can alter by carefully editing some of the tables in the main object database.

The user.radio.prefs table contains more than 50 items that you can edit to change Radio's behavior. Many of these can be edited from the desktop Web site, but others are available only by editing the database:

- browserBasedEditorSize: the number of rows in the text editor of the desktop home page (default: 9)

- flSystemEditor: a Boolean that equals true if an Edit This Page button should be displayed on all of the standard pages of the desktop Web site such as the Prefs and Events pages, making it possible to edit them with the Web browser (default: false, so no button is displayed)

- indexFileNames: a table containing the names that might be used for the main page in a folder of the desktop Web site (default: index.opml, index.txt, and index.html, in that order)

- passwords: a table containing the passwords that are created and managed with the Passwords and New Passwords preferences (no default)

CAUTION

Although permissible names start with a letter and contain alphanumeric characters and underscores, the Radio database is filled with names that break this rule.

The most common illegal names that turn up in the database are *directives*, preferences that begin with a pound character (#).

Illegally named items can be used in an address by surrounding them with brackets and quotation marks—for example, scratchpad.["Illegal Name"] refers to an item in the scratchpad table with the name Illegal Name.

NOTE

The passwords in the user.radio.prefs.passwords table show up as binary-encoded text in the Value column. To see the actual password, choose the item, press Ctrl+C or Cmd+C to copy it, and then paste it from the Clipboard using Ctrl+V or Cmd+V to a new outline or text document.

- rsdXmlFilePath: the relative URL of the XML file in the weblog that indicates its support for Really Simple Discoverability, a way for software to find out how to work with weblog publishing software (default: gems/rsd.xml)

- typesToRender: a table containing the MIME types for files that Radio should render as Web pages when upstreaming (default: text/plain and text/x-opml)

Summary

The first step in becoming a Radio UserLand developer is to explore Radio.root, the object database that comprises most of the program's core functionality.

The hierarchical, persistent database holds many kinds of data and scripts written in the UserTalk language.

In the database, thousands of lines of source code can be viewed and modified, enabling new programmers to learn from the techniques UserLand used to create the software's weblog publishing system, news aggregator, and other features.

Creating New Tables and Other Data

An object database in Radio UserLand is a one-size-fits-all container for information.

Any kind of data you might conceivably need can be stored in these loosely organized, hierarchical databases—individual elements, such as strings, characters, and integers, and more complex elements, such as scripts, outlines, and word processing text.

Every item in the database is an object that holds a value of a specific data type, but in most cases this type can be changed at any time—Radio's database, like the UserTalk scripting language used to work with it, is loosely typed.

For those who are unfamiliar with this distinction, a loosely typed programming language is one in which converting data into different forms is more important than controlling the range of values the data can express.

Everything in Radio's object databases is an object, which is assigned a data type that describes the value that it holds.

Editing the Object Database

An object database is opened for editing in Radio by choosing one of the commands on the Window menu. For example, to edit the main object database, open the application and choose Window, Radio.root.

A database is represented as a hierarchical outline with three columns: Name, the item's identifier; Value, the item's value or size; and Kind, the item's data type. An example is shown in Figure 11.1.

Name	Value	Kind
▷ examples	69 items	table
▷ age	41	number
▷ amplitude	255	number
▷ blue	91	number
▷ cleanupWindows	on disk	script
▷ counter	on disk	script
▷ countTables	on disk	script
▶ destTable	on disk	table
▷ dir	up	direction
▶ docs	on disk	table
▷ duration	2	number
▷ filterExample	on disk	script
▷ flag	true	boolean

Kind ▼   Sort ▼

FIGURE 11.1   Editing a database with Radio.

The object database consists of a main table, called the *root*, and a hierarchy of subtables that can be up to 25 levels deep.

Radio's outliner features can be used to make changes to the database. Items can be moved around, renamed, or deleted; tables can be expanded and collapsed; and items can be promoted or demoted.

There are a few exceptions: Unlike other outline items, the elements of a database cannot be hoisted, dehoisted, joined, or split.

The child items contained in a table can be expanded for display or collapsed away from view, making it possible to see as much or as little of the table hierarchy as desired. Collapsing a table hides everything below it in the hierarchy.

Each item in the database is marked by a small triangle icon. A table has a black triangle when it contains collapsed subheads (such as the destTable item in Figure 11.1) and a gray triangle when it has expanded subheads or no subheads at all (such as the examples item in the same figure).

Data can be placed at any level of a table. Figure 11.1 shows 12 child items contained within the examples table, including an age item with the numeric value 41, a dir item with the value up, and a flag item with the Boolean value of true. There also are subtables, such as destTable, and several scripts, which are executable UserTalk programs.

The Radio application can be used to create and edit each of the data types present in UserTalk, the software's scripting language.

The contents of an item's Value column depend on whether it can be edited with the table outliner. The database can hold scalar or non-scalar data types, and all but five of which hold their values in the Value column.

Scalars are data types that store a single unit such as a floating-point number, Boolean value, or character. *Non-scalars*, which are called *aggregates* in some programming languages, are data types that collect multiple units together. Examples include lists, x,y point coordinates, and RGB color values.

The values of all scalars and most non-scalars are displayed in the Value column of a database table.

If you see a value there, it can be edited directly: Click once in the column. A cursor appears at the spot clicked, enabling the existing value to be replaced. To save the new value, press the keyboard Enter key (Windows) or either the Return or keypad Enter keys (Mac OS).

When you are editing an item's value directly, Radio will only store values that can be represented by that data type.

For example, the number data type can hold long integers with a value ranging from a minimum of -2,147,483,648 to a maximum of 2,147,483,647. If the value of a number item was entered as 3000000000, Radio changes it to a permissible value, -1294967296.

Items can be added to a table in several ways. One is to use the commands of the Table menu. To add a new subtable to a table, follow these steps:

NOTE

Why -1,294,967,296? Like many programming languages, UserTalk handles out-of-bounds numbers by wrapping around to the other boundary—in this case going from 2,147,483,647 to -2,147,483,648—and counting further from there.

The value 3,000,000,000 is 852,516,352 too high to be represented as a long integer in UserTalk. Adding that number to the other boundary— -2,147,483,648—results in -1,294,967,296.

- Choose any of the items that belong to the parent table. Click an item's triangle icon or use the arrow keys to move to it.

  The selected item will be displayed in a black box with white text.

- Choose the menu command Table, New Sub-Table.

  A dialog box asks for a name to assign to the new table.

- You can keep the suggested name—newTable—or replace it with something else.

  Each item in a table must have a name that is unique to that table, starts with a letter, and contains only letters, numbers, and underscore characters ("_"). It can be up to 255 characters.

  Radio allows spaces and other characters to be used, but they're more difficult to refer to in UserTalk scripts and macros.

- Click OK to choose the name.

  The new subtable appears inside the parent table.

There are five non-scalar data types that are edited in their own windows: outlines, menu bars, scripts, tables, and wp text (the WP stands for *word processing*).

When these data types are present in a table, their Value columns contain the words on disk if they haven't been loaded from memory—for performance reasons, Radio only loads parts of the database when they are in use.

When one of these items has been loaded, the Value column displays its size: Tables show a count of their child items, outlines and scripts a line count, menu bars an item count, and word processing text a character count. This value cannot be edited.

Items can be added to the table in several ways:

- Choosing one of the menu commands of the Table menu.

- Using copy and paste:

    1. Choose the item to copy. Click the item's icon once or use the arrow keys to move to it.

    2. Copy it to the Clipboard. Press Ctrl+C (Windows) or Cmd+C (Mac OS).

    3. If the new item should be placed in a different table than the original, choose any item in the new table.

    4. Paste the new item from the Clipboard. Press Ctrl+V (Windows) or Cmd+V (Mac OS).

       If the item has the same name as something that's already in the table, a dialog box asks whether it should replace or duplicate the item. Click Duplicate to add the new item with a name of the form originalItemName #x.

- Adding a new item with an undefined data type:

    1. Choose an item that will be directly above the new item. Click the item's triangle icon once or use the arrow keys to move to it.

    2. Press the keyboard Enter (Windows) or Return (Mac OS) key.

       A new item will be added with the name item # followed by a number (to prevent two items from having the same name).

       The item will have the value (nil) and data type (none), as shown in Figure 11.2.

    3. Choose a data type for the item:

       - If it is a table, outline, script, menu bar, or wp text, double-click the item.

         A dialog box asks which of these data types should be used. Choose one and click the Zoom button. The item's editing window opens.

       - For any other data type, click the Kind button.

         A context menu displays each data type that can be assigned to the item. Select the desired type.

Name	Value	Kind
▷ examples	74 items	table
▷ age	41	number
▷ amplitude	255	number
▷ blue	91	number
▷ cleanupWindows	on disk	script
▷ counter	on disk	script
▷ countTables	on disk	script
▷ destTable	0 items	table
▷ item #1	(nil)	(none)
▷ dir	up	direction
▷ docs	1 item	table
▷ duration	2	number
▷ filterExample	on disk	script
▷ flag	true	boolean

Kind: ▼   Sort: ▼

Kind button

FIGURE 11.2   Adding unknown items to a table.

Creating Simple Data in the Outliner

A look at Radio's Table menu will illustrate how many data types can be stored in an object database.

The values of all but five of these data types are displayed in the Value column of a table outline and can be changed by clicking once in the column, using the keyboard to edit it, and then pressing Enter from the keyboard.

The simplest data to work with in the database are scalars:

- address (choose Table, New Scalar, Address), a pointer to an address in the database, which is preceding by an at character (@); example: @user.prefs.mailAddress.

- boolean (choose Table, New Scalar, Boolean), the boolean values true or false; Radio also will accept numeric values, converting 0 to false and any other value to true.

- char (choose Table, New Scalar, Character), a single character; example: M.

- date (choose Table, New Scalar, Date), a timestamp in the format 6/5/03; 2:18:57 PM; represented internally as a long integer containing the number of seconds since midnight on 1/1/1904.

- direction (choose Table, New Scalar, Direction), a literal that holds one of the following directional values: up, down, left, right, nodirection, flatup, flatdown, pageup, pagedown, pageleft, or pageright.

- double (choose Table, New Scalar, Float), a double-precision floating-point number accurate to about 19 digits; example: 3.1415926535897932.

- number (choose Table, New Scalar, Number), a long integer ranging from -2,147,483,648 to -2,147,483,648.

- string (choose Table, New Scalar, String), a string of characters.

The table outliner also can be used to edit several non-scalar data types:

> **CAUTION**
>
> Although strings are classified as scalars in Radio, they can contain more than one line of text in some instances. Only one line is visible at any time in the Value column—use the up and down arrow keys to see other lines, or more conveniently, convert the item from a string into wp text—select the item by clicking its triangle icon, click the Kind button, and then choose WP-Text from the pop-up menu that appears.

- binary (choose Table, New Special, Binary), a text encoding that enables binary data to be stored in the database; example: 0x42756C6C204D616E6375736F is the encoded form of the string "Bull Mancuso".

- filespec (choose Table, New Special, File Spec), a file path and name; example: C:\\Program Files\\Radio UserLand\\www\\index.txt.

- list (choose Table, New Special, List), a list of items of any scalar type surrounded by curly braces ("{" and "}") and separated by commas; examples: {1, 2, 3, 4, 5} and {"April", "May", "June"}.

- point (choose Table, New Special, Point), a set of two short integers that represent a point in an x,y coordinate system; example: 14,30.

- record (choose Table, New Special, Record), a list of scalar items similar to a list with an extra feature: each item can have a four-character name surrounded by quotation marks; example: {"city":"Jacksonville", "stat":"Florida"}.

- rect (choose Table, New Special, Rectangle), a set of four short integers that represent the top, left, bottom, and right extremes of a rectangle; example: 10,30,110,230.

- rgb (choose Table, New Special, Color), a set of three short integers that represent a color in the sRGB color space; hexadecimal values can be specified by preceding them with 0x; examples: 255,204,153 and 0xFF, 0xCC, 0x99, which are the same butterscotch hue.

- string4 (choose Table, New Special, String4), four-character string literals surrounded by single quotation marks; they are used internally by Radio as identifiers for object data types and other purposes; examples: 'JPEG', 'tabl', 'long'.

NOTE

Values can be converted easily from one data type to another, a process that Radio calls *coercion*.

Choose the item to convert by clicking its triangle icon, and then click the Kind button. The pop-up menu that appears shows you the data types to which the item can be coerced. Some menu commands will be enabled and others will be disabled.

Select a data type from the menu to convert the item.

Radio uses string4 identifiers to indicate the data type of encoded binary data, displaying this in the Kind column of a table outline alongside the word binary. Some examples are GIF graphics (GIFf), JPEG graphics (JPEG), strings (TEXT), RGB values (sRGB), and unknown data (????).

Users of the Mac OS versions of Radio have several additional non-scalar data types:

- alias (choose Table, New Mac Type, Alias), a shortcut to a file or folder; example: System:System Folder:Finder.

- card (choose Table, New Mac Type, Card), a card graphical user interface that works with MacBird, a card-based interface editor developed by UserLand for Mac OS.

- enumerator (choose Table, New Mac Type, Enumerator), four-character string literals comparable to the string4 data type.

- object spec (choose Table, New Mac Type, Object Spec), a text encoding comparable to the binary data type.

- pattern (choose Table, New Mac Type, Pattern), a 16-by-16 bitmap represented as a 16-digit hexadecimal number; this data type is rarely, if ever, employed.

Although menu options are present for these data types on the Windows version of Radio (and can be chosen), they work only on Mac OS.

Creating Outline-Based Data

In the object database, five data types are too complex to be created in a table's Value column. Instead, they are edited in a separate outliner window or text editor.

These data types are tables and four other non-scalars:

- Outlines (choose Table, New Outline), hierarchical lists of items edited with Radio's built-in outliner

- Scripts (choose Table, New Script), executable UserTalk scripts that also are edited as outlines

- WP Text (choose Table, New Text), word processing text in plain-text format

- Menu bars (choose Table, New MenuBar), drop-down menus that can be associated with the Radio application's menu bar

Outlines stored within a table are edited like any other outline, a process described during Chapter 8, "Creating Outlines." Scripts are covered in Part III, "Writing Scripts with UserTalk."

Creating Menus

Menu bars are drop-down and pop-up menus that appear across the top of the Radio application and in the Tools menu, which has an item for each enhancement program installed with the application.

As you might have noticed while using the application, Radio has an extremely fluid menu bar. There are fixed menus that always appear, such as the File and Help menus, and modal menus that appear only when they are needed. An example of the latter is the Outline menu, which appears only when the outliner is open.

You can extend the functionality of Radio by adding your own modal menus and making changes to the existing menus (although the latter requires editing parts of the object database that belong to UserLand, such as the system table, which is problematic because your work can be wiped out whenever UserLand updates the database).

Menu bars are edited as outlines, as shown in the examples.web window in Figure 11.3.

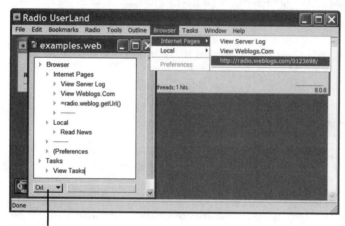

Shortcut key button

FIGURE 11.3   Editing a menu bar.

As menu bars are being created, they appear immediately on the application's menu bar for testing. In Figure 11.3, the menu being edited in the examples.web window creates the Browser menu shown to its right.

The text of each outline item forms the name of a menu element, with a few special wrinkles thrown in for unusual menu items.

The hierarchy of the menu bar outline determines the placement of menus and their items. If a menu is used on the application's menu bar, items in the root of the outline become elements on the bar—for example, the Browser and Tasks items in Figure 11.3.

Children of root items form the main drop-down menus for these items. Levels below that become additional pop-up menus, nested as deep as desired.

If a menu item consists of a single hyphen, it will be displayed as a separator. In Figure 11.3, one appears on the Browser menu below the Local element.

Menu items preceded with an open-paren-thesis character ("(") will be disabled. (Presumably, they will be enabled through a UserTalk script when appropriate.)

A menu item that is preceded with an equals character ("=") is replaced with the result of the UserTalk expression that follows it. This is comparable to expand-ing macros in templates—the output of a UserTalk statement or script call will be used as the menu element's text.

The example menu in Figure 11.3 contains one expression-based menu item:

```
=radio.weblog.getUrl()
```

The `radio.weblog.getUrl()` script returns the URL of your weblog's home page. In the example shown in the aforementioned figure, the menu item `http://radio.weblogs.com/0123698/` was created with this expression.

When an expression appears in a drop-down menu, it will be evaluated each time the menu is opened. When it appears on the application's menu bar, it is evaluated only once—at the point at which the menu is added to the menu bar.

Command keys, which can be used to choose a menu command with the keyboard instead of the mouse, can be associated with each menu item. Choose the item in the outline, click the Command Key button at the bottom-left corner of the outliner window, and then choose Set Command Key.

When you set a command key for a menu item, the key appears on the menu next to that element. By pressing the key while pressing the Ctrl key (Windows) or Cmd key (Mac OS), you can access the associated menu command.

Radio doesn't ensure that a command key is used only once in the menus of the application. Instead, when a key is pressed it looks at the menus from right to left, applying the key to the first command that matches.

A UserTalk script is associated with each menu item to make something happen when it is selected. Scripts can be executed for any element other than separators and the menu titles on Radio's menu bar.

To begin creating a script for a menu element, double-click its triangle icon in the outliner or select the item and press Enter (Windows) or Cmd+Enter (Mac OS). A script window opens, as shown in Figure 11.4.

FIGURE 11.4   Editing a menu element's UserTalk script.

The script for a menu element often is just a single line that calls another script in the database. In Figure 11.4, the `radio.menuCommands.openPage()` script is being called to cause Radio to open a Web page with the default Web browser.

There's no limit to the number of lines a menu script can contain. The disadvantage to creating an elaborate script for a menu element is that there's no way to call this script in other UserTalk scripts or in a Web page macro—it has no address in the database.

CAUTION

There might be times that Radio does not display a modal menu that you need. To correct this problem, choose Tools, Developers, Fresh Menus.

Creating Text

Text can be created in Radio using the data type wp text, which is short for word processing text.

When you double-click a wp text item's triangle icon, an editor opens with the contents of the document, as shown in Figure 11.5.

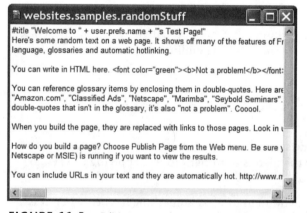

FIGURE 11.5   Editing a text document in Radio.

The editor differs in the two versions of Radio—Mac OS Classic users have alignment and tab stop features that are absent from Windows and Mac OS X. In all cases, it's a simple word processor without a lot of formatting features beyond the capability to set the font, size, and margins.

Formatting applied to text does not control how it will be presented on a Web page—HTML markup must be used to specify fonts and other presentation effects.

When the editor is open, the WP menu appears on the application's menu bar and offers these features:

- Choose WP, Uppercase or WP, Lowercase to change the capitalization of selected text.

- Choose WP, Fix Hard Returns to add blank lines between paragraphs in selected text.

- Choose WP, Margins Fit Window to rearrange all text so that the right margin is inside the right edge of the window.

- Choose WP, Save as Plain Text to save the text in a file outside of the database.

The Edit menu can be used to adjust the font and size of text.

For font changes, select the text that should be displayed in a new font, choose Edit, Font, and then choose one of the fonts installed on your computer.

Choose the commands of the Edit, Size menu to set text to 9, 10, 12, 14, 18, or 24 point. For other sizes, choose Edit, Size, Custom, and then enter the desired size in the dialog box that appears.

Several font-and-size shortcuts are available on the Edit, Common Styles menu, which has commands for common font and point sizes.

Unlike other word processors, Radio saves changes automatically. When you close the editor, the text is committed to the database.

The editor also supports several editing keys:

- Cut, copy, and paste with Ctrl+X, Ctrl+C, Ctrl+V (Windows) and Cmd+X, Cmd+C, and Cmd+V (Mac OS).

- Moving from word to word: Hold down Ctrl (Windows) or Option (Mac OS) and use the left and right arrow keys.

Summary

Radio UserLand object databases hold objects that store values of more than two dozen data types, ranging from simple scalars, such as points and strings to complex non-scalars, such as outlines, menu bars, and scripts.

Because Radio and the UserTalk programming language are loosely typed in their management of data, it's easy to convert any item from one data type to another. This approach values the capability to transform data, which is consistent with the organizational structure of the database itself.

Once you have become familiar with all the different kinds of information the database can hold, you'll be ready to begin creating and manipulating that data in UserTalk scripts.

PART III

Writing Scripts with UserTalk

Editing a New Script

12

Although Radio UserLand offers an impressive array of weblog publishing, information aggregation, content management, and database features, the killer app is the programming platform upon which these features was built.

At its core, Radio is an environment for the rapid development of Internet software: Web applications, XML-RPC and SOAP Web services, and client/server programs that make use of HTTP, FTP, SMTP, POP, and other common protocols.

Software designed for Radio is written in UserTalk, a programming language developed by UserLand Software.

Almost all of Radio's functionality is delivered with UserTalk using scripts stored in the main object database. These scripts serve as one of the best learning tools for new adopters of the language, because their source code can be freely viewed (and even modified).

Creating Scripts

Software is developed with Radio using the UserTalk programming language.

UserTalk, which is shared by Radio and Frontier, is a compiled procedural programming language that is especially well-suited for Internet programming and the control of programs that support scripting.

Scripts are a distinct data type in UserTalk and are stored in object databases.

Most of Radio's functionality is implemented with scripts in the main object database, which users can view and modify.

These scripts are located in the database's `system` table, which is reserved for the use of UserLand Software. Although you can change these scripts at any time, and it's relatively common for experienced UserTalk programmers to do so, there's a catch—UserLand can overwrite your changes at any time with one of its nightly updates to the database.

CAUTION

Although Radio's source code can be modified, UserLand Software offers no open- or shared-source license that would grant permission to create or distribute modified versions of these scripts. For this reason, new Radio scripts and tools intended for public release should be developed from scratch.

UserLand sends bug fixes and new feature updates to individual scripts as often as three or four times a week—if one includes a script that you have changed, your replacement will be wiped out by the upgrade to the script.

There are hundreds of scripts written by UserLand that you can call in your own programs to accomplish specific tasks. These scripts are often called *verbs*, which simply indicates that they were developed by UserLand and are considered part of the language's core functionality. There's no technical difference between a verb and scripts of your own creation.

Scripts are addressed like any other database element: a series of table names separated by dot characters (".") ends with the name of the script, such as `string.upper` or `xml.rss.readService`.

The name of the script indicates its location in the database.

Because scripts use the same address shortcuts as other forms of data, UserTalk verbs have longer names than the ones normally used to call them. Most verbs are contained within the `system.verbs.builtins` table—for instance, `string.upper` is at `system.verbs.builtins.string.upper`.

The address of a script is followed by parentheses to differentiate it from references to other database items. You can place one or more parameters within the parentheses and separated by commas.

Several examples follow:

```
radio.weblog.getUrl();
```

```
dialog.alert("Welcome to UserLand. Population: You.");
```

```
dialog.notify( clock.now() );
```

Every script returns a value expressed as one of Radio's data types. The third example uses the value returned by `clock.now()`—a date object representing the current date and time—as a parameter to `dialog.notify()`.

Writing a Script with an Outliner

A UserTalk script is a set of commands that are executed one at a time, in top-to-bottom order, until the end of the script is reached.

Scripts are written in Radio by using the software's outliner, so it's necessary to learn its functionality before you begin writing UserTalk programs.

Chapter 8, "Creating Outlines," describes how to use the outliner and the commands of the Outline menu.

Knowing the outliner's capabilities is important because indentation of outline items is significant in UserTalk programming.

UserTalk statements are grouped into blocks by indenting them at the same level under a common parent. These blocks determine how, or if, groups of related statements are executed.

A fragment of a script will illustrate this principle:

```
if year == 2004
  if month == 1
    if day == 7
      for i = 1 to 5
        dialog.notify("Happy birthday, Millard Fillmore!")
```

The example assumes that local variables named year, month, and day have been created and hold the values for the current day. Local variables are temporary storage places for information—in a UserTalk script, they cease to exist after the script finishes running.

This code displays a dialog box containing a birthday greeting for President Fillmore five times on Jan. 7, 2004. On any other day, no dialog box is displayed.

The selective execution of some statements and the repeated execution of others are accomplished with the if and for keywords and the use of indentation to group blocks of statements together.

The for keyword causes a block to be executed a specific number of times. In this example, the block is composed of one statement: a call to the dialog.notify() verb, which displays a message in a dialog box.

The if keyword causes a block to be executed only if an associated expression is true.

You can add a script object anywhere in a database:

1. Choose an existing item in the table where the script should be added: Click its triangle icon.

A good place to store new scripts is the workspace table, which UserLand offers as a work area for your own projects.

2. Choose Table, New Script. A dialog box appears asking for a name to give the script.

3. Enter a name and click OK.

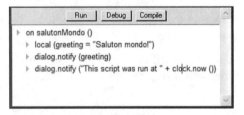

FIGURE 12.1   Editing a new script.

The script is added to the table. Double-click its triangle icon to open the script in an editing window, as shown in Figure 12.1.

Radio begins a new script with a few lines of boilerplate text: the keyword on followed by the name of the script and a blank line indented so that its parent is the on statement.

The on keyword defines a handler method, which is a form of script within a script.

A handler method enables a script to be called externally by other scripts with one or more parameters. The handler method must have the same name as the script.

If the parentheses of the method are empty, it is called with no parameters. Otherwise, parameter names and default values, separated by commas, will be placed within the parentheses. This is covered in Chapter 13, "Writing Statements and Calling Verbs."

When the script is called, the handler method is executed and any other statements at the top level of the outline are ignored.

FIGURE 12.2   Writing a script.

An example script is shown in Figure 12.2.

UserTalk scripts can take two forms. The outline version shown in Figure 12.2 is suitable for outliners. The second format, in a text editor, is described later in the chapter.

This script accomplishes four tasks, using syntax that will be described fully in subsequent chapters:

- The script's handler method is defined. Because no parameters appear within the parentheses of the method, it takes no parameters.

- A local variable named greeting is created and given an initial value: the string "Saluton mondo!" ("Hello world!" in the artificial language Esperanto).

- The `dialog.notify()` verb is called with the variable as a parameter. This verb opens a dialog box that contains the text sent to it as a parameter.

- The verb is called again with two strings combined with the + operator: the text `"This script was run at"` followed by a space and the value returned by the verb `clock.now()`.

A script is run by clicking the Run button at the top of the script window.

If this is done at the current point in the development of the `salutonMondo()` script, Radio displays a dialog box explaining that the script "has no statements in its body" and cannot be run. This occurs because running a script is different than calling it externally from another script.

When Run is clicked, Radio executes each line at the top level of the script's outline. The only top-level line of `salutonMondo()`, the on statement, defines a method but doesn't call it, so nothing happens when the script is executed.

This script as written can run only externally, either by calling it in another script or using Radio's Quick Script feature:

1. Choose Tools, Developers, Quick Script or press Ctrl+; (Windows) or Cmd+; (Mac OS). The Quick Script dialog box opens.

   This feature is used to run one or more UserTalk statements, see the results of an expression, and set or retrieve the values of database items. When it is used to execute multiple statements, there must be a semicolon at the end of each line (other than the last). This lets Radio know where one statement ends and the next one begins.

2. Type `workspace.salutonMondo()` in the text area of the dialog box—no semicolon is needed—and then click the Run button.

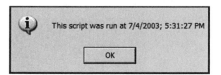

FIGURE 12.3   Displaying the time in a dialog box.

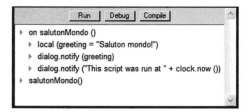

FIGURE 12.4   Calling a script's own handler method.

Radio runs the script, displaying `"Saluton mondo!"` in a dialog box. When the dialog box's OK button is clicked, the window shown in Figure 12.3 appears.

To make it possible to run the script with the Run button, add the statement `salutonMondo()` at the end of the script, putting it at the same indentation level as the on statement (see Figure 12.4).

When Run is clicked, Radio executes the on handler, which defines a method called `salutonMondo()`, and then proceeds to the statement that calls the method.

TIP

A script that takes no parameters does not need a handler method, although there's no harm in using one. When a script has no handler method and is called without parameters, the statements at the top level of the script's outline are executed.

UserTalk scripts are compiled before they are executed. There can be two different compiled versions of a script—one that is compiled by the Run button and another that is compiled by the Compile button.

To see this in action, create a script object named `workspace.surprise` that contains Listing 12.1.

LISTING 12.1 The Full Text of `workspace.surprise`

```
1: on surprise() {
2:    dialog.alert ("Madam I'm Adam");
3: };
4: surprise()
```

After creating the script, follow these steps:

1. Compile and run the script. Click the Compile button, and then click Run.

   The script displays the palindrome "Madam I'm Adam" in a dialog box and plays an alert sound.

2. Change the text to "Able was I ere I saw Elba" and click Run without clicking Compile first.

   The script displays the new palindrome.

3. Now for the surprise: Open a Quick Script dialog box and run the script. Enter the statement `workspace.surprise()` and click the dialog box's Run button.

   The script displays "Madam I'm Adam" again, even though the script window for `workspace.surprise()` no longer contains that text.

Because of this behavior, it's important to know the difference between these two compiled forms of a UserTalk script and how they were created.

When you click the Compile button immediately before clicking Run, the compiled versions of a script are identical.

When you only click Run, the compiled version of the script executes the statements in the editing window—so what you see is what you get.

If any other script calls this script or it is called from the Quick Script window, a different version of the script will be executed—the last one compiled with the Compile button.

As scripts are created in Radio, the software is merrily doing other things. Weblog entries are posted, RSS feeds are scanned and loaded into the `aggregatorData.root` database, and many other scripts are being called.

There might be times when Radio calls a script as you are editing it to fix a bug or enhance the functionality in some way.

By offering two compiled forms of a script, Radio supports the following development process:

1. You edit a script, testing your changes by clicking Run but never clicking Compile. The compiled version executed is the one you see in the window.

2. As you work, if any other scripts call that script, they execute the one that was last produced by the Compile button. This prevents them from executing code while it's being edited and might not be complete.

3. When your script has been tested and works correctly, you click Compile. Now the Run button and external scripts will execute the same code.

The easiest way to avoid confusion regarding this matter is to always click Compile before clicking Run. However, once your scripts have been put to use and are actively being used by other scripts, this can result in some subtle or not-so-subtle problems.

Writing a Script with a Text Editor

Radio's outliner is one of the best of its kind, so there's little reason to work on scripts with a text editor, aside from the occasional times that statements should be executed in the Quick Script dialog box.

NOTE

In previous versions of UserTalk employed in Frontier, script lines were limited to 255 characters, so programmers used a backslash character (\) at the end of a line to indicate that it continued on the next line. This limitation is not present in Radio, although the line-continuation character can still be used to improve the readability of a script.

However, outlines are not a common presentation format on the World Wide Web and email. You'll often see UserTalk scripts presented in a text format, so it's worthwhile to learn the syntax required to organize scripts in that manner.

Listing 12.2 contains the text version of the `workspace.salutonMondo()` script.

LISTING 12.2 The Full Text of `workspace.salutonMondo`

```
1: on salutonMondo() {
2:   local (greeting = "Saluton mondo!");
3:   dialog.notify(greeting);
4:   dialog.notify("This script was run at " + clock.now() )
5: }
6: salutonMondo()
```

Radio automatically formats a script for text presentation when you copy it from the outliner to the Clipboard and paste it into a text editor or a wp text object.

You can also manually format a script for text presentation using the following rules:

- Block statements—which are normally grouped together under a common parent and the same level of indentation—must be placed within left brace ("{") and right brace ("}") characters.

- When a statement is followed by another at the same indentation level, the first line must end with a semicolon.

NOTE

This book uses the text format for scripts to make the organization of blocks explicit. If you are typing examples into Radio's outliner as you read, you can include or omit the braces and semicolons at your discretion. The script will function successfully in either case as long as the line indentation is correct.

Documenting a Script in the Outliner

In Radio's outliner, each line of a script is a statement to execute, a blank line, or a *comment*, a place to document what a script is doing at a particular spot in the script.

To turn a line into a comment, follow these steps:

1. Select the line. Click its triangle icon or press the keypad Enter key.

   The line is displayed with white text in a black selection box.

2. Make it a comment. Choose Outline, Toggle Comment or press Ctrl+\ on Windows or Cmd+\ on Mac OS.

   The line's icon changes to a chevron character ([«]).

   If the line has any lines subordinate to it in the outline, they become comments as well.

Comments will be ignored when the script is executed, making them a useful place to document a script, keep track of changes, and hide code from being executed.

UserLand Software practices a style convention for its comments that's worth emulating. Each script begins with a hierarchy of comments that document the changes to the script in reverse-chronological order.

The top item in this hierarchy is called "Changes," and all changes are children of this item.

> **TIP**
>
> In my experience, UserTalk programming involves a lot of *refactoring*, the practice of rewriting code and moving statements around to make the code work better or run more efficiently. As I refactor a script, I often make discarded statements into comments so that they are still around until I can be assured that they are no longer needed.

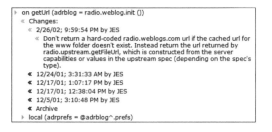

FIGURE 12.5   Documenting changes to a script.

An example is shown in Figure 12.5—a getUrl() script last edited by UserLand developer Jake Savin (who signed it with his initials, JES).

When UserLand programmers make changes, they add a timestamp and their initials as a comment. To create one of these signatures, press Ctrl+4 on Windows or Cmd+4 on Mac OS. Lines describing the change are added as children of this signature.

You can expand the Changes item to show this documentation or collapse it to hide the information.

Summary

Aside from a small kernel implemented in C that handles startup, shutdown, and features with a need for speed, Radio UserLand is implemented with UserTalk scripts in the main object database.

Much of UserTalk's own functionality is written with the language, making it difficult to determine where the language ends and applications begin.

UserTalk enables Radio to be used as a rapid application-development platform for Web applications, XML-RPC and SOAP Web services, and other Internet client and server software.

Writing programs with the language requires familiarity with Radio's outliner and UserTalk *verbs*, scripts written by UserLand that are stored in the system table of the main database.

Writing Statements and Calling Verbs

The UserTalk language includes hundreds of scripts that support general-purpose programming and Internet development.

UserLand Software frequently offers upgrades and bug fixes to these scripts, adds new scripts to support additional features in Radio UserLand, and makes other improvements.

The built-in scripts, which are called *verbs*, comprise almost all of the programming capabilities that are available when you begin writing your own UserTalk scripts. Most of these scripts are written with UserTalk, making it difficult to define where the language ends and its software begins.

A new UserTalk programmer can accomplish a lot by learning how to use the language's operators, store information in local variables and the main object database, and call verbs.

Writing a Statement

A UserTalk script is a series of statements evaluated in top-to-bottom order. Each statement can be used to accomplish these tasks:

- Assign a value to a local variable or database object

- Call a script, such as one of the verbs in the main object database

- Determine the execution of a statement or block of statements that follow it

Local variables and database objects are storage places for information.

Variables are temporary, lasting only as long as a script or a portion of a script.

Database objects are persistent; anything saved in the main object database or another database will stay there until it is replaced or deleted.

Both kinds of storage are described extensively in the next two chapters. They differ only in the way they store information; both are objects that hold any of UserTalk's data types.

A local variable is declared by following the local keyword with parentheses that contain its name, as in the following example:

```
local (x);
```

You can declare more than one variable at the same time by using a comma-separated list:

```
local (x, y, z);
```

You can give objects values through the use of one of the assignment operators.

A value can be given to a variable with the main assignment operator, =. The name of the object is followed by = and a value produced by an expression, script call, or literal.

You can do this as part of a local statement or in a separate statement:

```
local (x = 12, y = "xymurgy", z);
z = radio.weblog.getUrl();
```

The data type of the object is determined by UserTalk at the time a value is assigned to it. This can change at any time—there's no restriction that a variable must always hold the same type of information after its creation.

If an object holds a numeric value, the increment operator, ++, increases it by 1. The decrement operator, --, decreases it by 1. Examples:

```
local (x = 12, y = 10);
x++;
y--;
```

After these statements are executed, x equals 13, and y equals 9.

A statement that produces a value is called an *expression*.

The result of an expression can be assigned to an object.

Mathematical expressions can be created with five operators: addition (+), subtraction (-), multiplication (*), division (/), and modulus (%), which is used to determine the remainder of a division.

```
local (x = 5, y, z);
x = 5 + 1;
y = 10 - 2;
z = y / x - 1;
```

In these examples, x ends with a value of 6, y with 8, and z with 0, a result that might be unexpected. The value of z is determined by the data type produced by the expression and the order in which its division and subtraction operators are evaluated.

The result of a mathematical operation depends on the data types of its *operands*, the values on each side of the operator.

UserTalk is a loosely typed language, assigning data types to new objects based on the data assigned to them. When the data assigned to an object changes, its data type can change accordingly.

In an expression, if both operands are the same data type, the result will be of that type.

Dividing two integers results in an integer, so if y equals 9 and x equals 6, y divided by x equals 1.

Dividing two floating-point numbers results in a floating-point value, so if y equals 9.0 and x equals 6.0, y divided by x equals 1.5.

When the operands are of different data types, the result is the more complex type.

> **NOTE**
>
> This rule extends to the use of the addition operator to combine strings. When a string is an operand in an addition operation, the result of the expression will be that string combined with the string value of the other operand.

When a mathematical expression uses more than one operator, multiplication, division and modulus operations are evaluated first in left-to-right order, followed by addition and subtraction in left-to-right order.

You can change the order of evaluation by placing portions of an expression in parentheses—everything within the "(" and ")" will be evaluated before the expression that contains it.

Here's an example:

```
local (x = 9, y = 5, z = 2, result);
result = 9 * (y - z);
```

The result variable equals 27. If the parentheses had been absent from the last statement, the result would have been equal to 43.

You can compare the values of objects and other data using logical operators: equals (==), not equals (!=), greater than (>), less than (<), greater than or equals (>=), and less than or equals (<=).

These expressions produce the Boolean value `true` if the comparison is true or `false` otherwise. There's also a negation operator, ! or `not`, that does the opposite. For example:

```
local (x = 4, y = 13, z = y - x);
if (x < y)
  dialog.notify("x is less than y");
if (y < z)
  dialog.notify("y is less than z");
if not (x > z)
  dialog.notify("x is not greater than z");
```

This example makes use of the `if` statement, which causes one or more lines of code to be executed if an expression is true. It's covered in Chapter 16, "Working with Loops and Conditionals."

Executing this code causes two dialog boxes to open: one with the message "x is less than y" and another with the message "x is not greater than z."

Calling a Verb

Radio's main object database includes more than 300 UserTalk scripts that can be called to perform specific tasks. These scripts are dubbed *verbs* to recognize that they are an official part of the UserTalk language, but they are no different than any scripts that you create.

This chapter and the remainder of the book describe dozens of these scripts, focusing primarily on the most useful general-purpose and Internet verbs. UserLand Software offers official documentation for verbs on the DocServer Web site at `http://docserver.userland.com`.

CAUTION

The DocServer site isn't fully up to date with the current release of Radio—it was created for a previous version of Frontier. However, most of the existing documentation is still suitable for UserTalk programming, because UserLand avoids making changes that would cause a verb to stop working. A verb call that ran correctly four years ago should continue to work today.

Scripts are stored in an object database and called using their address followed by parentheses.

All of UserTalk's verbs are stored in subtables of the system table (primarily `system.verbs.builtins` and `system.verbs.globals`).

Because both of these tables are part of `system.paths`, the table that contains shortcuts for referring to database items, the scripts they contain can run without you having to specify `system.verbs.builtins` or `system.verbs.globals` as part of the address.

Some verbs take no parameters, so they are run simply by following their address with parentheses. One handy example is `clock.now()`, which returns a date object representing the current date and time. The following statement saves this value in a local variable named `when`:

```
local (when = clock.now() );
```

A script can have one or more parameters that are used to send values to the script. Presumably, these values will be used by the script in some way. For example, the `file.readWholeFile()` verb takes one parameter—the path and name of a file that should be read from disk:

```
local (textOfFile = file.readWholeFile("C:\\web\\header.txt"));
```

Some scripts are written to use one or more optional parameters. When an optional parameter is omitted, its default value is used.

The `string.replaceAll()` script is an example of a verb that takes multiple parameters, some of which are optional. This script can be called with the following parameters:

- `s`, a string containing text that should be replaced
- `searchfor`, a string containing the text to replace
- `replacewith`, a string containing the replacement text
- `flCaseSensitive`, an optional Boolean value that's `true` if the search for matching text should be case-sensitive, or `false` otherwise

Here's an example that calls the script:

```
workspace.hText = "<h1>Table of Contents</h1>";
workspace.hText = string.replaceAll(workspace.hText, "h1>", "h2>")
```

The example changes the value of `workspace.hText`, a string item in the main object database, from "`<h1>Table of Contents</h1>`" to "`<h2>Table of Contents</h2>`".

It accomplishes this with a call to the `string.replaceAll()` verb with all three of its required parameters: `s`, `searchfor`, and `replacewith`.

The order is significant. Parameters should be ordered in a specific manner in UserTalk scripts.

Required parameters, which must be specified for the verb to run, come first and are called without referring to their names.

You can specify optional parameters when calling a script in two ways:

- If every parameter preceding the parameter is being called, no name is needed.

- If one or more optional parameters have been omitted, any remaining parameter must be specified with its name.

A parameter's name is specified with a semicolon followed by the value of the parameter. The order of named parameters is not significant—they can be included in any order and still end up in the right place when a script is called.

The following example includes an optional parameter to the `string.replaceAll()` verb, `flCaseSensitive`:

```
workspace.hText = string.replaceAll(workspace.hText, "h1>", "h2>",
➥flCaseSensitive: false);
```

This example doesn't actually need the optional parameter's name, because the three parameters that precede it are included in the call to the verb.

The `tcp.httpClient()` verb, which saves the contents of a URL as a string, takes 21 parameters. All of them are optional. For this reason, it's rarely called without referring to some parameters by name.

Here's an example:

```
tcp.httpClient ("POST", "www.metafilter.com", 80, "/login/Login_action.cfm",
➥data: getData (@workspace.postFormGateway.login), datatype:
➥"application/x-www-form-urlencoded", cookiesOn: "true", debug: false);
```

This statement logs in to a Web site by providing data to a form on the site. The first four parameters are specified without names because they are the first four parameters of the script. The `data` parameter requires a name because it follows four parameters that are not specified—`proxy`, `proxyPort`, `proxyUserName`, and `proxyPassword`. All subsequent parameters require names as well.

Writing a Script

Most scripts are written to be called externally in one or more places—inside another UserTalk script, in a macro placed in a weblog template, or with Radio's Quick Script dialog box.

As described in the preceding chapter, "Editing a New Script," a UserTalk script can be called externally with one or more parameters if the script includes a handler method taking the same name as the script.

The handler method's on statement indicates the name and order of the parameters that can be specified when calling the script. It also can be used to assign default values to those parameters.

Listing 13.1 contains a script that uploads a file from your computer to an FTP server.

LISTING 13.1 The Full Text of `workspace.uploadFile`

```
 1: on uploadFile (filename, host, username, password, path) {
 2:    « create local variables
 3:    local (connect, file, name);
 4:    « make a connection to the FTP server
 5:    connect = tcp.ftp.openConnection (host, username, password);
 6:    « copy the file into a local variable
 7:    file = file.readWholeFile (filename);
 8:    « upload the file to the FTP server
 9:    tcp.ftp.writeFile (connect, file, path);
10:    tcp.ftp.closeConnection (connect);
11:    return true};
12: uploadFile ("C:\\Program Files\\Radio UserLand\\www\\rss.xml",
➥"example.com", "notrealuser", "notrealpass", "/web/rss.xml")
```

A script also can define *local handlers,* which are methods that are called within the script.

These handlers are defined like a script's main handler method—the on keyword is followed by the name of the method and the parameters that it takes.

A local handler can be created at any place in a script. Listing 13.2 contains a script that uses a local handler.

LISTING 13.2 The Full Text of `workspace.rollThreeDice`

```
1: on rollThreeDice() {
2:   on roll() {
3:     return random(1, 6)
4:   };
5:   local (total = roll() + roll() + roll());
6:   dialog.alert("Total: " + total)
7:   };
8: rollThreeDice()
```

Using Verbs in Expressions

Radio includes several hundred verbs that will be useful in your own scripts.

The remaining chapters of the book cover many of them, others are described on the DocServer Web site at `http://docserver.userland.com`, and the rest must be discovered by other means—you can find some by examining the source code of verbs.

The following verbs take care of some handy mathematical and `date/time` functions:

- `abs(`*number*`)`: Returns the absolute value of the `number` parameter, which should be an integer, floating-point number, or character.

- `clock.now()`: Returns a date that holds the current date and time, which can be displayed as a string of the form `8/5/03; 11:03:23 AM`.

- `clock.waitSeconds(number)`: Pauses a script for the specified `number` of seconds.

- `random(lower, upper)`: Returns a randomly generated integer that can be any value ranging from the integers `lower` to `upper` (including those values).

Summary

UserLand provides hundreds of verbs that support HTTP networking, FTP file transfer, XML-RPC and SOAP Web services, and many other aspects of software development in an Internet client/server environment.

These verbs are documented on the DocServer Web site, a reference that's a few years old but still extremely useful for people writing software with Radio UserLand.

During nightly updates that you can enable or disable from a user preference, UserLand offers updates to its scripts as often as several times a week.

Because you can accomplish so much simply by calling verbs, they are the best starting place for a new UserTalk programmer.

Reading and Writing to the Database

One of the best reasons to learn UserTalk programming is the convenience of database access.

Unlike languages in which data access requires special connectivity or query syntax, UserTalk makes it as easy to work with an object database as with variables.

This functionality, like the loosely typed data supported by Radio UserLand, can be extremely useful as long as you're careful how you work with database addresses in assignment statements.

Working with Data in an Object Database

Data can be stored or retrieved in an object database simply by referring to a database address in a statement or expression, as in this example:

```
workspace.helloMessage = "Saluton Mondo!";

dialog.alert (user.radio.prefs.wwwfolder);
```

The first statement uses the assignment operator to store the text "Saluton Mondo!" in the main object database's workspace table in a string object named helloMessage.

The second opens a dialog box displaying the contents of user.radio.prefs.wwwfolder, a string that holds the full path and name of Radio's www subfolder.

The addressing scheme is the same for database objects as it is for verbs.

Data stored in the database is stored persistently, remaining at that address for use by scripts until it is deleted or replaced with something else.

These rules apply when storing data in an object database:

- All tables and subtables referred to in the address must exist.

  The preceding example works because workspace is one of the built-in root-level tables in Radio. The following statement will fail with a runtime error if the workspace.example table does not exist:

  ```
  workspace.example.Hello = "Saluton Mondo!";
  ```

- If nothing exists at the database address, it will be created to hold the data.

- If data already is being stored at that address, the new data will not be saved if the address holds one of the five complex data types—tables, outlines, scripts, menu bars, and wp text.

  UserTalk prevents the assignment operator from being used to replace these types with simple types such as strings, displaying a runtime error like the one shown in Figure 14.1.

  The reason for this prohibition is that it otherwise would be easy to accidentally wipe out large swaths of the database. Consider the following statement:

  ```
  workspace = "Saluton mondo!";
  ```

  This statement, if not prohibited, would replace the entire workspace table with a single string item, removing any of the scripts and data stored there.

```
Assignment over existing table object "test" is not
allowed.  Delete the object first, or use table.assign to
override protection.                                    Go To
```

FIGURE 14.1   Preventing the replacement of database tables.

The address of a database item should start with a letter and can contain letters, numbers, and underscore characters ("_"). Each table or item name in the address is limited to 255 characters.

To use different characters and punctuation, a portion of an address can be placed within "[" and "]" brackets and specified as a string literal:

```
workspace.["data folder"] = "Data Files";
```

This statement creates an item named data folder in the workspace table, in spite of the fact that this statement breaks Radio's naming rule for database items. Whenever this item is referenced in a UserTalk script, the brackets must be used around the item name.

The brackets also can be used to calculate a database address as a script runs.

In the address, place an expression, script call, or local variable within "[" and "]" brackets. The bracketed portion will be evaluated before the assignment operator and then replaced with the value it produces. For example:

```
workspace.[user.prefs.initials] = user.prefs.name;
```

This statement creates an item in the workspace table with your initials (the string stored in the database at user.prefs.initials). The value of the item is your name (from user.prefs.name). In my copy of Radio, the following two statements are identical:

```
workspace.[user.prefs.initials] = user.prefs.name;
workspace.RC = "Rogers Cadenhead";
```

The following example uses a verb to determine a portion of the database address:

```
workspace.[radio.weblog.getURL()] = clock.now();
```

Name	Value	Kind
getVialnfo	on disk	script
helloMessage	Saluton Mondo!	string [14]
http://www.cadenhead.org/workbench/	7/2/2003; 3:29:19 PM	date
importBlog	on disk	script
incomingMail	on disk	table

Kind: ▼   Sort: ▼

FIGURE 14.2   Calculating database addresses with UserTalk code.

A table containing the result of this statement is shown in Figure 14.2.

Several useful UserTalk verbs work on specific database objects. Each of these verbs takes one parameter: the address of an object.

The defined() verb ensures that the specified object exists at that address. For example:

```
local (lastUpdate = "none");
if defined (@workspace.lastUpdate) {
    lastUpdate = workspace.lastUpdate
};
dialog.alert(lastUpdate)
```

TIP

Brackets also can be used to get around another database address prohibition—UserTalk keywords and constants cannot normally serve as database tables or item names in an address.

```
workspace.loop = true; // not allowed
workspace.["loop"] = true; // allowed
```

This verb can be used to check for the existence of an object no matter how it is addressed. It works with database objects, local variables, and individual array elements.

The delete() verb removes the specified object from the database.

There must be an object at that address when the verb is called. Otherwise, the statement will fail with an error.

The following statement deletes the object at the address workspace.lastUpdate:

```
delete(@workspace.lastUpdate)
```

The parentOf() verb returns the address of the object's parent, as in this example:

```
dialog.alert(parentOf(user.prefs.initials))
```

The parent of the top-level tables in the main object database is root. The parent of a top-level table in another database is the address of the database file, which includes a full reference to the folder in which it is contained.

A UserTalk script can access any open object database by referring to the full address of an item that it contains, as in the following example:

```
dialog.alert(weblogData.prefs.title);
```

This verb opens a dialog box displaying the name of your weblog. The weblogData table is at the top of the weblogData.root database.

Databases that are currently open are listed in the Window menu below the list of open windows.

Storing Addresses to Use as Pointers

Up to this point, database addresses have been used as a means of storing and retrieving data. When UserTalk encounters an address expressed as a literal or with code in "[" and "]" brackets, it is interpreted as an effort to work with the value stored at that address.

An address is also a data type in UserTalk that can be stored in the database and within local variables for use as a pointer.

FIGURE 14.3   Displaying a database address and its value.

References to addresses intended for this use are prefaced with an at sign @, as demonstrated here:

```
dialog.alert(workspace.helloMessage + cr + cr
+ @workspace.helloMessage);
```

The output of this statement is shown in Figure 14.3.

The top line of Figure 14.3, `Saluton Mondo!`, displays the value of the database item stored at `workspace.helloMessage`. The bottom line displays the text of the address itself.

When working with addresses as data, it must be a place where data can be stored immediately—the tables referred to in the address must exist.

For example, a reference to `@scratchpad.result` works because the `scratchpad` table exists as a standard part of the main object database. Even if there isn't an item currently in the database at `scratchpad.result`, the address reference will work.

A reference to `@scratchpad.result.score` will cause a script to fail with a runtime error if the `scratchpad.result` table does not exist.

Addresses are used often as parameters to UserTalk verbs. They can indicate where to find data used by the verb or where to store data that it creates.

The verb `xml.compile()` creates a database table that contains the contents of well-formed XML data. It takes two parameters:

- A string that contains the XML data
- The address in the database where the data should be stored

Here's an example:

```
xml.compile(tcp.httpReadUrl("http://www.cadenhead.org/workbench/rss.xml"),
➥@scratchpad.rssxml);
```

The `tcp.httpReadUrl()` verb returns the contents of an XML document stored on the Web, which is used as the first parameter to `xml.compile()`. The second parameter, `@scratchpad.rssxml`, indicates the address of the table that should hold the XML data. If this address does not exist, it will be created. If it does exist, the existing data will be overwritten.

The table is shown in Figure 14.4.

Name	Value	Kind
▶ rssxml	3 items	table
▶ ?xml	1 item	table
▶ /comment	RSS generated by Radio UserLand v8.0.8 on Thu, 03 J...	string [73]
▶ rss	2 items	table
▶ /atts	1 item	table
▶ channel	23 items	table
▶ title	Workbench	string [9]
▶ link	http://www.cadenhead.org/workbench/	string [35]
▶ descri...	Programming and publishing news and comment	string [43]
▶ langu...	en-us	string [5]
▶ copyri...	Copyright 2003 Rogers Cadenhead	string [31]

Kind: ▼   Sort: ▼

FIGURE 14.4 Storing data by using an address as a pointer.

This example demonstrates a capability of addresses: They can be used to return multiple values from a script (such as a verb) or a local handler.

Using addresses as parameters enables a script or local handler to return more than one value.

Normally, the only thing returned is the value expressed in a `return` statement. An address sent as a parameter can indicate where additional data should be stored.

When an address is stored in a local variable, it can be used to refer to the data stored at that address.

The `local` keyword creates a local variable, which can then be used to store the same range of data types as an object database.

One way to use `local` is to follow it with the names and initial values of one or more variables between parentheses:

```
local (name, street, city, state, zip);
```

The following statement creates a local variable and uses the assignment operator to give it a value:

```
local dataAdr = @scratchpad.data;
```

Because of the @ sign preceding the address, the `dataAdr` variable holds the address `scratchpad.data` and has the address data type. Without it, `dataAdr` would hold the contents of `scratchpad.data`, if anything exists at that address.

The carat character (^) enables a variable's contents to be used as an address or part of an address. It must appear after the name of the variable.

The following two statements accomplish exactly the same thing, setting a date object at `workspace.now` to the current time and date:

```
workspace.now = clock.now();

local (nowAdr = @workspace.now);
nowAdr^ = clock.now();
```

Before an address containing a carat is evaluated, UserTalk replaces each carat-containing portion of the address with an actual address. So the statement `nowAdr^ = clock.now()` becomes `workspace.now = clock.now()` and then is executed. This conversion process is called *dereferencing*.

Storing addresses in local variables makes them easier to work with in scripts. The following example uses an address stored in a variable to display several items in the `user.radio.prefs.defaultCloud` table, which holds information about the Web service used to publish a weblog:

```
local (prefAdr = @user.radio.prefs.defaultCloud);
dialog.notify (prefAdr^.server + cr + prefAdr^.port + cr +
[ic:ccc]prefAdr^.path);
```

Three table items are being displayed:

- `user.radio.prefs.defaultCloud.server`
- `user.radio.prefs.defaultCloud.port`
- `user.radio.prefs.defaultCloud.path`

When a script is being called by an address that will be dereferenced, the parentheses follow the ^, as in this example:

```
local (weblog = @radio.weblog.getUrl);
dialog.notify (weblog^());
```

There can be more than one carat to dereference in an address. UserTalk resolves the address from left to right, replacing each caret-containing portion and then reevaluating the address.

This should be clearer with a demonstration:

```
scratchpad.myAddr = @user.prefs.initials;
local (addr = @scratchpad);
local (initials = addr^.myAddr^);
dialog.notify (initials);
```

This code displays your initials in a dialog box. The third statement, which sets the value of the `initials` variable, is dereferenced twice:

- First, `addr^.myAddr^` becomes `scratchpad.myAddr^`, because `addr` contains the address `scratchpad`.
- Next, `scratchpad.myAddr^` becomes the contents of the address `user.prefs.initials`, a string object that holds your initials.

The addition or omission of a "^" can introduce logic errors in a script—subtle problems that don't stop a script from being compiled or executed.

In the preceding example, changing `addr^.myAddr^` to `addr^.myAddr` causes `initials` to contain the address `user.prefs.initials` instead of the string stored at that address.

Becoming comfortable with dereferencing is important because it's used so often in UserLand's own scripts for verbs and other elements of Radio.

Using with to Shorten Addresses

Because a database address in an object database can be nested up to 25 levels deep, there can be some addresses that are so long that they become cumbersome to reference in a script.

One way to deal with this is to use local variables to hold addresses.

Another way is to use the with keyword, which forms a block in which a database address can be referenced with a shorter name.

The with keyword is followed by one or more addresses of database tables separated by commas. Any lines of the script indented as a block below the keyword will use the with keyword to determine where to look first in the database for addresses.

Here's an example that uses this shorthand form of reference to call the xml.rss.readService() and xml.rss.compileService() verbs:

```
with xml.rss {
  readService("http://www.scripting.com/rss.xml", @scratchpad);
  compileService(@scratchpad.["http://www.scripting.com/rss.xml"]);
  dialog.notify("Changes: " + scratchpad.["http://www.scripting.com/rss.xml"]
➥.ctChanges)

}
```

When more than one table is specified, the with keyword looks for the internal table inside the external one. The following example works exactly like the one that precedes it:

```
with xml
  with rss {
    readService("http://www.scripting.com/rss.xml", @scratchpad);
    compileService(@scratchpad.["http://www.scripting.com/rss.xml"]);
    dialog.notify("Changes: " + scratchpad.["http://www.scripting.com/rss.xml"]
➥.ctChanges)

  }
}
```

Summary

The database-programming capabilities of Radio UserLand are extremely handy, enabling data to be stored, retrieved, and organized as easily as local variables are manipulated.

UserTalk scripts can use the @ operator to create address data, the "[" and "]" operators to calculate addresses programmatically, and the ^ operator to dereference addresses.

This power comes with one cautionary piece of advice: Addressing mistakes can unwittingly cause large parts of an object database to be removed or replaced, so it's important to back up databases regularly and review data-handling code carefully.

Using Variables and Arrays

15

IN THIS CHAPTER

- ▶ Creating and Using Variables
- ▶ Assigning Values to Variables
- ▶ Storing Data in Arrays
- ▶ Working with Other Types of Data

There are several good reasons to store most of the data required in a UserTalk script within Radio UserLand's main object database:

- The database is available at all times from any script.
- It stores data persistently.
- It can be accessed simply by using addresses and the @ operator.
- Two database tables, scratchpad and temp, are available for temporary data.

For the times when data should be represented in a temporary form, you can use local variables. Anything that can be stored in an object database can be represented by these variables, which can hold collections of data in sophisticated arrays such as lists, records, and binaries.

Creating and Using Variables

Two kinds of objects can be given names and put to use in a UserTalk script:

- Persistent objects stored in an object database, which are accessed with their address, such as user.prefs.mailHost
- Temporary objects that exist within a particular script or block of a script, which are accessed with a name, such as htmltext

Temporary objects are called *local variables*, or simply variables. They are local to the script or block in which they were created and cannot be directly accessed by other scripts.

They can be created simply by using them in a script, like so:

```
product = "Clay Basket";
```

This statement creates a local variable named product which holds the string "Clay Basket". Because UserTalk is a loosely typed language, the data type of a variable is determined by its usage and can be changed at any time. In this case, the quote marks around the literal text "Clay Basket" cause it to be stored in a variable as a string.

Although you can create variables in this casual manner, it's risky behavior that can easily cause objects in the system or root table to be overwritten. The reason is that Radio can't tell database object addresses and variable names apart.

Although objects are likely to have longer names that consist of several table names separated by dots and an identifier, it's also possible for objects to be referenced by names that look exactly like local variables.

For instance, open the Quick Script dialog box (Tools, Developers, Quick Script) and execute this call:

```
dialog.notify(gold)
```

FIGURE 15.1   Referring to an object with a simple identifier.

The dialog box and resulting output are shown in Figure 15.1.

Although gold looks like a reference to a local variable, it's interpreted by Radio as a reference to system.verbs.colors.gold, one of 141 constants that holds RGB color values represented as three hexadecimal numbers for use on Web pages. The value FFD700 is a shade of gold.

This happens for the reason described in Chapter 13, "Writing Statements and Calling Verbs"—when Radio can't find a local variable matching a name, it looks for objects using each of the addresses in the system.paths table, choosing the first match that it finds.

One of the addresses in system.paths is system.verbs.colors, a table that contains a string object named gold. The shorthand reference gold is interpreted as a reference to that object.

The following line appears to be creating a local variable named gold and assigning it a value:

```
gold = 120;
```

However, if it was used in a script, it would assign the number 120 to the object system.verbs.colors.gold, introducing a subtle error in the system table that might completely escape notice.

To actually create a variable named gold in a script and avoid the risk of overwriting objects at any time, the local statement can be used to declare that a local variable is being created.

The local keyword is followed by one or more variables in parentheses, each separated by commas:

```
local (gold, porkBellies, silver);
```

> **CAUTION**
>
> This is one of the less damaging examples of how a name collision between objects and variables can affect the main object database; others are more catastrophic.
>
> Radio prevents database tables from being overwritten because they share a name with a local variable, but any other data types can be replaced with an assignment statement.
>
> A good backup procedure is a necessary part of UserTalk programming because of issues like this. Chapter 9, "Backing Up Data," covers how to save the object database and other important files periodically.

This statement creates three local variables named gold, porkBellies, and silver. Like object references, variable names are case-insensitive, so porkBellies is the same thing as porkbellies.

As an option, any local variable can be given an initial value with the = operator, as in this example:

```
local (gold = 120, porkBellies = 80, silver);
```

An alternative way to declare local keywords is to indent them under a local keyword:

```
local {
  gold = 120;
  porkBellies = 80;
  silver
}
```

> **CAUTION**
>
> There's a bug in Radio that occurs when the last item indented in a local declaration has been changed into a comment: Radio erroneously reports the line as a syntax error and won't allow it to be compiled.

The placement of the local statement within a script determines its *scope*, the portion of a program in which a variable exists and can be used in the code.

A variable's scope in UserTalk is determined by its indentation level and parent in the outliner.

After the variable is created, any statements at the same level or lower in the same part of the outline can refer to the variable. When execution proceeds back to the level of its parent, the variable and its value cease to exist.

This is demonstrated by a short example that uses the `bundle` statement to group several lines together:

```
bundle {
  local (days = 31);
  msg(days)
}
msg(days)
```

In this example, the first `msg(days)` statement works but the second triggers a runtime error, "Can't evaluate the expression because the name 'days' hasn't been defined."

The error occurs because the scope of the local variable days is the block that has `bundle` as a parent. When execution exits that block, days no longer exists and cannot be referenced.

> **NOTE**
>
> The scope of local variables is demonstrated by the lookup feature of Radio's debugger, which displays the contents of `system.compiler.stack`, the database table that holds the names and values of all local variables while they are in scope. This is covered in Chapter 19, "Handling Errors and Debugging Scripts."

Assigning Values to Variables

Local variables can hold any of the data types that can be represented in an object database.

UserTalk is a loosely typed programming language, a distinction that values the capability to convert data into different types over rigid control of a variable or object's contents.

The data type of a local variable is determined when it is created and can be changed at any time.

A local variable created without an initial value is given the value of `nil` (a constant in UserTalk that represents nothing) and the unknown data type.

A local variable created with an initial value, such as one returned by a script or stored in a database object, takes the data type of that value.

When a variable is assigned a value using a literal, the following rules apply:

- Text surrounded by double or smart quotation marks is a string (example: `local (lang = "Kvikkalkul")`).

- A single character surrounded by single quotation marks is a character (`local (upKey = 'W')`).

- Text with no quotation marks that is preceded by an at sign (@) is an address (`local worktable = @scratchpad.temp)`).

- Four characters surrounded by single quotation marks is a `string4` code (`local (target = 'optx')`).

- A number with no decimal point is a long, provided that it ranges from -2,147,483,648 to 2,147,483,647 (`local (jenny = 8675309)`).

- A number with a decimal point is a double (`local (pi = 3.14)`).

- The `true` and `false` literals are Booleans (`local (newGame = true)`).

- Comma-separated values of any data type surrounded by curly brackets are a list (`local (vacation = {"April", "May"})`).

- A list with strings identifying each element is a record (`local (vitals = {"height": 75, "weight": 215, "aged": 36})`).

The data type of a variable or object can be determined by calling the `typeof()` verb with it as the only parameter, as in this example:

```
local
  item = user.prefs.mailhost;
  itemType = typeOf(item);
dialog.notify (item + " is a " + itemType);
```

This code opens the dialog box shown in Figure 15.2.

FIGURE 15.2 Checking a variable's data type.

In Figure 15.2, the word TEXT is a `string4` identifier that indicates the object at `user.prefs.mailhost` is a string.

The `typeOf()` verb uses `string4` codes to identify each of the data types supported by UserTalk—for example, strings are `'TEXT'`, characters are `'char'`, and unknown data is `'????'`.

Many of these identifiers aren't particularly memorable, such as `'exte'` for doubles and `'QDpt'` for points. Fortunately, there are more descriptive nicknames that can be used in place of the `string4` identifiers.

Table 15.1 lists several of the ways each of the data types can be identified in UserTalk scripts and menu commands, including `string4` identifiers and nicknames.

TABLE 15.1

Working with Data Types

NICKNAME	IDENTIFIER	VERB	MENU COMMAND
addressType	addr	address()	New Scalar, Address
aliasType	alis	alias()	New Mac Type, Alias
binaryType	data	binary()	New Special, Binary
booleanType	bool	boolean()	New Scalar, Boolean
charType	char	char()	New Scalar, Character
dateType	date	date()	New Scalar, Date
directionType	dir		New Scalar, Direction
doubleType	exte	double()	New Scalar, Float
enumeratorType	enum	enum()	New Mac Type, Enumerator
filespecType	fss	filespec()	New Special, File Spec
fixedType	fixd	fixed()	
listType	list	list()	New Special, List
longType	long	long()	New Scalar, Number
menubarType	mbar		New MenuBar
objspecType	obj	objspec()	New Mac Type, Object Spec
outlineType	optx		New Outline
patternType	tptn		New Mac Type, Pattern
pictureType	pict		
pointType	QDpt	point()	New Special, Point
recordType	reco	record()	New Special, Record
rectType	qdrt	rect()	New Special, Rectangle
rgbType	cRGB	rgb()	New Special, Color
scriptType	scpt		New Script
shortType	shor	short()	
singleType	sing	single()	
stringType	TEXT	string()	New Scalar, String
string4Type	type	string4()	New Special, String4
tableType	tabl		New Sub-Table
unknownType	????		
wptextType	wptx		New Text

The verbs listed in Table 15.1 are used to convert a local variable or database object from one data type to another—a process called *coercion.*

Each of the coercion verbs takes one parameter: the variable or object to be converted. If the value can successfully be coerced, the verb returns it in that form.

The following code employs the `dialog.ask()` verb to take input from the user, and then attempts to convert it to a double:

```
dialog.ask("Enter a value to convert to a double", @scratchpad.value);
local (d = double(scratchpad.value));
dialog.notify(d)
```

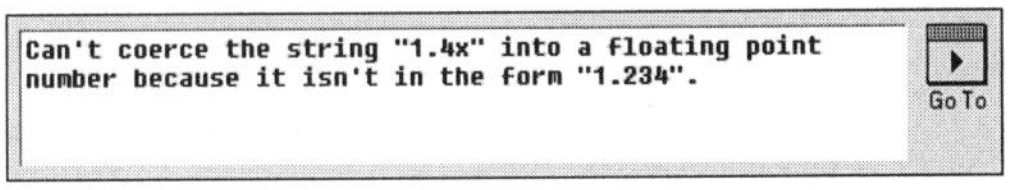

Can't coerce the string "1.4x" into a floating point number because it isn't in the form "1.234".

Go To

If the input is a valid double value, it will be displayed in a dialog box using the `dialog.notify()` verb.

Otherwise, script execution stops and an Error Info dialog box describes the error, which will be something like the one shown in Figure 15.3.

FIGURE 15.3 Viewing an error message.

Errors like this can be handled in a script by using a `try-else` statement, which is described in Chapter 19.

Storing Data in Arrays

Arrays, collections of data that are related to each other, can be represented as local variables in UserTalk with five data types: lists, records, tables, strings, and binary objects.

> **NOTE**
>
> Radio also includes two data types used internally by UserLand: codeType (`'code'`) for compiled script code and tokenType (`'tokn'`) for tokens used by the compiler.

A table is a database table stored in a local variable rather than an address in an object database.

A string is a collection of characters, which can be created by placing them between double quotation marks or curly quotation marks:

```
local (title = "Home Page");
```

When a string is delineated by double quotation marks, quotation marks can be included in a string by prefacing them with the escape character—a backslash ("\"), as in this example:

```
local (quote = "\"Hemlock is poison?\" — Socrates");
```

Table 15.2 lists the escape sequences that can be used in a string, constants that contain their character equivalents, and their ASCII character codes.

TABLE 15.2
Escape Characters

ESCAPE	DESCRIPTION	CONSTANT	ASCII
\'	Single quote	none	39
\"	Double quote	none	34
\\	Backslash	none	92
\n	Linefeed	lf	10
\r	Return	cr	13
\t	Tab	tab	9

Any character with an ASCII code can be placed in a string by following \x with the code in hexadecimal, such as \x1B for the escape character (ASCII code 27).

A list is a collection of data grouped together between opening and closing curly brackets ("{" and "}") and separated with commas:

```
local (folders = {"stories", "categories", "2003"});
```

A record is a list with string identifiers associated with each element:

```
local (player = {"id":6700, "name":"borg", "score":47500});
```

Lists, records, and tables do not need to contain the same data type for all elements—they can hold any data type. UserTalk's normal rules for assigning a data type are used for each element.

An individual element of any array can be accessed with an index number, beginning with 1 for the first element. The following code creates a list and displays br, its second element:

```
local (okTags = {"p", "br", "i", "b", "img"});
dialog.notify(okTags[2]);
```

Here's an example that displays the first character of a string:

```
local (url = "http://www.userland.com");
msg(url[1]);
```

A record also can be retrieved by using its string4 identifier in place of an index number:

```
local (rec = {"name":"Puddin N. Tane", "id":20});
dialog.notify(rec["name"])
```

The number of elements in an array can be determined with the sizeof() verb, which equals a count of elements and the index position of the last element.

Two for loops will be described in the next chapter, "Working with Loops and Conditionals," that can iterate through the contents of an array.

As a preview, the next example uses both kinds of loops to display each element of an array, pausing one second after each one:

```
local (okTags = {"p", "br", "i", "b", "img"});

for i = 1 to sizeof (okTags) {
  msg(okTags[i]);
  thread.sleepfor(1)
}

for item in okTags {
  msg(item);
  thread.sleepfor(1)
}
```

Working with Other Types of Data

Although most of the data types in UserTalk can be manipulated with coercion verbs and the new keyword, a few require additional verbs to properly utilize.

A binary object holds raw binary data that is further identified with an internal data type that describes the format or purpose of the data. This internal type is expressed as a string4 identifier.

If this identifier is one of UserTalk's data type identifiers, the object holds the encoded binary form of that data.

This is not a requirement, however. The identifier can be any string4 value.

Binaries can be used for any kind of binary representation—two of the most common in Radio's database are GIF and JPEG files, which have the binary types GIFf and JPEG, respectively.

A binary can be created from other data by calling the pack() verb with two parameters: the data and the database address where it should be stored. Like this:

```
local (password = "swordfish");
pack(password, @scratchpad.login);
```

This code stores the binary encoding of the string "swordfish" in the main database, as shown in Figure 15.4.

Name	Value	Kind
▶ examples	on disk	table
▶ scratchpad	26 items	table
▶ httpClientUrls	on disk	table
▶ httpCommand	on disk	wp text
▶ httpResult	on disk	wp text
▶ incomingMail	on disk	table
▶ linkDirOutline	on disk	outline
▶ login	0x73776F726466697368	binary [TEXT]

Kind ▼   Sort ▼

FIGURE 15.4   Storing binary data in the database.

The data type and internal data type are shown in the Kind column in Figure 15.4—TEXT is the string4 identifier for strings.

Binary data can be decoded into other data types by calling unpack() with two parameters: the database address of the binary data and the address where it should be stored. For example:

```
local (password = unpack(@scratchpad.login,
  @scratchpad.pass));
```

The data type of the decoded binary is determined by its internal data type, which should be one of the UserTalk data types.

The internal type of a binary can be determined by calling the getBinaryType() verb with the binary as a parameter.

The type can be set by calling the setBinaryType() verb with two parameters: the database address of the object and its string4 identifier or nickname.

CAUTION

When displaying binary data with verbs such as msg() and dialog.notify(), keep in mind that UserTalk will coerce data to a form suitable for display. If scratchpad.login from Figure 15.4 was displayed, the text "swordfish" would be shown instead of the binary data 0x73776F726466697368. Because the binary's internal type indicates that it is a string, the data is implicitly coerced to that form before being shown.

A wp text object holds text that is edited in its own window, a simple text editor comparable to Windows Notepad or SimpleText on Mac OS.

The contents of a wp text object or local variable can be retrieved by coercing its data type to a string.

Call the string() coercion verb with the wp text object as the parameter:

```
local (s = string(examples.lunchReminder));
dialog.alert(s)
```

Creating a wp text object and filling it with text requires the use of several new verbs: wp.setText(), target.set(), and target.get().

The two target verbs are used to control an aspect of the Radio application's user interface: the window that has the focus which is currently being edited.

Up to this point, windows have been under your direct control in the Radio application. When a wp text object or one of the other non-scalars was opened in the database, a window appeared and you could edit the contents of that object. The window with the focus is the one on top; clicking another window gives it the focus and brings it to the front.

UserTalk can be used to handle the same kinds of interactions, even to the point of opening windows and making changes as you observe the process.

There are several dozen verbs that open, close, and manipulate the windows used to edit outlines, scripts, wp text, and menu bars. They're described on the DocServer Web site at `http://docserver.userland.com`.

These verbs operate on the target window—the one that has the focus and is ready for editing.

Before making a wp text or outline object the focus, the existing target should be stored in a local variable:

```
local (oldTarget = target.get());
```

Next, the target can be set to the object that should be edited. This example makes a new wp text object the focus:

```
new (wpTextType, @scratchpad.virginia);
target.set(@scratchpad.virginia);
```

Once a wp text object is the target window, the `wp.setText()` verb can be called with one parameter—the string that should become the contents of the object:

```
wp.setText("Free the bound periodicals!");
```

It's good practice to restore the original target when you're done:

```
target.set(oldTarget);
```

The UserTalk data type with the richest potential for manipulation is the outline. Scripts can take advantage of the capabilities of Radio's outliner using verbs that work directly with a target outline:

- `op.attributes.getOne(string, address)`: Get one of the OPML attributes of the current item. The first parameter is the attribute's name and the second is the address of a database object or local variable where the attribute's value should be stored.

- `op.attributes.setOne(string, string)`: Set one of the OPML attributes of the current item, using the first parameter as the name of the attribute and the second as its value.

- `op.collapse()`: Collapse all subheads under the current item.

- `op.expand(integer)`: Expand the subheads under the current item to the level indicated by the specified integer—1 just for subheads, 2 to add their subheads also, and so on. Use infinity in place of a number to expand all subheads below the item.

- `op.firstSummit()`: Move the current position in the outline to the first top-level heading.

- `op.getLineText()`: Retrieve the text of the current item in the outline.

- `op.go(integer, integer)`: Move the outline one or more lines in a specific direction. The first parameter indicates the direction and can be one of the following constants—up, down, left, or right to move within the current subhead and its related items, or flatup and flatdown to move up and down as if the outline had no levels. The second parameter indicates the number of lines to move.

- `op.insertAtEndOfList(string)`: Insert the specified string after the last child item in the current group.

- `op.outlineToXml(address)`: Create a string that contains the OPML text representation of the outline.

- `op.sort()`: Sort the current item and its related subheads in alphabetical order.

- `op.xmlToOutline(string, address, boolean)`: Use text formatted as OPML to create an outline and store it at the specified address. The third parameter, `flNewOutline`, determines whether to create a new outline (`true`) or add to an existing outline (`false`). The default is `true`.

A UserTalk script that uses the `op` outline verbs is presented in Chapter 17, "Developing Web Services with XML-RPC."

Summary

Although Radio UserLand's main object database is an extremely convenient place to store persistent and transitory data, local variables offer an alternative for data used briefly in a particular script.

These variables, which can be any kind of data type stored in the object database, are created with the `local` statement and can be assigned an initial value using literals, the value returned by verbs, or database items.

The variables exist only within their *scope*, the portion of the program in which they can be referenced, and cannot be referenced in other scripts.

This makes them the most useful place to store completely transitory data. The main object database's `scratchpad` and `temp` tables can be used for this purpose, but there's always a chance some other script might modify items in these tables unexpectedly.

Working with Loops and Conditionals

16

IN THIS CHAPTER

▶ bundle **Statements**

▶ if **and** if-else **Conditionals**

▶ case **and** case-else **Conditionals**

▶ for **loops**

▶ while **and** loop **Loops**

▶ **Scanning Folders with** fileloop

Because Radio UserLand's script editor is an outliner, it makes use of indentation to form *blocks*, statements that have been grouped together at the same level under the same parent.

Blocks are most useful in UserTalk scripts when they are placed inside loops and conditionals, two techniques to control the execution of a block.

A loop is a statement that executes a block a specific number of times or until a particular condition has been met. The condition is represented by a Boolean or an expression that produces a Boolean value.

A conditional is a statement that executes a block only if a condition is true.

bundle **Statements**

Radio's outliner makes it easy to expand and collapse sections of a script to view the structure of the code. To take advantage of the outliner, it's often convenient to form a block without associating it with a loop or conditional.

The bundle keyword is used to group statements together strictly for organizational purposes. It appears alone on a line, followed at a lower level by the statements that comprise the block.

The following example uses a `bundle` keyword to group several statements that manipulate a list:

```
bundle { // swap items
  local (inputList = {1, 12, 7});
  local (temp = inputList[1]);
  inputList[1] = inputList[2];
  inputList[2] = temp;
  dialog.notify(inputList)
}
```

The `//` operator causes the rest of a line to be interpreted as a comment. It's often used with `bundle` to make the purpose of the block apparent.

`if` and `if-else` **Conditionals**

In any UserTalk script, the primary example of logic is the `if` conditional, which executes a block only if a condition has been met. Here's an example:

```
if score > highScore {
  dialog.alert ("You broke the record!");
  highScore = score;
  if lives < 5
    lives++
}
dialog.alert ("Your score: " + score);
```

This code compares the value of two variables to determine whether a player has set a new high score in a game.

If score is equal to or less than `highScore`, the block contained within the `if` statement is ignored.

If score is greater than `highScore`, the block is executed: a dialog box announces `"You broke the record!"`, the high score is changed to the current score, and another conditional is evaluated to determine whether the `life` variable should be incremented.

An `if` statement can be followed immediately by an `else` statement with its own block. One block will be executed and the other will not, as in this example:

```
if playerLives < 1
  dialog.alert ("Game over.");
else
  dialog.alert ("Lives remaining: " + playerLives);
  playerLives--;
```

case and case-else Conditionals

A wider range of conditions than true or false can be tested with the case or case-else statements, which compare a variable, object, or value to a list of possible values.

These statements take the following form:

```
case solution
  test1
    << block 1
  test2
    << block 2
  test3
    << block 3
else
 << block 4
```

In a case statement, both the *solution* and each of the *test* cases can be a variable, object, or literal value. Each test must be indented one level below the case statement and can contain a block of code.

Starting at the top, if *solution* equals a test case, the next block is executed and the rest of the statement is ignored.

If none of the test cases matches the solution, the else block is executed (if one is present).

More than one test can be grouped together, which causes them to share the next indented block of code:

```
case solution
  test1
  test2
    << block 1
  test3
    << block 2
else
 << block 3
```

In this example, the code in block 1 will be executed if either *test1* or *test2* matches the solution.

Here's an example that asks a user to choose one of four timezones—EST, CST, MST, or PST—and resets a timestamp accordingly:

```
local (month = 4, day = 13, year = 1967, hour = 14);
local (when = date.set (day, month, year, hour, 0, 0));
```

```
dialog.alert (when);
dialog.ask ("Time Zone", @scratchpad.timeZone);
case scratchpad.timeZone {
  "EST" {
    hour = hour - 5};
  "CST" {
    hour = hour - 6};
  "MST" {
    hour = hour - 7};
  "PST" {
    hour = hour - 8}};
else {
  dialog.alert ("That is not a valid timezone.")
}
when = date.set (day, month, year, hour, 0, 0);
dialog.alert (when)
```

A case statement tests for equality and quits when it finds the first test case that matches the solution.

By using the Boolean value true as a solution, each test can be a conditional expression, as in this school-grading example:

```
dialog.ask ("Grade average (1 to 100)", @scratchpad.grade);
scratchpad.grade = number (scratchpad.grade);
case true {
  scratchpad.grade < 70 {
    grade = "F"};
  scratchpad.grade < 80 {
    grade = "C"};
  scratchpad.grade < 90 {
    grade = "B"}}
else {
  grade = "A"};
dialog.alert ("Letter grade: " + grade)
```

CAUTION

At the time of this writing, there appears to be a bug in Radio that prevents case statements from working correctly if one or more of their test cases has been turned into a comment. In some situations, this will stop the compiler with a syntax error. In others, the case statement will be evaluated in an unpredictable manner.

for **loops**

Loops are used to execute a block of statements either a fixed number of times or until a condition has been met.

Two for loops execute a block using an iterator variable that counts upwards or downwards by 1 during each trip through the loop:

```
for i = 1 to 10 {
  << block ...
}
```

This loop executes a block 10 times, using an iterator named i that begins with a value of 1 and ends with a value of 10.

```
for i = 10 downto 1 {
  << block ...
}
```

This loop also executes a block 10 times, but i starts at 10 and ends at 1.

The variable used as an iterator will be created for the loop (if necessary) and continues to exist after the loop completes, enabling it to be used when counting how many times a loop was executed.

The values that define the start and end boundaries of the loop should be integers or objects that can be coerced into integers.

An unusual aspect of UserTalk's for loop is the way the iterator variable can be changed in value without affecting the progression of the loop from start to finish. Any change is disregarded with the next trip through the loop, as demonstrated by the following example:

```
local (output)
for i = 1 to 10 {
  if i == 5 {
    i = 11
  };
  output = output + i + " "
}
```

After execution, the value of output is 1 2 3 4 11 6 7 8 9 10, not 1 2 3 4 11, as you might expect.

A for loop can be used to loop through the contents of arrays (lists, records, and tables) by using 1 and the sizeof() verb as the boundaries of the loop.

For example, the following code loops through the entire workspace table of the main object database, displaying the name and data type of each item in the About Radio UserLand dialog box:

```
for i = 1 to sizeof (workspace) {
  msg (nameof (workspace[i]) + " " + typeof (workspace[i]));
  thread.sleepFor (1)
}
```

The call to thread.sleepFor() pauses one second through each trip through the loop, slowing things down enough for the output to be viewed.

A more compact way to loop through arrays is to use the for-in loop, which loops once for each value and has no iterator variable.

The loop is created by providing the source of the array and the name of a variable where each of its items will be stored, using the form for *variable* in *source*.

When using for-in with tables, both the *variable* and *source* are addresses, as in this example:

```
for item in @workspace {
  msg (nameof (item^) + " " + typeOf (item^));
  thread.sleepFor (1)
}
```

This code is a rewrite of the preceding example, displaying the name and data type of each item in the workspace table.

When using for-in with lists and records as the *source*, *variable* will be used for any data type that lists and records might contain.

The following example displays the value and data type of each item in a list:

```
local (data = {1, 2, "xyzzy"});
for item in data {
  msg (item + " " + typeOf (item));
  thread.sleepFor (1)
}
```

A for loop can skip a loop or stop completely through the use of the continue and break statements.

The continue statement causes for loops to immediately skip to the next iteration of the loop, ignoring any other statements in the block.

The following code uses continue each time the iterator variable is evenly divisible by 2:

```
local (output);
for i = 1 to 10 {
  if i % 2 == 0 {
    continue
  };
  output = output + i + " "
}
dialog.notify(output)
```

The value of output produced by this example is 1 3 5 7 9.

The break statement ends a for loop prematurely, as in this example:

```
local (output);
for i = 1 to 10 {
  if i > 5 {
    break
  };
  output = output + i + " "
}
dialog.notify(output)
```

The output variable equals 1 2 3 4 5.

The continue and break statements affect only the loop in which they are placed. When one loop is placed inside another, they affect only the innermost loop.

Both of these statements can be used with any of the loop statements in UserTalk.

while and loop Loops

The various for loops are used primarily to loop a specific number of times.

When a block should keep looping until a condition has been met, a while loop can be used.

To create the loop, the while keyword is followed by a Boolean variable or an expression that evaluates to a Boolean. (This includes numbers, because UserTalk coerces 0 to false and any other number to true.) The loop continues until the expression is no longer true.

The following example displays the current date and time in the About Radio UserLand dialog box until roughly 10 seconds have passed:

```
local (now = clock.now());
while clock.now() - now < 10 {
  msg (clock.now())
}
```

NOTE

The while loop and several others introduced in this chapter can loop endlessly if the condition is never met, a circumstance called an *infinite loop*. Click the Kill button on top of the script window to stop the execution of a script trapped in a loop.

The block within the while loop executes until the condition expression is false. For times when it would be easier to look until it is true, the not operator can be used. Here's a rewrite of the preceding example using not:

```
local (now = clock.now());
while not (clock.now() - now > 10) {
  msg (clock.now())
}
```

A loop loop, when specified without a conditional, will loop until a break statement is executed.

The following code loops until about 10 seconds have passed:

```
local (now = clock.now ());
loop {
  if clock.now() - now > 10 {
    break
  };
  msg (clock.now ())
}
```

Another way to use loop is to loop a fixed number of times in a manner more complex than a for loop.

These loop statements take the form loop (*initialization*; *condition*; *increment*).

Each part of the loop is a statement that serves a different purpose, separated by semicolons:

- The *initialization* is a statement that creates an iterator variable and gives it an initial value.

- The *condition* is an expression that must be true for the loop to continue.

- The *increment* is a statement that is executed after each trip through the loop, presumably to change the value of the iterator variable.

The following code loops through a range of floating-point values from 0.1 to 3.4, incrementing the iterator by 0.1 each trip:

```
loop (local (i = 0.1); i < 3.5; i = i + 0.1) {
  msg (i)
}
```

Unlike `for` loops, changes to the iterator variable will affect the loop as it progresses. The *condition* statement will be evaluated each time through the loop with the present value of the iterator.

Scanning Folders with `fileloop`

UserTalk includes a specialized loop, `fileloop`, that iterates through a file folder to see what it contains.

The `fileloop` keyword takes the form `fileloop` (*variable* in *folder*) or `fileloop` (*variable* in *folder*, *depth*).

Each file or folder that is found in the specified folder will be stored as a string in the variable, which is created automatically if it doesn't already exist. The depth, which is optional, enables subfolders to be explored.

A `fileloop` statement identifies the folder to explore. The following code displays every folder and file contained in Radio's main folder:

```
local (progroot = file.folderFromPath (Frontier.getProgramPath ()));
fileloop (filename in progroot) {
  msg (filename);
  thread.sleepFor (1)
}
```

The `Frontier.getProgramPath()` verb returns the full path and filename of the Radio application, `Radio.exe`. This can be used as a parameter to the `file.folderFromPath()` verb, which identifies the folder when given a full path and filename, to determine the location of the folder where Radio was installed.

A `fileloop` also can specify the depth of subfolders to explore as a second parameter to the statement.

If the `infinity` constant is used, it will loop recursively through all subfolders looking for files. Otherwise, a positive integer represents the depth of the search—1 for the main folder only, 2 for the main folder and its subfolders, and so on.

Here's a rewritten example that displays all files in a hierarchy topped by the main Radio folder:

```
local (progroot = file.folderFromPath (Frontier.getProgramPath ()));
fileloop (filename in progroot, infinity) {
  msg (filename);
  thread.sleepFor (1)
}
```

This second form of `fileloop` works differently than the first: It only finds files. Subfolders will be opened and explored, but they are not placed in the variable identified by the `fileloop` statement.

The following code uses a recursive handler called `viewFolders()` to get around this limitation, identifying each folder in a specified hierarchy:

```
on viewFolders (folder) {
  fileloop (filename in folder) {
    if file.isFolder (filename) {
      msg (filename);
      viewFolders (filename)
    }
  }
};
local (progroot = file.folderFromPath (Frontier.getProgramPath ()));
viewFolders(progroot)
```

Summary

In spite of their simplicity, conditionals and loops provide most of the brains of any UserTalk script, determining if or how often a block of statements should run.

The conditionals `if` and `if-else` execute a block based on the value of an expression or Boolean object.

The conditionals `case` and `case-else` execute a block when one tested case is true out of a list of possibilities. They can be used to compare variables, objects, and literals.

The `for`, `for-in`, and one form of the `loop` statement execute a block a specific number of times.

The `while` statement and another form of `loop` execute a block repeatedly, either waiting for a condition to be true or for a `break` statement to be executed.

The `fileloop` statement iterates through a folder, storing each of its files and folders to a common variable.

Developing Web Services with XML-RPC

17

A driving force in Web application development in recent years has been the introduction of *Web services*, protocols that enable software to call other programs over the Internet and receive data in response.

One of the most popular protocols is XML-RPC, a remote procedure call protocol that works by exchanging data over HTTP, the protocol that delivers World Wide Web content.

UserLand Software co-created XML-RPC, publicly released the first draft of the protocol, and offers the main support site, so it should come as no surprise that Radio UserLand is a robust platform for Web services.

Radio functions as both an XML-RPC client and a server, enabling developers to consume Web services offered by others and offer some of their own.

Using XML-RPC

There have been many attempts to offer a standard for remote procedure calls (RPC), protocols that enable one program to call a procedure in another over the Internet and other networks.

XML-RPC, developed and released in 1998 by Dave Winer of UserLand Software and Microsoft, was originally implemented in Frontier, UserLand's content-management and Web hosting software. Fredrik Lundh of PythonWare quickly followed with XML-RPC for Python, a library that spurred considerable activity and became a standard part of the Python language with version 2.2.

XML-RPC, which was designed to be extremely simple, was supported quickly by RedHat, Microsoft, and numerous UserTalk and Python developers. At this time, there are client/server implementations of XML-RPC available for most platforms and programming languages in widespread use. UserLand Software offers a directory of implementations on its XML-RPC.Com Web site at `http://www.xmlrpc.com`.

The protocol exchanges information using a combination of HTTP and XML, structuring everything as either a client request or a server response. Clients and servers exchange XML-RPC data using HTTP to transport the information and XML to encode the data.

The process requires six steps:

1. An XML-RPC server waits for a client to send an HTTP POST request to a designated URL and port number.

   For example, I run an XML-RPC server on `cadenhead.org` port 4413. Any POST request to the URL `http://cadenhead.org:4413` will be received by the server.

2. When a request is received, the XML contents of the request are parsed to determine the procedure name and parameters of the remote procedure call.

   Procedure names in an XML-RPC request consist of one or more identifiers separated by periods and do not include parentheses.

   These names do not necessarily correspond with the name of a program or service—the XML-RPC server maps each name to a real program and procedure it can access.

   My server currently accepts two procedures:

   - `dmoz.getRandomSite`, which takes no parameters and returns information about a random site from the database of the Open Directory Project (`http://www.dmoz.org`).

   - `dmoz.getMatchingSite`, which takes one string parameter—a search key—and returns information about a random Open Directory Project site with a description that contains the key.

3. The XML-RPC server calls the procedure with any parameters that have been specified.

   For security reasons, XML-RPC servers are set up to only call remote procedures that have been registered with the server. Any requests to call procedures other than `dmoz.getRandomSite` and `dmoz.getMatchingSite` are ignored by my server, as are requests with the wrong number of parameters.

4. The XML-RPC server receives the return value (or values) of the procedure.

   Both of the procedures on my server return four strings: "ok" followed by the URL, title, and description of a site from the Open Directory Project database.

5. The XML-RPC server converts values returned by the procedure into a response formatted as XML data.

6. The response is sent to the XML-RPC client.

An XML-RPC procedure call can contain more than one parameter and always returns at least one value.

The same data types are supported for procedure calls and return values:

- `array`, a data structure that holds multiple elements of any of the other data types, including arrays

- `base64`, binary data in Base64 format

- `boolean`, the number 1 (`true`) or 0 (`false`)

- `dateTime.iso8601`, a string containing the date and time in ISO8601 format, such as 20030607T15:01:22 (which is June 7, 2003, at 3:01:22 pm)

- `double`, a signed floating-point number with double precision

- `int`, signed integers ranging in value from –2,147,483,648 to 2,147,483,647

- `string`, characters of text

- `struct`, name-value pairs of data whereby the name is a string and the value can be any of the preceding data types

These data types are implemented by the software and software libraries that support XML-RPC, so there's usually no need to work directly with them.

One of the biggest selling points of Web services is platform- and language-independence—programs written in different languages on different operating systems can communicate over XML-RPC.

> **NOTE**
>
> Radio offers verbs that support XML-RPC internally, translating the XML response and request data into UserTalk data types. For more information on the specifics of the XML-RPC protocol and the XML dialect that it employs, read Appendix D, "XML-RPC."

Calling Remote Procedures with XML-RPC

The UserTalk verb `xml.rpc()` can be used to call a remote procedure with XML-RPC in Radio.

This verb takes the following parameters (with default values in parentheses):

- `rpcServer("localhost")`, a string that contains the domain name or IP address of the XML-RPC server

- `rpcPort(user.inetd.config.http.port)`, a number that contains the port number of the server; the default value is usually 80

- `procedureName("")`, a string that contains the remote procedure name; the default value is likely to cause an error on most XML-RPC servers

- `adrparamlist(nil)`, the address of a list that contains the parameters to be called with the procedure

- `fldebug(false)`, when `true`, this Boolean causes Radio to create wp text copies of the XML-RPC request in `scratchpad.httpCommand` and the response in `scratchpad.httpResult`

- `ticksToTimeOut(user.betty.prefs.rpcClientDefaultTimeout)`, a number that contains the ticks (1/60th of a second) before the remote request is cancelled and an error is generated; the default value is usually 3,600

- `flShowMessages(true)`, when `true`, this Boolean causes Radio to display information about the request in the About Radio UserLand dialog box

- `rpcPath(nil)`, a string that contains the path for XML-RPC requests on the server; when `nil`, the value of `user.betty.prefs.rpcClientDefaultPath` is used, which is usually `"/RPC2"`

- `flAsynch(false)`, a Boolean that determines whether the procedure call will be synchronous (`true`) or asynchronous (`false`)

- `adrCallback(nil)`, an address that identifies a UserTalk script to call when an asynchronous procedure call is completed; if `nil`, no script is called

- `extraInfo(nil)`, a data type of any kind that should be made available to the script identified in `adrCallback`

- `adrErrorCallback(nil)`, an address that identifies a UserTalk script to call when an asynchronous procedure call fails; ignored if `nil`

- `username("")`, a string that contains the username for HTTP authentication, if required

- `password("")`, a string that contains the password for HTTP authentication

- `protocol("xml-rpc")`, a string that identifies the remote procedure call protocol to use, which is either `"xml-rpc"` or `"soap"`

- `soapAction("")`, a string used by SOAP that is disregarded for XML-RPC

The default values are usually acceptable for most of these parameters, aside from the first four.

The `xml.rpc()` verb translates UserTalk data types and XML-RPC data types transparently, enabling you to work with remote procedures simply by using data in expected forms.

Procedure parameters are specified as a list in which each element can be an object of any UserTalk data type.

The return value of a procedure can be a list or any of the XML-RPC data types—use the typeof operator with any list element to identify its data type.

Listing 17.1 contains odpdemo1.txt, a Web page that displays the results of 10 calls to the dmoz.getRandomSite remote procedure.

LISTING 17.1   The Full Text of odpdemo1.txt

```
1: #title "XML-RPC Demo 1"
2:
3: <p>Random <a href="http://www.dmoz.org">Open Directory Project</a> sites:
4:
5: <ul>
6: <%local (htmltext = "");
7:   for i = 1 to 10 {
8:     local (resp = xml.rpc("cadenhead.org", 4413, "dmoz.getRandomSite"));
9:     local (flStatus = resp[1]);
10:    if (flStatus == "ok") {
11:      local (url, title, description);
12:      url = resp[2];
13:      title = resp[3];
14:      description = resp[4];
15:      htmltext = htmltext + "<li><a href=\"" + url + "\">" + title;
16:      htmltext = htmltext + "</a>: " + description + "</li>";
17:    }
18:    else {
19:      htmltext = htmltext + "<li>Could not get site</li>";
20:    }
21:  };
22:  return (htmltext)%>
23: </ul>
```

When the Web page is rendered, the UserTalk statements in lines 6–22 are executed. The return statement in line 22 causes the contents of the htmltext string to be displayed as output.

The dmoz.getRandomSite procedure takes no parameters and does not require HTTP authentication, so the xml.rpc verb can use it with three arguments (line 6):

```
local (resp = xml.rpc("cadenhead.org", 4413, "dmoz.getRandomSite"));
```

The procedure returns four strings when successfully executed: "ok" followed by the URL, title, and description of a Web site.

The verb returns a list containing the data returned by the procedure. Each list element can be accessed by an index (remember that the first list element in UserTalk is a 1, not a 0), as in line 9:

```
local (flStatus = resp[1]);
```

The rendered Web page is shown in Figure 17.1.

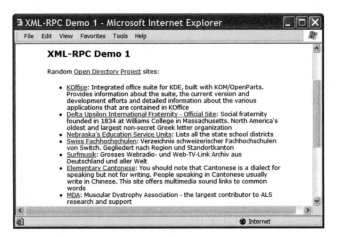

FIGURE 17.1 Displaying XML-RPC data on a Web page.

When an XML-RPC procedure should be called with parameters, they are stored in order in a list and specified as the fourth argument to xml.rpc.

Listing 17.2 contains odpdemo2.txt, a Web page that calls the dmoz.getMatchingSite remote procedure with one parameter, a word that should be present in the description of the randomly selected site.

LISTING 17.2 The Full Text of odpdemo2.txt

```
1: #title "XML-RPC Demo 2"
2:
3: <p>Random <a href="http://www.dmoz.org">Open Directory Project</a> sites:
4:
5: <ul>
6: <%local (htmltext = "");
7:   for i = 1 to 10 {
```

LISTING 17.2   Continued

```
 8:     local (params = {"sports"});
 9:     local (resp = xml.rpc("cadenhead.org", 4413, "dmoz.getMatchingSite", @params));
10:     local (flStatus = resp[1]);
11:     if (flStatus == "ok") {
12:       local (url, title, description);
13:       url = resp[2];
14:       title = resp[3];
15:       description = resp[4];
16:       htmltext = htmltext + "<li><a href=\"" + url + "\">" + title;
17:       htmltext = htmltext + "</a>: " + description + "</li>";
18:     }
19:     else {
20:       htmltext = htmltext + "<li>Could not get site</li>";
21:     }
22:   };
23:   return (htmltext)%>
24: </ul>
```

The parameter list is created and then used in the call to xml.rpc (lines 8–9):

```
local (params = {"sports"});
local (resp = xml.rpc("cadenhead.org", 4413, "dmoz.getMatchingSite",
➥@params));
```

Offering Web Services with XML-RPC

Radio functions as an XML-RPC server, as well as a client. Surprisingly enough, it's easier to offer Web services with the software than it is to call them.

To offer an XML-RPC Web service in Radio, save a UserTalk script that returns a value as a text file in the software's Web Services folder.

That's all there is to it. Radio will find the procedures in the file, registering each as an XML-RPC procedure.

Listing 17.3 contains a simple service.

LISTING 17.3 The Full Text of `secondsUntilChristmas.txt`

```
on secondsUntilChristmas () {
  return (html.data.standardMacros.secsToChristmas());
}
```

Each procedure is identified on Radio's XML-RPC server by using `radio.` followed by the procedure name, so in this example it is `radio.secondsUntilChristmas`.

Radio looks for remote procedure calls on port 5335, the same port it uses to serve the desktop Web site, at the file path `/RPC2`.

The script saved in the `Web Services` folder can be a full UserTalk script or simply a call to a script in the main object database.

The script can take parameters, which will be translated from XML-RPC data types into UserTalk data types when it is called. Likewise, the return value of the procedure will be translated automatically.

A Web page that calls this Web service is contained in Listing 17.4.

LISTING 17.4 The Full Text of `xmas.txt`

```
1: #title "Ho Ho Ho"
2:
3: <p>Seconds until Christmas:
4:
5: <p><%xml.rpc ("127.0.0.1", 5335, "radio.secondsUntilChristmas")%>
```

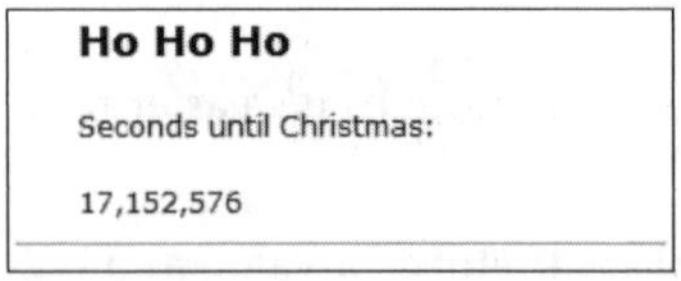

FIGURE 17.2 Using remote procedure calls on the Web.

NOTE

Because the Web service is being called from the same computer as Radio in Line 5, no user authentication is required.

Radio Web services also can be called over the Internet if remote access is enabled (click Prefs on any desktop page, and then click the Remote Access and Security link).

The rendered Web page is shown in Figure 17.2.

The IP address 127.0.0.1 is a reference to your computer (the string `"localhost"` also can be used for this purpose).

The next example script is a more complex Web service that adds a bookmark to an existing link directory outline.

One of the uses of Radio's outliner is the creation of bookmark outlines, a service comparable to the Favorites folder in Internet Explorer and the `bookmark.html` file in Mozilla and Netscape Navigator.

Each item in a Radio outline can have a URL linked with it, which can be clicked to open that page in a Web browser.

A link directory outline can have headings, subheadings, and items with links, which are identified by arrow icons (see Figure 17.3).

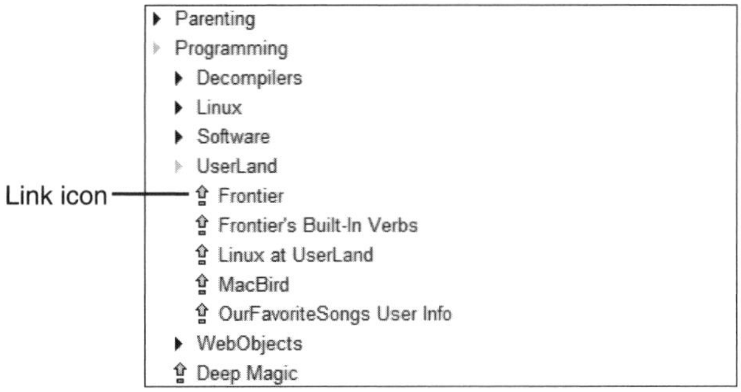

Link icon

FIGURE 17.3   Editing a link directory outline.

Radio stores outlines in OPML, an XML protocol that has been adopted by other software developers and is described in Appendix B, "OPML."

Listing 17.5 contains addBookmark.txt, a UserTalk script that adds a bookmark to an existing OPML link directory file.

This script contains one main procedure: addBookmark(). Save the file in Radio's Web Services folder to make the procedure available over XML-RPC under the name radio.addBookmark.

LISTING 17.5   The Full Text of addBookmark.txt

```
 1: on addBookmark(destFile, url, title, category, flSort = false) {
 2:   on addItem() {
 3:     op.insertAtEndOfList(title);
 4:     op.attributes.setOne("type", "link");
 5:     op.attributes.setOne("url", url);
 6:     if (flSort) {
 7:       op.sort()
 8:     };
 9:     success = true
10:   };
11:   local (success = false);
12:   local (pc = file.getPathChar);
13:   if destFile == "" {
14:     destFile = user.radio.prefs.wwwfolder + "gems" + pc + "bookmarks.opml"
```

LISTING 17.5   Continued

```
15:   };
16:   local (text = file.readWholeFile(destFile));
17:   op.xmlToOutline(text, @scratchpad.linkDirOutline, flNewOutline: true);
18:   local (oldTarget = target.get());
19:   target.set(@scratchpad.linkDirOutline);
20:   op.firstSummit();
21:   if category == "" {
22:     addItem()
23:   }
24:   else {
25:     local (level = string.countFields(category, "/"));
26:     for i = 1 to level {
27:       local (key = string.nthField (category, "/", i));
28:       local (found = op.findNext(key, true));
29:       if found {
30:         if i == level {
31:           local (type = "none");
32:           op.attributes.getOne("type", @type);
33:           if type == "none" {
34:             op.expand(1);
35:             addItem()
36:           }
37:         }
38:       }
39:     }
40:   };
41:   target.set(oldTarget);
42:   text = op.outlineToXml(@scratchpad.linkDirOutline);
43:   file.writeWholeFile(destFile, text);
44:   return (success)
45: }
```

The addBookmark script uses `file` and `xml` verbs to read and write the OPML link directory file. The outline is searched and edited using op verbs. These verbs were covered in preceding chapters of Part III and are also documented by UserLand on the Web at http://docserver.userland.com.

The Web service is called with five parameters:

- destFile, a string that contains the location and name of the link directory; the default is bookmarks.opml in Radio's gems folder

- `url`, a string that contains the link of the new bookmark

- `title`, a string that contains the text to associate with the link

- `category`, a string that names the parent item under which the bookmark should be saved, which can be specified in three ways:

    - As an empty string, which stores the bookmark in the outline's top level.

    - As an item name, which stores the bookmark under the top-level heading matching that name. Using Figure 17.3's outline as an example, using Programming as the category saves the bookmark as a sibling to the Decompilers and Linux items.

    - As several item names separated by slash characters (/), which stores the bookmark under the last subheading in the list. Also from Figure 17.3, using Programming/UserLand as the category stores the bookmark as a sibling to the Frontier and MacBird items.

- `flSort`, when `true`, this Boolean causes the bookmark item's siblings to be sorted after it is added to the outline; the default is `false`.

The `addBookmark` Web service can be called by an XML-RPC client. The following code is an example of how to call it with UserTalk:

```
params = {"c:\\bookmarks\\bookmarks.opml", "http://www.inessential.com",
➥"Brent Simmons", "Weblogs"};
xml.rpc ("127.0.0.1", 5335, "radio.addBookmark", @params)
```

Summary

XML-RPC, which is transmitted over HTTP and uses XML as the format for client requests and server responses, has become extremely popular since its initial release in 1998.

Part of the reason for its popularity is the protocol's simplicity: One of the design goals of XML-RPC was to be as simple as possible so that any developer could make use of remote procedure calls.

Radio UserLand supports this goal as both an XML-RPC client and a server. You have to learn only one new technique in order to call the Web services of others and produce your own—the UserTalk verb `xml.rpc()`.

Everything else uses the techniques required for general UserTalk programming: calling scripts, using parameters, and handling UserTalk data types.

Sending and Receiving Email

18

In addition to supporting new forms of Internet data exchange, such as XML-RPC Web services, Radio UserLand supports one of the oldest: electronic mail.

Radio scripts can retrieve email and attached files, storing them in a table in an object database. Each header is saved as a string in the table and a subtable holds one or more attached files.

Scripts also can send files using strings and a table to define the headers of the message.

Receiving Email from a POP Server

The UserTalk verb tcp.getMail() reads all of the email for an account on a POP server, storing the results in a table. Mail can be deleted or left on the server after being read.

Each retrieved email is stored in a numbered subtable that contains strings for each header, as shown in Figure 18.1.

There's also a text item containing the body of the mail and a msg item containing the entire mail (the headers followed by a blank line and the body).

This verb takes the following parameters (with default values in parentheses):

- host (no default), a string that identifies the host-name or IP address of the POP server

- username (no default), a string that contains an existing account on that server

- password (no default), a string that contains the password for that account

- adrMsgTable (no default), the address of a table in which received email should be stored; anything presently at that address will be deleted

- deleteMessages (user.prefs.getMail.deleteMessages), a Boolean that is true if messages should be deleted on the POP server after being received; the default value is true when Radio is installed

- timeOutTicks (user.prefs.getMail.timeOutTicks), a number that contains the ticks (1/60th of a second) before the request is cancelled and an error is generated; the default is set to 600

- flMessages (user.prefs.getMail.flMessages), when true, this Boolean causes Radio to display information about the request in the About Radio UserLand dialog box

Name	Value	Kind
▶ newMail	1 item	table
▶ 0001	11 items	table
▶ Date	Fri, 20 Jun 2003 18:33:01 -0400	string [31]
▶ From	root <root@localhost.localdomain>	string [33]
▶ fullHeader	+OK 1759 octets\r\nReturn-Path: <root@localhost.localdomain>...	string [445]
▶ Message-Id	<200306202233.h5KMX1q02400@localhost.localdomain>	string [49]
▶ msg	+OK 1759 octets\r\nReturn-Path: <root@localhost.localdomain>...	string [1779]
▶ Received	(from root@localhost) by localhost.localdomain (8.11.6/8.11.6) i...	string [124]
▶ Return-Path	<root@localhost.localdomain>	string [28]
▶ Status		string [0]
▶ Subject	localhost.localdomain 06/20/03:18.33 system check	string [49]
▶ text	\r\n\nUnusual System Events\r\n=-=-=-=-=-=-=-=\r\nJun 20 ...	string [1325]
▶ To	logcheck@localhost.localdomain	string [30]

Kind: ▼ Sort: ▼

FIGURE 18.1   Viewing an individual email's table.

Retrieving mail is error-prone due to network connectivity and account authentication problems, so the verb can be enclosed within try and else statements:

```
try {
    tcp.getMail ("example.com", "bull", "mancuso", @scratchpad.email)
}
else {
    scriptError (tryError)
};
```

This approach enables a script to take advantage of Radio's built-in error reporting capabilities. When a statement causes an error within a try block, a message describing the error is stored in the tryError variable.

Calling scriptError() opens the familiar error dialog box in Radio and displays a string specified as a parameter.

Listing 18.1 contains workspace.readMail(), a script that reads incoming mail and turns the 15 most recently received items into an RSS feed that can be read with Radio's news aggregator.

LISTING 18.1   The Full Text of workspace.readMail

```
 1: on readMail(host, username, password, rssfile = "mailrss.xml") {
 2:    on add(line) {
 3:      add a line to the RSS file
 4:      if indentlevel < 0 {
 5:        indentlevel = 0
 6:      };
 7:      xmltext = xmltext + string.filledstring("  ", indentlevel) +
➥line + "\r\n"
 8:    };
 9:    on encode(line) {
10:      « encode text so that it can be XML data
11:      if system.environment.isMac {
12:        return (xml.entityEncode(string.macToLatin(line), true))
13:      }
14:      else {
15:        return (xml.entityEncode(line, true))
16:      }
17:    };
18:    local (indentlevel = 0);
19:    local (mail = @scratchpad.["mail-" +host+"-"+username]);
20:    local (out = @workspace.["mail-" +host+"-"+username]);
21:    « create recent mail table in workspace (if necessary)
22:    if not defined(out^.items) {
23:      new (tableType, out);
24:      new (tableType, @out^.items)
25:    };
26:    if not defined(out^.count) {
27:      out^.count = 0
28:    };
29:    « retrieve current mail, storing it in a scratchpad table
30:    try {
31:      tcp.getMail(host, username, password, mail)
32:    }
33:    else {
34:      scriptError(tryError)
35:    };
36:    « loop through current mail
37:    for i = 1 to sizeof(mail) {
```

LISTING 18.1   Continued

```
38:    if defined(mail^[i]) {
39:      « retrieve current mail item
40:      local (when = mail^[i].date);
41:      local (subject = mail^[i].subject);
42:      local (text = mail^[i].text);
43:      « add HTML paragraph and line breaks
44:      text = string.replaceAll(text, "\r\n \r\n", "<p>");
45:      text = string.replaceAll(text, "\r\n", "<br>");
46:      local (from = mail^[i].from);
47:      from = string.replaceAll(from, "<", "");
48:      from = string.replaceAll(from, ">", "");
49:      « add the item to recent mail table
50:      local (ct = string.padWithZeros(out^.count, 8) );
51:      new (tableType, @out^.items.[ct]);
52:      out^.items.[ct].title = subject + " from " + from;
53:      out^.items.[ct].description = text;
54:      out^.count = out^.count + 1;
55:      « delete an old item when more than 15 items exist
56:      ct = string.padWithZeros(out^.count - 16, 8);
57:      if defined (out^.items.[ct]) {
58:        delete (@out^.items.[ct])
59:      }
60:    }
61:    };
62:    « create RSS file of all recent mail
63:    local (xmltext = "");
64:    add ("<?xml version=\"1.0\"?>");
65:    add ("<rss version=\"2.0\">");
66:    indentlevel++;
67:    add ("<channel>");
68:    indentlevel++;
69:    add ("<title>Incoming mail</title>");
70:    add ("<link>" + radio.weblog.getUrl() + "gems/" + rssfile + "</link>");
71:    add ("<description>Incoming mail</description>");
72:    for i = sizeof(out^.items) downto 1 {
73:      add ("<item>");
74:      indentlevel++;
75:      add ("<title>" + encode (out^.items[i].title) + "</title>");
76:      add ("<description>" + encode(out^.items[i].description) +
➥"</description>");
77:      indentlevel—;
```

LISTING 18.1 Continued

```
78:    add ("</item>")
79:    };
80:    indentlevel—;
81:    add ("</channel>");
82:    indentlevel—;
83:    add ("</rss>");
84:    local (pc = file.getPathChar() );
85:    local (f = file.folderFromPath(Frontier.getProgramPath()) +
➥"www" + pc + "gems" + pc + rssfile);
86:    file.writeTextFile(f, xmltext)
87: }
```

The script is called with the host, username, and password of a POP server account. A fourth parameter, rssfile, can be used to specify a name for the RSS file. The default name is mailrss.xml.

The RSS files generated by this script are stored in Radio's www/gems folder, causing them to be upstreamed automatically each time the script runs.

Comments in the script describe most of its functionality.

Because the email is being presented with an RSS newsreader, line and paragraph breaks are changed into HTML tags so they will display properly:

```
text = string.replaceAll(text, "\r\n \r\n", "<p>");
text = string.replaceAll(text, "\r\n",
"<br>");
```

Also, because email From headers often contain "<" and ">" characters that would cause the header to be displayed incorrectly using HTML, they are removed:

> **TIP**
>
> An alternative solution: Call the string. cleanMailAddress() verb with an email address as the only parameter. This verb displays the address in the form *Name* (*username@example.com*).

```
from = string.replaceAll(from, "<", "");
from = string.replaceAll(from, ">", "");
```

Two local handlers are used in the script: add(), which adds a line to the RSS file and indents it properly, and encode(), which makes sure that all elements of the RSS file contain properly encoded XML data.

In order for a string to be used as character data in XML, some characters must be encoded as entity references. For example, the "<" and ">" characters are replaced in data with the entities < and >.

The verb `xml.entityEncode()` returns a version of a string that's properly encoded. It takes two parameters:

- `unencodedString`, the string to encode

- `flAlphaEntities` (default: `false`), a Boolean that's `true` if the characters "<", ">", "&", and double-quote marks should be converted to entity references

On Macs, two steps are required to properly encode a string for XML. First, `string.macToLatin()` is called to convert from the Mac OS to the Latin character set, and then the string is XML-encoded.

After the script has been compiled, the `scheduler.addTask()` verb can be used to schedule it to run repeatedly. This verb takes three parameters:

- `taskTime`, a date that represents the time at which it should next be run

- `scriptString`, a string that contains the call to the script

- `minutesBetweenRuns`, a number that determines how many minutes will pass between each run of the script

The `clock.now()` verb returns a date that represents the current time, making it a convenient value for the first parameter to `scheduler.addTask()`.

Here's an example that can be executed in the Quick Script dialog box (choose Tools, Developers, Quick Script) that runs the script once an hour:

```
scheduler.addTask (clock.now(), "workspace.readMail(\"example.com\",
➥\"bull\", \"mancuso\", \"bullmail.xml\")", 60)
```

Each scheduled task is an item in the `user.scheduler.tasks` table with a name of the form `taskx`, as shown in Figure 18.2.

Name	Value	Kind
▶ task1	5 items	table
▶ ctRuns	10	number
▶ error		string [0]
▶ minutesBetweenRuns	60	number
▶ script	on disk	script
▶ taskTime	6/21/2003; 1:55:00 PM	date

| Kind ▼ | Sort ▼ |

FIGURE 18.2   Editing tasks in the main object database.

These values can be edited. The `taskTime` date represents the approximate time at which the script will next be run, `minutesBetweenRuns` is the same as the parameter, and `script` holds the script that will be called.

Sending Email to an SMTP Server

The UserTalk verb tcp.sendMail() sends an email to one or more addresses using an SMTP server. It takes the following parameters:

TIP

If you want a script to be called at a specific time each hour or day, determining the first parameter of scheduler.addTask() can be cumbersome. Usually, I schedule tasks with clock.now() as the first parameter, and then edit the task's table manually to set up the desired time.

- recipient (""), a string that contains the email address of the recipient

- subject (""), a string that contains the subject of the email

- message (""), a string that contains the body of the email

- sender (user.prefs.mailAddress), a string that contains the sender's email address; the default is the address used when Radio was installed

- cc (""), a string containing a comma-separated list of email addresses for carbon copy (CC) recipients

- bcc (""), a string containing a comma-separated list of blind carbon copy (BCC) recipients (CC addresses are disclosed to recipients and BCC addresses are not)

- host (user.prefs.mailHost), a string that identifies the name or IP address of the SMTP server used to deliver the message; the default is Radio's Outgoing (SMTP) Mail Server preference

- mimeType ("text/plain"), a string identifying the MIME type of the email, which is usually "text/plain" for text and "text/html" for HTML email

- adrHdrTable (nil), the address of a table that holds headers for the email; standard headers that appear in this table take preference over those defined as other parameters

- timeOutTicks (3600), a number that contains the ticks (1/60th of a second) before the request is cancelled and an error is generated; the default is 60 seconds

- flMessages (true), when true, this Boolean causes Radio to display information about the request in the About Radio UserLand dialog box

Like tcp.getMail(), this script can be called within a try block to deal with connectivity and access problems sending the email.

Listing 18.2 contains workspace.writeMail(), a script that emails items from an RSS newsfeed.

LISTING 18.2   The Full Text of `workspace.writeMail`

```
1: on writeMail(recipient, service, maxItems = 15) {
2:   on add (line) {
3:     «add a line to the e-mail
4:     mailtext = mailtext + line + "\r\n"
5:   };
6:   «get addresses of tables in aggregatorData.root
7:   local (adrdata = xml.aggregator.init ());
8:   local (adrservice = @adrdata^.services.[service]);
9:   local (adritems = @adrservice^.compilation.items);
10:   local (count = 0,  title, description, link, mailtext);
11:   «get the RSS service's title and URL
12:   title = adrservice^.compilation.channeltitle;
13:   link = adrservice^.compilation.channellink;
14:   add ("Current items from <a href=\"" + link + "\">" + title + "</a>");
15:   «look for items from most recent backwards
16:   for i = sizeof (adritems^) downto 1 {
17:     «add each item to body of e-mail
18:     add ("<p>" + adritems^[i].title);
19:     add ("<p><hr><p>");
20:     count++;
21:     «quit when the maximum is reached
22:     if count >= maxItems {
23:       break
24:     }
25"  };
24:   «attempt to send the e-mail
25:   try {
26:     tcp.sendMail ( recipient, "New items from " + title, mailtext,
➥mimeType: "text/html" )
27:   }
28:   else {
29:     scriptError (tryError)
30:   };
31:   return (true)
32: }
```

Rather than retrieving RSS files over the Internet, the `workspace.writeMail()` script uses RSS data that the Radio news aggregator has already collected.

The writeMail() script can be called with three parameters:

- recipient (no default), the recipient's email address

- service (no default), a string containing the URL of an RSS newsfeed to which you subscribe

- maxItems (15), the maximum number of items that should be retrieved from the newsfeed

The script uses data in aggregatorData.root, a database in Radio's Data Files folder that holds the data collected by the news aggregator for each of your subscriptions.

Each time the aggregator checks one of your RSS subscriptions, it creates a compilation subtable containing all of the items in that newsfeed, as shown in Figure 18.3.

Name	Value	Kind
▸ http://www.cadenhead.or...	13 items	table
▸ compilation	10 items	table
▸ changesUrl	http://www.weblogs.com/rssUpdate...	string [45]
▸ channeldescription	Programming and publishing news a...	string [43]
▸ channellanguage	en-us	string [5]
▸ channellink	http://www.cadenhead.org/workbench/	string [35]
▸ channeltitle	Workbench	string [9]
▸ cloud	on disk	table
▸ format	RSS2	string [4]
▸ itemHistory	on disk	table
▸ items	10 items	table
▸ 00001	3 items	table
▸ comments	http://www.pycs.net/system/comme...	string [139]
▸ permalink	http://www.cadenhead.org/workbenc...	string [55]
▸ title	<a href="http://www.cadenhead.org/...	string [455]
Kind: ▾ Sort: ▾		

FIGURE 18.3 Using RSS data stored by the aggregator.

The address of the aggregator database, RSS subscription (also called a *service*), and its items are determined by the following statements:

```
local (adrdata = xml.aggregator.init ());
local (adrservice = @adrdata^.services.[ser-
vice]);
local (adritems =
@adrservice^.compilation.items);
```

The xml.aggregator.init() verb, which initializes values in the aggregator database when they are not present, returns the address of the database.

The service variable, which is passed as a parameter to workspace.writeMail(), contains the URL of an RSS newsfeed.

Receiving Emailed File Attachments

File attachments for email are currently supported in one direction—they can be received by tcp.getMail() but not sent by tcp.sendMail().

If an email message includes one or more attached files, they will be stored in a parts table of the message with each file in its own subtable, as shown in Figure 18.4.

Name	Value	Kind
▸ mail-cadenhead.org-photohead	1 item	table
▸ 0001	15 items	table
▸ Content-Type	multipart/mixed; boundary="10874617-PO...	string [50]
▸ Date	Mon, 23 Jun 2003 12:27:54 -0400	string [31]
▸ From	Rogers Cadenhead <rogers@cadenhead.or...	string [39]
▸ fullHeader	+OK 172266 octets\r\nReturn-Path: <roger...	string [910]
▸ Message-Id	<20030623162756.BZJS16268.imf24aec.b...	string [54]
▸ Mime-Version	1.0	string [3]
▸ msg	+OK 172266 octets\r\nReturn-Path: <roger...	string [172288]
▸ parts	3 items	table
▸ 0001	2 items	table
▸ 0002	2 items	table
▸ Content-Type	Content-Type: image/jpeg; name="harrypot...	string [146]
▸ data	/9j/4AAQSkZJRgABAgEASABIAAD/7Rky...	string [87384]

Kind ▾   Sort ▾

FIGURE 18.4   Receiving attached files with an email.

Each file's subtable has two items: a `Content-Type` string that identifies the file type, name, and encoding used to send the file and `data`, a string that contains the file encoded as a string using Base64 encoding.

A Base64-encoded string containing a graphic can be decoded in three steps:

- Call the UserTalk verb `base64.decode()` with the string as a parameter.

- Call the `binary()` verb with the decoded string as a parameter.

- Set the binary type to the four-digit character code identifying the graphic (such as "GIFf" for GIF and "JPEG" for JPEG graphics). Call `setBinaryType()` with two parameters—the binary object and its four-digit code.

The following statements turn a string object holding an attached JPEG graphic (at the address `part^.data`) into a binary object that can be written to disk as a file.

```
part^.data = base64.decode (part^.data);
part^.data = binary (part^.data);
setBinaryType(@part^.data, "JPEG");
```

Listing 18.3 contains `workspace.photokeeper()`, a script that stores graphics sent as email attachments in a Radio folder where they can be upstreamed.

LISTING 18.3   The Full Text of `workspace.photokeeper`

```
1: on photokeeper (host, username, password, folder = "photoalbum") {
2:    local (mail = @scratchpad.["mail-" +host+"-"+username]);
3:    «retrieve current mail, storing it in a scratchpad table
4:    try {
5:      tcp.getMail (host, username, password, mail,  timeOutTicks: 60*60*10)
6:    }
```

LISTING 18.3   Continued

```
 7:   else {
 8:     scriptError (tryError)
 9:   };
10:   «loop through current mail
11:   for mailitem in mail {
12:     «retrieve current mail item
13:     if defined (mailitem^.parts) {
14:       «retrieve any attachments
15:       for part in @mailitem^.parts {
16:         «ignore attachments without a defined content type
17:         if defined (part^.["Content-Type"]) {
18:           «only save image/jpeg and image/gif attachments
19:           local (cType = part^.["Content-Type"], imageType, ext);
20:           if string.patternMatch ("Content-Type: image/jpeg", cType) > 0 {
21:             imageType = 'JPEG';
22:             ext = ".jpg"
23:           };
24:           if string.patternMatch ("Content-Type: image/gif", cType) > 0 {
25:             imageType = 'GIFf';
26:             ext = ".gif"
27:           };
28:           if imageType == "" {
29:             continue
30:           };
31:           «retrieve current filename from content-type header
32:           local (pc = file.getPathChar() );
33:           local (folder = file.folderFromPath(Frontier.getProgramPath())
➡+ "www" + pc + folder + pc);
34:           local (name = "", pos);
35:           pos = string.patternMatch ("name=", cType);
36:           if pos > 0 {
37:             name = string.mid (cType, pos + 6, string.length (cType) - pos);
38:             pos = string.patternMatch ("\"", name);
39:             name = string.mid (name, 1, pos - 1)
40:           }
41:           else {
42:             «if all else fails, generate a unique name
43:             name = file.uniqueName ("picture" + ext, folder)
44:           };
45:           «decode and save the data to a file
46:           part^.data = base64.decode (part^.data);
```

LISTING 18.3   Continued

```
47:            part^.data = binary (part^.data);
48:            setBinaryType(@part^.data, imageType);
49:            local (f = folder + name);
50:            file.writeWholeFile (f, part^.data)
51:         }
52:      }
53:    }
54:  }
55: }
```

Because attached files take longer to retrieve, the default value of the timeOutTicks parameter, 10 seconds, is likely to be too short. The photokeeper() script waits up to 10 minutes before timing out with an error.

Summary

The tcp.getMail() and tcp.sendMail() verbs make it easy to incorporate email data exchange into Radio UserLand.

Radio can send and read email, as well as read files attached to an email. (Sending attached files is not presently supported.)

UserTalk's tcp verbs also include support for other Internet protocols such as File Transfer Protocol (FTP) and domain name service (DNS) lookups.

Handling Errors and Debugging Scripts

19

IN THIS CHAPTER

- ▶ **Running Scripts with the Debugger**
- ▶ **Viewing Information as a Script Runs**
- ▶ **Setting and Removing Breakpoints**
- ▶ **Examining Runtime Errors**
- ▶ **Stopping a Running Script**
- ▶ **Handling Errors in Running Scripts**

Radio UserLand programming becomes considerably easier through the use of its debugger, a tool that enables UserTalk scripts to be run interactively as their variables and other runtime conditions are inspected.

The debugger, which is available in the script-editing window, can be used to stop script execution at specific lines, step through scripts one line at a time, and view local variables and the object database before execution is resumed.

Users of other debuggers will find Radio's tool easy to pick up, because the functionality and terminology are comparable to debuggers offered for other programming languages.

Running Scripts with the Debugger

Even if this is your first experience with a debugger, the time spent learning its use should pay off quickly when you begin applying its bug-hunting techniques to your own UserTalk projects.

TIP

Before you get into any serious debugging, it's worth remembering one of the more invisible sources of bugs in a UserTalk script—the differences that can occur between a compiled version of a script and the one that's run with the Run button.

There are two versions of any UserTalk script that can be run: The explicitly compiled version, which is produced when the Compile button is clicked, and the implicitly compiled one, which is produced each time the Run button is clicked.

These can be different. If you open a script, change a line, and click Run, Radio implicitly compiles and runs the changed version. However, there's still an unchanged version that will run if the script is called using its address.

To clear up any confusion, always click Compile before clicking Run. The only time not to do this is when other Radio threads might call the script as you are still working on it. However, you can avoid that problem by working on a copy of the script in your workspace while it is being written, and then copying it to the correct location afterward.

Debugging is one of those "eat your vegetables" kinds of tasks that programmers often neglect, using more informal techniques, such as displaying the value of variables in a dialog box or saving them to a temporary table.

My own tendency has been to use Radio's `dialog.alert()` verb to display the contents of one or more variables and objects. The verb displays a string—its first argument—in a dialog box and plays an alert sound, as in this example from a script that uses the outliner:

```
dialog.alert(op.getLineText())
```

The output is shown in Figure 19.1.

This technique works, but it only shows you some runtime information about the script, always stops at the same point, and leaves issues in the script that must be removed later.

Another less intrusive way to provide additional information as a script runs is to use the `msg()` verb, which displays text in the About Radio UserLand dialog box, as in this example:

```
msg("Looking for " + entryPageUrl)
```

FIGURE 19.1   Displaying a dialog box.

Any information that's presented in either of these ways is also available when using the debugger, a feature that's available whenever a UserTalk script is being edited with Radio.

The debugger is an alternative way to run a script.

When a script is being edited, there are Run, Debug, and Compile buttons atop the script window.

To run a script with the debugger, click the Debug button. The debugger gets ready to run the program and displays a new toolbar atop the editing window with seven buttons, as shown in Figure 19.2.

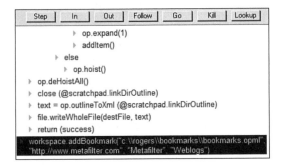

FIGURE 19.2   Editing a script.

Radio is in debugger mode for as long as these buttons are visible.

The line that will be run next by the debugger is selected in the script outline. In Figure 19.2, it's a call to `workspace.addBookmark()`.

Most of the buttons on the debugger's toolbar are navigational. They dictate how much of the script to run before pausing and whether to open other scripts in the debugger as they are called.

The Kill button stops running the script and closes the debugger.

The In button jumps into the next script encountered by the debugger. When In is clicked, the debugger runs the script without interruption until it encounters a line that calls a new script or reaches the end of the script. When a new script is encountered, the debugger opens the script in an editing window and pauses at the first line.

For example, Figure 19.3 shows an active debugging session.

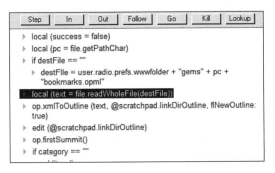

FIGURE 19.3   Debugging a script as it runs.

The selected line in Figure 19.3 assigns a local variable to the result of the file.readWholeFile() script.

If In was clicked at this point, the debugger would open the readWholeFile() script, select its first line, and pause. Two scripts would be open at this point—the original script and readWholeFile().

The Out button jumps out of the present script, running the script until it completes. If the script is one that had been jumped into, the script window closes and the debugger returns to the calling script.

The practical result is that this button can be used to get out of the most recent use of In.

The Step button executes the next line of the script. You can step through the entire script one line at a time in this manner—the selected line changes with each step.

Figure 19.4 shows another point in the same debugging session.

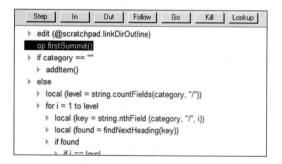

| Step | In | Out | Follow | Go | Kill | Lookup |

▸ edit (@scratchpad.linkDirOutline)
    op firstSummit()
▸ if category == ""
    ▸ addItem()
▸ else
    ▸ local (level = string.countFields(category, "/"))
    ▸ for i = 1 to level
        ▸ local (key = string.nthField (category, "/", i))
        ▸ local (found = findNextHeading(key))
        ▸ if found
            ▸ if i == level

FIGURE 19.4   Stepping through a script line by line.

CAUTION

When you run most scripts with the debugger, you might be surprised by what happens if the first thing you click is the Step button. UserTalk runs the script without pause and closes the debugger.

This occurs because Step doesn't descend into scripts or handler methods. Because the script is executed by running a test call to its handler, Step runs this call without interruption.

To begin debugging a script that has a handler method, as most do, click In rather than Step. Radio jumps into the handler and pauses before executing its first line.

If a script has no handler method, Step can be used to execute the first line and pause afterward.

The selected line executes one of the outliner verbs, op.firstSummit(). Clicking Step at this point executes that verb without opening the firstSummit() script and proceeds to the next line shown in Figure 19.4, an if statement.

The Go button executes the remainder of the script, closing the debugger when it reaches the end.

The Follow button is similar to Go, but it provides more information as it executes the script. Each line of the script is selected as it is being executed, enabling you to follow along (although it often runs more quickly than you can adequately track).

Both Go and Follow cause the Go button to change into a Stop button while the script is running. As you might have guessed, clicking this button pauses the execution of the script after the current line is finished.

Viewing Information as a Script Runs

When a UserTalk script is running, Radio will open windows and databases and can show data as it is being manipulated by the script.

A good example of this: any script that uses the op verbs to open, navigate, and change items in the outliner.

Watching a script run as it manipulates an outline is a unique experience if you're unfamiliar with Radio—the software opens the outliner by itself, expands and collapses nodes, and adds and removes items, functioning as if a ghost were manning the keyboard.

This trait of the software is helpful when you're running a script with the debugger, because you can observe the process and determine whether Radio is making use of its database and data windows correctly.

When a script is being run with the debugger, you can pause execution and look around, opening databases, viewing the contents of tables and individual item's values, and looking at each open window to see its contents and current state.

When the debugger is paused, the Lookup button opens a table that contains all local variables that exist at the currently selected line. This table is shown in Figure 19.5.

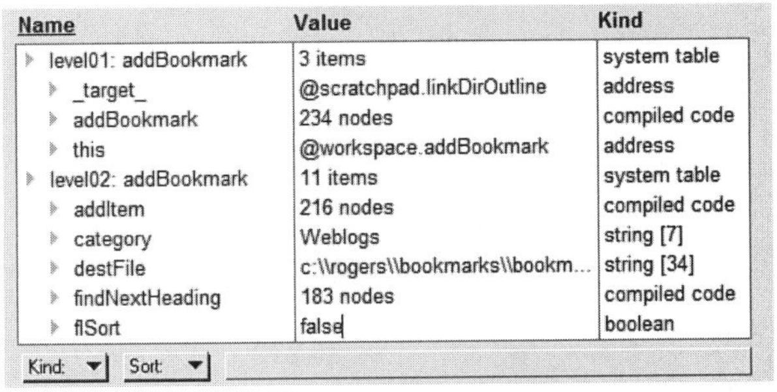

Name	Value	Kind
▷ level01: addBookmark	3 items	system table
▷ _target_	@scratchpad.linkDirOutline	address
▷ addBookmark	234 nodes	compiled code
▷ this	@workspace.addBookmark	address
▷ level02: addBookmark	11 items	system table
▷ addItem	216 nodes	compiled code
▷ category	Weblogs	string [7]
▷ destFile	c:\\rogers\\bookmarks\\bookm...	string [34]
▷ findNextHeading	183 nodes	compiled code
▷ flSort	false	boolean

Kind: ▼   Sort: ▼

FIGURE 19.5   Viewing the local variable stack.

The table opened by the Lookup button is `system.compiler.stack`, a table that holds the names and values of all local variables while they are in *scope*, the portion of the script in which the variable exists and can be used.

The stack is organized by script and level, as indicated by the names of each top-level table.

The level indicates variable scope, which is determined by the outline level at which a script variable was declared with a `local` statement.

When a variable is no longer in scope, it disappears from the stack table along with any other variables that exist at the same level.

The stack table isn't just read-only; variables can be changed by editing their entries in the `Value` column (for most data types) or double-clicking the item to open an editing window (for outlines, wp text, and the like).

Variable value changes are reflected in the script executed by the debugger.

You can look up objects from the script window while you are debugging or at any other time. Select the full name of the object, hold down the Ctrl (Windows) or Cmd (Mac OS) key, and then double-click the name. Radio opens the object or the table that contains it, depending upon its data type.

This even works for local variables as a script is being debugged. Double-clicking the variable's name while holding Ctrl or Cmd opens the stack table with the variable selected.

Setting and Removing Breakpoints

All of Radio's debugging functions can be affected by the placement of *breakpoints*, lines that have been marked to stop execution before they are executed.

A UserTalk script can contain numerous breakpoints, each of which is displayed with a stop icon in place of the triangle icon, as shown in Figure 19.6.

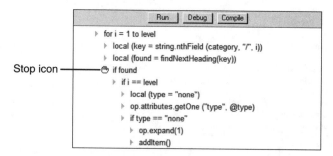

FIGURE 19.6   Stopping script execution with breakpoints.

When the debugger reaches a line with a breakpoint set, it selects the line and pauses execution. Breakpoints are ignored when the script runs normally; they don't have to be removed.

The breakpoint stops execution regardless of which debugger function was used to reach that point in the script. Because it can be tedious to step through a program one line at a time or jump into and out of scripts, breakpoints are often the easiest way to focus on the code where an error is occurring.

To set a breakpoint, select the line where it should be placed and choose Script, Toggle Breakpoint or use the shortcut (Ctrl+K or Cmd+K). To signify the breakpoint, the line's icon changes from a triangle to a stop icon. The same command is used to remove a breakpoint later.

A breakpoint works only if it is set on a line that actually executes, so it shouldn't be placed on a comment. Also, a few UserTalk keywords are not by themselves executable, so they don't work with breakpoints—bundle, case values, else, local statements that do not assign any values, and on.

Examining Runtime Errors

When a UserTalk script generates a runtime error, it halts the execution of the program if the erroneous line was not placed within a try block.

Runtime errors are displayed in an error dialog box alongside a GoTo button, as shown in Figure 19.7.

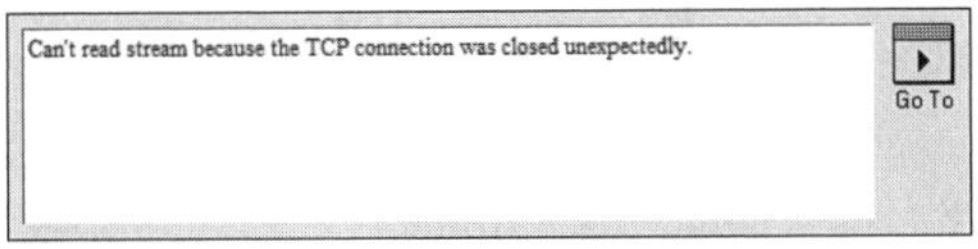

FIGURE 19.7   Examining a runtime error.

Click Go To to see the line of the script where the error occurred. Radio opens the script with the line selected.

This error isn't necessarily in your own code; UserTalk verbs can generate runtime errors if an unexpected condition occurs, such as the TCP/IP network connectivity problem shown in Figure 19.7.

To see how the script got to the point at which the error happened, you can view the entire chain of script calls that brought the script there. Instead of clicking Go To, hold the button down until you see a pop-up menu listing one or more scripts, as shown in Figure 19.8.

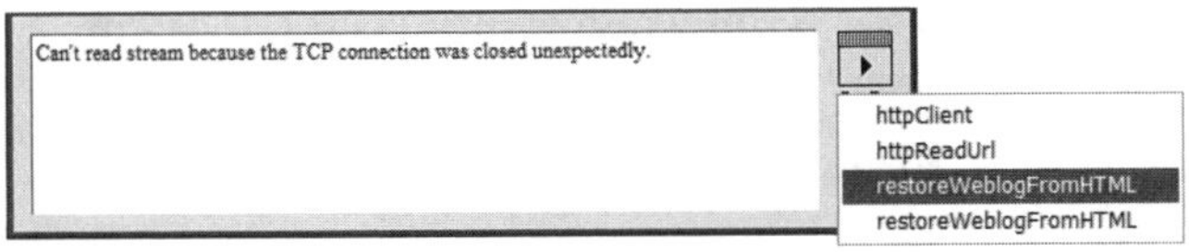

FIGURE 19.8   Viewing the script calling chain.

Choose one of the items to go to the line of that script where the call occurred.

The Go To pop-up menu goes backwards up the chain. In Figure 19.8, you can see that restoreWeblogFromHTML called restoreWeblogFromHTML, which called httpReadUrl, which called httpClient.

Here's the call chain matching that figure, beginning with the first line in the chain:

In the restoreWeblogFromHTML() script, the last line calls a handler in that script with the same name:

```
restoreWeblogFromHTML("http://blogs.salon.com/0002379/", "<br>
➥<div class=\"itemTitle\"><b></b></div>", "<font class=\"small\"
➥size=\"-1\" color=\"gray\">", "<font class=\"small\" size=\"-1\"
➥color=\"gray\">", "  <a href=\"..")
```

In that handler, a Web page is loaded by calling the tcp.httpReadURL() verb as part of a variable assignment:

```
local (weblogPage = tcp.httpReadURL(entryPageUrl))
```

In the httpReadUrl() script, the page is loaded over HTTP using the tcp.httpClient() verb in a complex return statement:

```
return (string.httpResultSplit(tcp.httpClient(server:urllist [2],
➥path:urllist [3])))
```

In most cases, it's likely that the runtime error is either caused by something in your script or must be dealt with there. Changing code in Radio's system table to fix an error will only resolve the problem temporarily.

When UserLand updates that portion of the object database in a future update, the fix will disappear.

Stopping a Running Script

Like most other programming languages, UserTalk scripts can have bugs that trap execution of the program in an *infinite loop*, a line or block of lines that loop endlessly because their exit condition will never be met.

To stop a running script, click the Kill button atop the script window or press the shortcut key Cmd+. (Mac OS) or Ctrl+. (Windows).

You might need to do this several times, even to the point of holding the shortcut key down.

Handling Errors in Running Scripts

During the execution of a script, there are numerous errors that can cause the program to halt with a runtime error.

The normal behavior of a script is to open an Error Info dialog box displaying the error message like the one in Figure 19.9.

FIGURE 19.9   Viewing a runtime error.

Click the Go To button in the Error Info dialog box to open the script where the error occurred at the line that triggered it.

In many cases, this is the desired response in the event of an error—the script stops when something occurs that would prevent it from running normally.

A script can respond to errors by enclosing them within a try or try-else block.

A try block encloses statements that might cause a runtime error. If an error occurs in one statement in the block, the script exits the block immediately, skipping the rest of the block.

The following statement calls the tcp.getMail() verb to retrieve email from a POP server:

```
tcp.getMail("example.com", "myusername", "mypassword", @scratchpad.mx)
```

There are many errors that can occur as mail is being retrieved—the username or password might be incorrect, the POP server might be offline or unreachable, and so on.

If tcp.getMail() is called and an error occurs, the script will halt execution and display an Error Info dialog box describing the problem.

To prevent the script from stopping in these circumstances, the verb can be called in a try block:

```
try {
  tcp.getMail("example.com", "myusername", "mypassword", @scratchpad.mx)
}
```

This try block causes the script to proceed without interruption whether or not the call to tcp.getMail() was successful.

A try-else block can be used to respond to both successful and erroneous execution of statements. The else block is executed only when an error occurs within the try block. A message describing the error is stored in a local variable called `tryError`, which is available within the scope of the else block.

Here's an example that displays the result of a call to `tcp.getMail()` whether it succeeds or fails:

```
local (result);
try {
  tcp.getMail("example.com", "myusername", "mypassword", @scratchpad.mx);
  result = "Mail retrieval complete."}
else {
  result = tryError
};
dialog.notify(result)
```

In the `else` block, a script can mimic Radio and halt execution with the display of an Error Info dialog box. Call the `scriptError()` verb with one parameter—the error message to display:

```
try {
  tcp.getMail("example.com", "myusername", "mypassword", @scratchpad.mx)}
else {
  scriptError(tryError)
}
```

Summary

The time spent mastering the particulars of a debugger pays dividends when you face the inevitable task of finding and fixing bugs in your own programs.

Radio UserLand's debugger is comparable in function to those available in other programming environments. You can step through a script one line at a time, jump in and out of scripts, set breakpoints, and look up the values of local variables.

The debugger also gives you a chance to stop execution of a script during a run so that you can look around the main object database and inspect the state of all windows that have been opened by the code.

Creating and Distributing Tools

Underneath the weblog publishing system and RSS news reader, Radio UserLand is a development environment that can be used to create a wide range of Internet-connected, information-gathering, and end-user software.

The way to extend Radio's capabilities is to offer a *tool*, add-on software that's packaged as a single object database comparable to Radio.root, Radio's primary database and its most important component.

Tools are installed simply by placing them in one of Radio's folders and can be upgraded by their users over the Internet.

Some of Radio's most interesting development is coming from users who have created their own tools.

Using Tools to Extend Radio's Functionality

Radio's Tools menu shows which tools have been installed with the application. Each tool has its own submenu with one or more commands.

Tools are packaged as individual object database files and can be installed with Radio simply by saving the file in Radio's Tools folder. They can be uninstalled just as easily: Simply delete or remove the file.

When a new tool is placed in the Tools folder, Radio should discover the new file automatically, handle any required setup, and add the tool to the Tools menu. (If the tool doesn't appear, exit and restart the application.)

NOTE

A term used often in conjunction with tools is *guest databases*. It refers to any object database that can be used with Radio aside from the main database, `Radio.root`. A tool's functionality is packaged into one guest database and it can use data from one or more additional databases.

The desktop Web site includes a Tools page that displays all of the currently installed tools. Click the Tools link to see it.

The Tools page can be used to deactivate a tool, causing it to stop functioning even though it is in the `Tools` folder. Choose the tool to deactivate, and then click Submit.

Tools can offer most of the functionality of the Radio application. Many tools offer their own preferences page. On the Tools page, click the name of the tool. The preferences page for the Manila-Blogger Bridge, a tool that enables Radio to post to weblogs that use Manila, Blogger, and other software, is shown in Figure 20.1.

This page is presented as part of the desktop Web site, even though it was provided by a tool. When a user changes a preference on this form, it will be received by Radio's built-in responder.

Manila-Blogger Bridge

On this page you can configure Radio 8 to automatically mirror posts to your Radio weblog to a news-item oriented Manila site, a Blogger site, or any centralized blogging tool that supports the Blogger API. See the docs on the Radio UserLand site for more information on how to configure this tool.

☐ Check this box to enable mirroring on the site described below.

Server:	bloggerapitest.manilasites.com
Port:	80
Path:	/RPC2
Blog ID:	http://bloggerapitest.manilasites.com/
Username:	publictestaccount@example.com
Password:	••••••••••

FIGURE 20.1   Editing a tool's preferences.

As this demonstrates, tools can replicate much of the functionality of the parent application—in addition to Web pages and a responder, they can offer scripts, data, a thread, scheduled tasks, node types, and Web services. Like Radio, a tool can be run with menu commands or by using its own desktop Web pages.

During tool installation, Radio supports the tool by adding calls in its database to the scripts and other data in the tool's database. These are removed automatically during uninstallation.

Creating a New Tool

Radio makes it easy to create a new tool by offering a default tool database file you can customize for your particular project.

To start a new tool, follow these steps:

1. Choose Tools, Developers, New Tool.

   A file dialog box opens with the Tools folder visible.

2. In the File Name text field, type a name that isn't already taken and give it the file extension .root.

   The name will be used as a name for the tool in the database and desktop Web pages, so pick something succinct and descriptive.

3. Click the Save button.

Radio creates the database for the new tool and opens it so that you can begin customizing it with your own data and scripts. The database also is added to the Window menu so that it can be opened for editing at any time.

A new tool starts out with 10 tables, each with a name prefixed by the name you chose for the tool. For instance, if the tool was named Web.root, tables begin with the prefix Web.

The following tables are included, with *x* in place of the tool's prefixed name:

- *x*Data, data used by the tool such as user preferences

- *x*Info, information about the tool and its author

- *x*NodeTypes, the tool's special node types

- *x*Responder, the tool's responder

- *x*RpcHandlers, the tool's XML-RPC handlers

- *x*SoapHandlers, the tool's SOAP handlers

- *x*Suite, the scripts that comprise the tool's primary functionality

- *x*Thread, a script that loops continuously

- *x*Website, the desktop Web pages that represent the tool's Web browser interface

- *x*WindowTypes, the tool's special window types

The tables that come with a new tool can be edited, or if you don't need some of the functionality for that tool, deleted.

Describing the Tool

The *x*Info table contains the basic facts about the tool: its name, description, and home page; the author's name and email address; and the tool's release date and version number.

With the exception of the home page, all of these items appear on the Tools page, providing users with a reminder of the tools they've installed and when they were last upgraded.

Defining the Tool's Functionality

The two tables likely to be used most often in a tool are *xData*, which is offered as a space for data, and *xSuite*, the place for scripts that deliver its core functionality.

The *xData* table is empty except for a `prefs` subtable that can be used to store user preferences.

The *xSuite* table also holds the status center message, scheduled tasks, menu, and callbacks for the tool.

The status center message is text that appears in the sidebar of the desktop home page, under the "Status Center" heading.

The message, which can contain HTML, is determined by editing the `xSuite.statusCenterMessage()` script and changing the string that it returns.

The script is called each time the home page is loaded, so it can be used to alert users to some facet of the tool's operation (for example, a tool that reads RSS newsfeeds can provide a count of newly received items).

Setting Up Tasks and Menus

Scheduled tasks are implemented by editing three scripts in the *xSuite.background* table: `everyHour`, `everyMinute`, and `everyNight`.

When created, these scripts do nothing—all that each contains is a comment. Radio executes these scripted tasks automatically at the designated frequencies.

The *xThread* table can be used to create a script that runs continuously and monitors some aspect of the tool or data that it manages. This table contains three items:

- `ct`, a number that can be used as a counter
- `enabled`, a Boolean that's `true` if the thread should be actively running or `false` if it should be shut down
- `script`, the thread's script

When a tool is first installed, the thread's script is active and running, but all it does is sleep for 10 seconds using the `thread.sleepFor()` verb.

The tool's menu is contained in the *xSuite.menu* menu bar, which begins with a single command—a `Hello World` demonstration item—as shown in Figure 20.2. This command, and any others at the same level, will appear on the Tools menu for that particular tool.

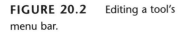

FIGURE 20.2 Editing a tool's menu bar.

To change the tool's name on Radio's main menu bar, edit the top-level item in the menu outline (Web in Figure 20.2).

A tool can have only one main menu bar, but there can be several levels of menus below that. Add a heading below the top level, and then give it menu commands or menus as child items.

Each menu command has a script associated with it, which can be edited by double-clicking the command. Typically, these scripts are one-line calls to scripts elsewhere in the tool's database, but that's not a requirement. They can contain full scripts, although you can't call them elsewhere because menu scripts lack their own database addresses.

Menu changes will not be reflected on the Tools menu until the tool is reinstalled. With the tool as the uppermost window in Radio, choose Tools, Developers, Re-install Front Tool.

Customizing with Callbacks

Tools can become strongly linked with the Radio application by tying into Radio's callbacks framework, a means of customizing the application's behavior in specific areas.

Rather than adding callbacks manually to the object database in scripts, they are placed in the subtables of the `xSuite.callbacks` table and added automatically during tool installation.

The `callbacks` table contains three subtables, each corresponding to a different part of Radio's main object database:

- `fileMenu`, callbacks triggered by the selection of File menu commands
- `radio`, callbacks that correspond to the `user.radio.callbacks` table, running when different events occur in Radio's weblog-publishing and news-aggregation features
- `user`, callbacks that correspond with the `user.callbacks` table and run as the Radio application is used

During tool installation, Radio looks at each of these subtables for scripts or addresses to place in its own `callbacks` tables. The value of the item can be either a script or the address of another script in the tool's database.

For example, if a script is placed in `xSuite.callbacks.radio.publishItem.new`, when the tool is installed (or reinstalled), an address will be added to the main database's `user.radio.callbacks.new.x` table, where `x` is the tool's name prefix:

```
@["C:\\Program Files\\Radio UserLand\\Tools\\x.root"].xSuite.callbacks.
➥radio.publishItem,new
```

Radio will provide the path and filename of the tool database, which will be different on Windows and Mac OS.

After it has been added to the main object database, a tool callback will be called whenever the relevant functionality of Radio is invoked. In the preceding example, whenever a weblog entry is published, a script associated with the tool's `publishItem` callback runs.

The `fileMenu` callbacks take the same name as items in the main object database's `user.tools.commandCallbacks` table:

- `new` (menu command File, New), called with no parameters

- `open` (File, Open), called with no parameters

- `openUrl` (File, Open URL), called with one parameter: a string containing the URL to open

- `close` (File, Close), called with one parameter: the address of the window that should be closed

- `save` (File, Save), called with two parameters: the address of the window to save, and a Boolean that's `true` if the window also should be closed

- `saveAs` (File, Save As), called with one parameter: the address of the window to save

- `saveAsHtml` (File, Save As HTML), called with three parameters: the address of the window to save as a Web page, the relative path of the folder where it should be stored, and a Boolean that's `true` if the page should be previewed instead of being saved

- `saveAsPlainText` (File, Save As Plain Text), called with one parameter: the address of the window to save as text

- `revert` (File, Revert), called with one parameter: the address of the window that should revert to its last saved version

- `viewInBrowser` (File, View in Browser), called with one parameter: a string containing the window to view with the computer's default Web browser

File menu callback scripts should return `true` if they have fulfilled the menu command or `false` if Radio should follow the callback with the normal behavior of that command.

NOTE

File callbacks are used to support new data types that are edited with tool scripts. An alternative technique, window types, is discussed later in this chapter.

Radio callbacks correspond to the `user.radio.callbacks` table and are associated with specific events that occur as Radio publishes weblog entries, reads RSS newsfeeds, and handles other tasks.

Two callbacks support the addition of extra fields to the desktop home page's weblog editor:

- beforeWeblogPostForm, a callback for Web form elements to display above the weblog editor on the desktop home page

- afterWeblogPostForm, a callback for form elements to display below the weblog editor

These callbacks are called by Radio when the weblog editor should be displayed and when an entry is posted.

The scripts both take a single parameter: the address of the table that holds the entry currently being edited, or nil if no entry is being edited.

They return the HTML text to display, which should contain one or more form elements, such as text fields and text areas.

Radio's responder puts form data in a table when a form is submitted. The address of this table is available by calling the verb html.getPageTableAddress(), as in this example:

```
local (pta = html.getPageTableAddress())
```

The table contains a method string that contains either GET or POST, depending on how the page was loaded. When retrieving form element data, always make sure it is POST.

In the form data table, a radioResponder.postArgs subtable holds strings containing each form element's value. The name given to each form element in HTML is used as its name in this subtable. For example, an element called streetAddress is stored in radioResponder.postArgs.streetAddress.

Listing 20.1 contains a callback script that adds "Via Source" and "Via Link" elements to the weblog editor, enabling you to credit the weblog where a link was originally found.

LISTING 20.1   The Full Text of afterWeblogPostForm

```
 1: on afterWeblogPostForm(adrpost) {
 2:    local (pta = html.getPageTableAddress ());
 3:    local (viasource = "", vialink = "");
 4:    if adrpost != nil {
 5:      if pta^.method == "POST" { // add the extra form data to the post table
 6:        if sizeOf(pta^.radioResponder.postArgs.viasource) > 0 {
 7:          adrpost^.viasource = pta^.radioResponder.postArgs.viasource
 8:        };
 9:        if sizeOf(pta^.radioResponder.postArgs.vialink) > 0 {
10:          adrpost^.vialink = pta^.radioResponder.postArgs.vialink
11:        }
12:      }
13:      else { // get the extra form data from the post table, if it exists
14:        if defined(adrpost^.viasource) {
```

LISTING 20.1   Continued

```
15:          viasource = adrpost^.viasource};
16:        if defined(adrpost^.vialink) {
17:          vialink = adrpost^.vialink
18:        }
19:      }
20:    };
21:    «prepare the HTML form elements
22:    local (htmltext);
23:    htmltext = "<table cellspacing=\"10\" cellpadding=\"0\">";
24:    htmltext = htmltext + "<tr><td>Via Source: </td>";
25:    htmltext = htmltext + "<td><input type=\"text\" name=\"viasource\"
➥size=\"20\" value=\"" + viasource + "\"></td></tr>";

26:    htmltext = htmltext + "<tr><td>Via URL: </td>";
27:    htmltext = htmltext + "<td><input type=\"text\" name=\"vialink\"
➥size=\"40\" value=\"" + vialink + "\"></td></tr>";

28:    htmltext = htmltext + "</table>";
29:    return (htmltext)
30: }
```

If the script is saved as *x*Suite.callbacks.radio.afterWeblogPostForm and the tool is reinstalled, the desktop Web site will have two new fields, as shown in Figure 20.3.

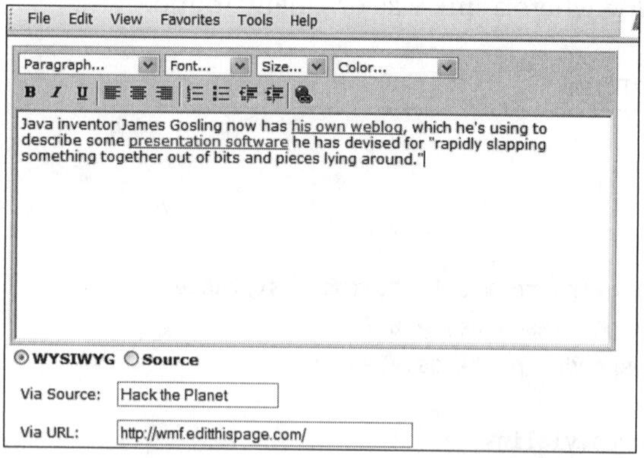

FIGURE 20.3   Customizing weblog editor fields.

Weblog entries are saved in a subtable of weblogData.root inside the weblogData.posts table. The afterWeblogPostForm callback script saves two new fields in an entry's subtable: viasource and vialink.

In order to display this new information for each weblog entry, the item template must be modified with UserTalk code or a macro call that retrieves and presents the viasource and vialink strings.

One solution is to create a script like the one in Listing 20.2, and save it in the workspace table.

LISTING 20.2   The Full Text of `workspace.getViaInfo`

```
1: on getViaInfo (paddedItemNum) {
2:    local (adrpost = @weblogData.posts.[paddedItemNum]);
3:    if defined(adrpost^.viasource) {
4:       return ("Via <a href=\"" + adrpost^.vialink + "\">" +
➥adrpost^.viasource + "</a>")
5:    }
6:    else {
7:       return ("")
8:    }
9: }
```

The `getViaInfo()` script takes one parameter: the value of the `<%paddedItemNum%>` macro that can be used in the item template.

To use this script, the following macro call is added to an item template where the "Via" information should appear:

`<%workspace.getViaInfo("<%paddedItemNum%>")%>`

Three callbacks are called as weblog entries are being authored:

- `postItem`, called when an entry is saved

- `publishItem`, called when an entry is published

- `deleteItem`, called when an entry is deleted

All three callbacks take one parameter, the address of the entry in the `weblogData.posts` table of `weblogData.root`, which is the database that holds weblog entries, category information, and related information.

Each entry is saved in a numbered table in the `posts` table that contains at least four items:

- `text`, a wp text object holding the contents of the entry

- `when`, the date and time it was posted (formatted like `6/13/2003; 8:40:43 PM`)

- `flNotOnHomePage`, a Boolean that's `true` if the entry is not published on the main weblog

- `categories`, a table that holds Boolean `true` items for each category to which the entry has been routed

If the weblog uses item titles and links, there also will be `title` and `link` strings containing this information.

TIP

Footbridge, a Radio tool released as shareware by Mark Paschal, uses these callbacks to mirror Radio weblog entries to Advogato diaries, LiveJournal journals, and weblog publishing systems that use the original Blogger API, including Movable Type weblogs. The software is available from `http://markpasc.org/code/radio/footbridge`.

The names of items in the `categories` table correspond to items in the `weblogData.categories` table, which holds information about each category.

The `when` timestamp does not change after an entry is first saved. To determine whether it has been updated, call the `timeModified()` verb with text as the only parameter—it returns the date and time the entry's text was last revised.

These callbacks are used by several tools to route Radio weblog entries to other servers and services, such as the Manila-Blogger Bridge tool that's included when the software is installed.

Listing 20.3 contains `postFormGateway.publish()`, a script that mirrors a weblog's last five entries from the home page to a CGI script that requires login and cookie-based user authentication.

The CGI script, part of the community weblog MetaFilter at `http://www.metafilter.com`, updates a user's profile page, which includes a space where the weblog entries can be displayed.

LISTING 20.3 The Full Text of `postFormGateway.publish`

```
1: on publish() {
2:   on getData(adrtable) {
3:     «adrtable: table containing post data
4:     local (postdata = "");
5:     for adr in adrtable {
6:       if typeof(adr^) == scriptType {
7:         postdata = postdata + nameof(adr^) + "=" + adr^() + "&"
8:       }
9:       else {
10:        postdata = postdata + nameof(adr^) + "=" + adr^ + "&"
11:      }
12:    };
13:    return (postdata)};
14:    «log in to Web site to get authentication and session cookies
15:    tcp.httpClient ("POST", "www.metafilter.com", 80, "/login/
➥Login_action.cfm", data: getData (@WebSuite.postFormGateway.login),
➥datatype: "application/x-www-form-urlencoded", cookiesOn: true,
➥debug: false);
16:    «post to the site's user profile page via POST
17:    tcp.httpClient ("POST", "www.metafilter.com", 80, "/contribute/
```

LISTING 20.3 Continued

```
➥customize_action.cfm", data: getData (@WebSuite.postFormGateway.
➥post), datatype: "application/x-www-form-urlencoded", cookiesOn:
➥true, debug: true);
18:   «log out from Web site to conserve its resources
19:   tcp.httpClient ("GET", "www.metafilter.com", 80, "index.mefi?
➥delcookie=yes", cookiesOn: true, debug: false);
20:   return (true)
21: }
22: publish()
```

This script makes use of the `tcp.httpClient()` verb, which is used to request a Web resource and post information to a Web server using either HTTP GET or HTTP POST. Full documentation for the verb is available from UserLand's Web site at `http://docserver.userland.com/tcp/httpClient`.

The `httpClient()` verb takes care of the hardest parts of communicating with a CGI script—it can provide username and passwords for HTTP authentication, save cookies sent by the server, and send them back for subsequent client connections.

The bulk of the work required to use it for HTTP GET and POST requests is to encode the data that will be sent to the CGI script.

CGI data is encoded as a set of *name=value* pairs separated by ampersand characters (&), as in this example:

```
username=rcade&userpass=lilabner&group=13
```

Name	Value	Kind
▶ postFormGateway	3 items	table
▶ post	23 items	table
▶ base_ref	same	string [4]
▶ blurb	on disk	script
▶ font_family	Times New Roman,serif	string [21]
▶ font_size	12	string [2]
▶ small_font_family	Times New Roman,serif	string [21]
▶ small_font_size	10	string [2]
▶ link_days	3	string [1]
▶ theme	1	string [1]
▶ timezone	0	string [1]
▶ titles	0	string [1]

Kind: ▼   Sort: ▼

FIGURE 20.4 Preparing form data in a table.

The data is URL-encoded, which makes it safe to appear in a Web URL (for a GET request) or in the body of a POST request.

In this script, the data for each request is prepared in a table that contains two kinds of items: strings and scripts. An example, a `postFormGateway.post` table, is shown in Figure 20.4.

The `getData()` handler in lines 2–13 of Listing 20.3 assembles the data required for a request by looking in a table like the one in Figure 20.4. The name of each item must match its name on the Web form that calls the CGI script.

When the item is a string, the string is added to the request data (for example, base_ref=same and font_size=12).

When the item is a script, the string returned by the script, when called with no parameters, is used.

Listing 20.4 contains an example of a script that could be used in the post table, postFormGateway.post.blurb().

LISTING 20.4   The Full Text of postFormGateway.post.blurb

```
 1: on blurb() {
 2:    local (htmltext = "");
 3:    local (posts = weblogData.posts, itemCount = 0);
 4:    htmltext = htmltext + "<h4 align=\"center\">Recent posts from";
 5:    htmltext = htmltext + " <a href=\"" + radio.weblog.getUrl();
 6:    htmltext = htmltext + "\">my weblog</a></h4>";
 7:    for i = sizeof(posts) downto 1 {
 8:      if posts[i].flNotOnHomePage {
 9:      continue
10:      }
11:      local (posttext = string(posts[i].text))
12:      htmltext = htmltext + "<blockquote>" + posttext;
13:      htmltext = htmltext + " <h5 align=\"right\"> ";
14:      htmltext = htmltext + posts[i].when + " ¦ <a href=\"";
15:      htmltext = htmltext + radio.weblog.getUrl();
16:      htmltext = htmltext + date.year(posts[i].when) + "/";
17:      htmltext = htmltext + string.padWithZeros(date.month(posts[i].when), 2);
18:      htmltext = htmltext + "/" + string.padWithZeros(date.day(posts[i].
➥when), 2);
19:      htmltext = htmltext + ".html#a" + number (nameof(posts[i]));
20:      htmltext = htmltext + "\">permalink</a></h5></blockquote>";
21:      itemCount++;
22:      if itemCount > 10 {
23:        break}
24:      };
25:    htmltext = string.replaceAll(htmltext, "<p>", "",
➥flCaseSensitive: false);
26:    htmltext = string.replaceAll(htmltext, "</p>", "",
➥flCaseSensitive: false);
27:    return (string.urlEncode (htmltext))
28: }
```

The `blurb()` script returns HTML text that contains the last five entries from a weblog, formatted in a manner similar to the way entries are arranged with Radio's item template.

After the text has been prepared, the `string.urlEncode()` verb is used to encode it, replacing characters that cannot be used as part of a URL or in the body of a POST request.

The final step in creating the CGI gateway callback is to make it one of the tool's Radio callbacks by creating a short script as *xSuite.callbacks.radio.publishItem*:

```
on publishItem (adrpost) {
  xSuite.postFormGateway (adrpost);
  return (false)}
```

Note that *xSuite* should be replaced with the actual name of the tool's suite table.

The following Radio callbacks can be defined to add information to the RSS newsfeeds associated with a weblog and its categories:

- `writeRssNamespace`, called to add a namespace declaration to an RSS newsfeed's top-level RSS element

- `writeRssChannelElement`, called to add new elements in a namespace under the `channel` element

- `writeRssItemElement`, called to add new elements in a namespace to each `item` element

The `writeRssNamespace` callback takes one parameter: a table that contains name-value pairs represented by string items. Each name should be a namespace's local name and the value of its global identifier, which is usually an URL.

The `writeRssChannelElement` callback takes one parameter also: a table containing the names and values of the element (or elements) to add inside the RSS newsfeed's `channel` element.

The last callback, `writeRssItemElement`, takes two parameters: a table containing name-value pairs and the address of the weblog post used to create the item.

Summary

Tools extend Radio UserLand's capabilities and customize its functionality.

Tools are packaged as individual object database files and installed by being saved in Radio's Tools folder. They also can be reinstalled with the menu command Tools, Developers, Reinstall Front Tool.

By using features such as callbacks and custom menus, tools can be integrated so closely into Radio that it won't be apparent to users where the main application ends and a tool begins.

Tools are an appropriate stopping point for *Radio UserLand Kick Start* because they best demonstrate the true nature of this deceptively simple and strangely named program.

Although Radio UserLand is a highly popular weblog editor, RSS news aggregator, and content-management system, the software is best described as a development environment upon which all of those features—and many more—can be built.

Radio, through the use of its object database and UserTalk scripting language, can be used to rapidly create applications that take advantage of Internet protocols and Web services.

The software functions as an Internet client/server, Web site editor, Web services platform, outliner, text editor, file server, email gateway, and scripting platform. It supports an entire alphabet full of buzzworthy acronyms: HTTP, HTML, XML, FTP, SMTP, POP3, XML-RPC, SOAP, RSS, and TCP.

Because the software is such a robust platform for development and is updated frequently by UserLand Software, there doubtlessly will be new features introduced after this book goes to press.

You can keep up with these changes and discuss the subjects covered in *Radio UserLand Kick Start* on the author's own weblog, Workbench, at `http://www.cadenhead.org/workbench`.

Radio UserLand belongs to an emerging class of software that combines common data formats such as XML, RSS, and XML-RPC with the dynamic collaborative environment of weblogs, making it possible for individuals to create new relationships, services, and software.

As these programs kick-start another revolutionary stage of World Wide Web publishing, it promises to be a wild ride.

> "Let's not limit the dreams of people who use our tools."
>
> —UserLand Software founder Dave Winer

PART IV

Appendices

RSS

Radio UserLand is both a consumer and producer of RSS, the most popular format for sharing content between different Web sites.

Radio's news aggregator downloads RSS files once an hour from selected Web sites and other sources, presenting new items for quick browsing.

Radio's weblog editor produces RSS files, making content available to news aggregator users and other audiences.

This appendix describes the history and format of RSS, a simple XML dialect created by Netscape and UserLand Software. Learning the particulars of RSS is a good way to discover the different ways it can be used.

Syndicating Content with RSS

RSS was created with a specific purpose in mind: sharing content from one Web site with others, usually in the form of headlines linking to content on the originating site.

For example, a daily newspaper can use RSS to offer headlines and links to the 15 most-recently published stories on its Web site, enabling other sites to offer those headlines to their users. Both sites benefit; one gets more traffic and the other gets frequently updated content to offer visitors.

RSS files, which are called *newsfeeds* or simply *feeds*, use an XML dialect that is supported today by numerous products and software libraries.

Learning about RSS can be confusing because of how it was developed. Three entities have offered versions of RSS that aren't all compatible with each other.

There are four versions in wide use today:

- RSS 0.91, published by Netscape in 1999

- RSS 0.92, an upgrade offered by UserLand in 2000

- RSS 1.0, an upgrade to RSS 0.91 by the RSS-DEV Working Group

- RSS 2.0, a release introduced by UserLand that follows RSS 0.92

The two "current versions" of RSS are 1.0 and 2.0, which were developed independently and are not fully compatible with each other.

Radio reads files that use all four of those RSS versions (along with others), so a news aggregator user doesn't normally need to be concerned with the RSS version employed by a feed.

Radio weblogs produce RSS 2.0 feeds.

NOTE

The differences between RSS versions 1.0 and 2.0 even extend to the RSS acronym itself. RSS stands for Rich Site Summary to the RSS-DEV Working Group and stands for Really Simple Syndication to the authors of RSS 2.0.

The first appearance of a format that became RSS was in 1997, when Dave Winer of UserLand Software began offering the latest items from his Scripting News weblog in a simple XML dialect of his own creation.

The dialect, which became known as <scriptingNews> format, was created to encourage the development of software that could read Web content presented as XML. Other sites adopted the <scriptingNews> format for their own headlines and news items.

In 1999, Netscape introduced RSS 0.9, an XML dialect for content sharing that it used on the My.Netscape home page service.

With the service, Netscape users could choose from a variety of information providers, putting their headlines on a personalized home page. It was intended for use by sites that wanted to appear on My.Netscape, an attractive proposition because Netscape.Com was the home page for millions of Netscape Navigator users.

Although both formats were based on XML and could be used to exchange headlines, RSS 0.9 was a more complex protocol that made use of the Resource Description Framework (RDF), an XML dialect created by the World Wide Web Consortium for making information more understandable and useful to software.

UserLand followed with My.UserLand, a service for reading feeds that used the company's syndication format, and expanded the <scriptingNews> format to include descriptions for each item and other new elements.

In 1999, Netscape released RSS 0.91, an updated version that dropped support for RDF and adopted some features of UserLand's latest format.

One year later, after Netscape stopped actively supporting RSS, UserLand adopted the format and introduced version RSS 0.92 as the successor to both of the existing syndication formats: <scriptingNews> and RSS 0.91.

Every new feature of RSS 0.92 was optional, making an RSS 0.91 feed fully compatible with the newer version.

During the same year, the 12-member RSS-DEV Working Group introduced RSS 1.0, a different format based on RSS 0.9. The group's goal was to produce a format with more room to grow as RSS is adopted for new uses beyond headline syndication. Towards this end, it adopted the RDF support from version 0.9 and was not compatible with any other RSS. It also makes use of XML namespaces, a protocol for extending XML data with optional modules that support new uses for the data.

By this time, hundreds of sites were offering RSS feeds, especially news providers and weblog publishers. UserLand Software's Manila, a server-based weblogging tool, offered built-in support for RSS feeds. Hundreds of webloggers began Manila sites that offered feeds, helping to further popularize the format.

In 2002, UserLand released RSS 2.0, an upgrade from RSS 0.92 that supports several new elements to further describe a newsfeed item, including item categories, publication dates, and unique identifiers.

RSS 2.0 also supports the extension of the format through XML namespaces, offering partial compatibility with RSS 1.0's optional modules.

In July 2003, UserLand transferred the RSS 2.0 specification to the Berkman Center for Internet and Society at Harvard Law School and established an advisory board to oversee its future development. That board includes Winer, NetNewsWire developer Brent Simmons, and *InfoWorld* columnist Jon Udell.

This brings the convoluted history of RSS to the present. Both the RSS 2.0 advisory board and the RSS-DEV Working Group continue ongoing work in support of their flavors of RSS, so it's a good idea to bookmark the primary Web sites for these protocols:

- RSS 1.0:
  http://web.resource.org/rss/1.0

- RSS 2.0:
  http://backend.userland.com/rss

NOTE

There's even a third effort underway to create a syndication format and related protocols that will compete with both versions of RSS.

Information about the format, developed by a group led by Sam Ruby of the Apache Software Foundation, is available from Ruby's Intertwingly weblog, which is published at http://www.intertwingly.net.

Reading RSS Feeds

The first RSS format a Radio user should learn is version 2.0, Radio's preferred format for incoming RSS feeds and the only format it uses on outgoing feeds.

RSS 2.0 is an XML dialect that adheres to the XML 1.0 specification. The first line of the feed must be a processing instruction establishing this fact:

```
<?xml version="1.0"?>
```

The feed must contain one root element named rss that has a version attribute identifying the implemented RSS version:

```
<rss version="2.0">
```

The rss element must contain one channel element describing the feed and an item element for each news item in the feed.

Using URLs in an RSS Feed

Several elements in an RSS 2.0 feed make use of URLs for specific resources on the Internet, such as Web addresses and FTP-hosted files. Whenever an URL is expected as an element or attribute, the first non-whitespace character must be the start of an URL addressing scheme.

The most common schemes are ftp://, http://, https://, mailto:, and news://.

RSS 2.0 also allows any of the addressing schemes approved by the Internet Assigned Numbers Authority. For a list, visit http://www.iana.org/assignments/uri-schemes.

Describing a Feed

The channel element identifies the source of the RSS feed and determines how news aggregators and other clients can use it.

It must contain three elements—a title, link, and description.

The title element contains the name of the feed or the site providing the feed.

The link element contains the URL of the site providing the feed.

The description element contains a phrase or sentence that describes the feed.

An example from my own weblog:

```
<channel>
  <title>Workbench</title>
```

```
<link>http://www.cadenhead.org/workbench/</link>
<description>Programming and publishing news and commentary by Rogers
➥Cadenhead.</description>
</channel>
```

Optional Elements

The `channel` element also can contain 16 kinds of optional elements: `category`, `cloud`, `copyright`, `docs`, `generator`, `image`, `language`, `lastBuildDate`, `managingEditor`, `pubDate`, `rating`, `skipDays`, `skipHours`, `textInput`, `ttl`, and `webmaster`.

category

There can be one or more `category` elements that each categorize the channel in some manner. The `category` element contains the name of the category and can contain a `domain` attribute that names, describes, or locates the categorization system it uses.

Feed categorization systems are not established by the protocol—it's an opportunity for outside groups to provide some kind of meaningful categorization of RSS feeds. One categorization system is offered by `Weblogs.Com`, the UserLand site that lists recently updated weblogs at `http://www.weblogs.com`.

Participation in this system is supported through the following `category` element:

```
<category domain="http://www.weblogs.com/rssUpdates/changes.xml">
➥rssUpdates</category>
```

cloud

There can be one or more `cloud` elements that support publish-subscribe notification, a way for servers to notify RSS-reading clients that a feed has changed.

If an RSS feed produced by Radio supports this kind of notification, it will contain the following element:

```
<cloud domain="radio.xmlstoragesystem.com" port="80" path="/RPC2"
➥registerProcedure="xmlStorageSystem.rssPleaseNotify" protocol="xml-rpc" />
```

The attributes of the `cloud` element identify an XML-RPC, SOAP, or HTTP Web service that supports publish-subscribe notification.

When a Radio user subscribes to an RSS feed containing this element, the `pleaseNotify` method of the XML-RPC server at port 80 of `radio.xmlstoragesystem.com` will be called. This method tells the server that the user's copy of Radio should be notified whenever the feed changes.

When the feed changes, the server will contact each client that asked to be notified, using the XML-RPC or SOAP method requested when `pleaseNotify` was called.

Requests for notification show up in the Radio event log as "Please notify" events with a list of every RSS feed you monitor using publish-subscribe (see Figure A.1).

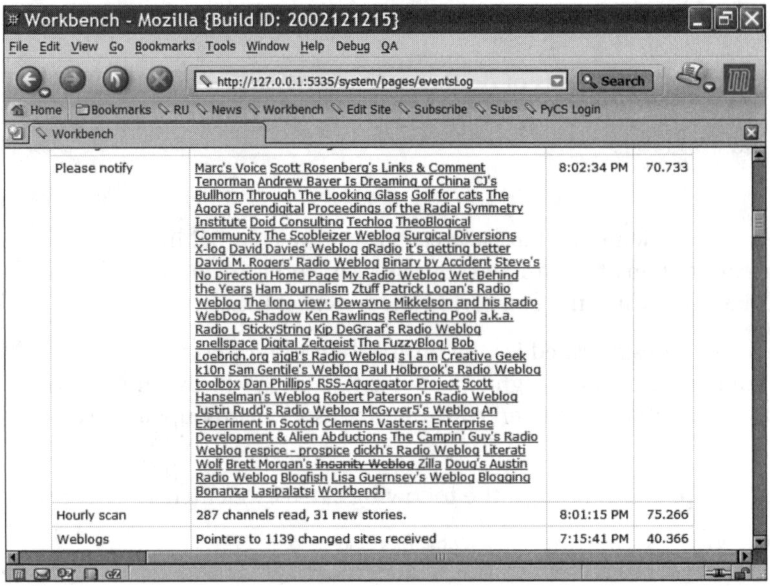

FIGURE A.1.   "Please notify" events.

When any of the monitored feeds changes, `radio.xmlstoragesystem.com` calls an XML-RPC method on your copy of Radio, causing the news aggregator to immediately request that feed.

A Radio weblog's RSS feed will not contain a `cloud` element if it is published using FTP.

`copyright`

The `copyright` element contains the feed's copyright notice. For example:

```
<copyright>Copyright 2003 Rogers Cadenhead</copyright>
```

`docs`

The `docs` element contains an URL that links to documentation for the RSS format used by the feed. For RSS 2.0 feeds, it is the following:

```
<docs>http://backend.userland.com/rss</docs>
```

generator

The generator element contains the name of the software that created the RSS feed. For example:

```
<generator>Radio UserLand v8.0.8</generator>
```

image

The image element identifies a GIF, JPEG, or PNG graphic associated with the feed. It was used by the My.Netscape and My.UserLand services to display a Web site's logo along with items from its RSS feed. Both of these services have been discontinued and it does not appear that they are being used elsewhere. Radio does not include this element in the RSS feeds that it generates.

An image element must contain three elements: link, title, and url. It also can contain three optional elements: description, height, and width.

The link and title elements should be the title and link of the feed—the same information identified in the link and title elements contained inside channel.

The url element contains the URL of the graphic.

The height and width elements contain the display dimensions of the graphic, which can be no larger than a height of 144 pixels and a width of 400 pixels. If these elements are not specified, the default values are a height of 88 pixels and width of 31 pixels.

The description element contains a description that can be presented with the graphic.

Here's an example:

```
<image>
  <title>Workbench</title>
  <link>http://www.cadenhead.org/workbench</link>
  <url>http://www.cadenhead.org/workbench/images/logo.gif</url>
  <height>44</height>
  <width>272</width>
</image>
```

language

The language element identifies the language used by the feed, as in this one for English:

```
<language>en-us</language>
```

More than 190 language codes can be used with this element. The full list is available from UserLand's Web site at http://backend.userland.com/rss.

lastBuildDate

The `lastBuildDate` element contains the date and time the RSS feed was last created, such as the following:

```
<lastBuildDate>Fri, 15 Aug 2003 04:32:25 GMT</lastBuildDate>
```

All timestamps in RSS 2.0 follow the rules of RFC 822, an Internet standard for text messages such as email, except for one difference: RSS 2.0 accepts two- or four-digit years even though RFC 822 requires four digits.

managingEditor

The `managingEditor` element identifies the email address of the person in charge of the feed's editorial content. For example:

```
<managingEditor>editor@example.com</managingEditor>
```

pubDate

The `pubDate` element contains the publication date of the items in the feed. This is intended for use by publications whereby the feed might have been published at a different time than the stories it contains. For example, a daily newspaper that publishes stories each morning at 9 a.m. EST could use an element such as the following:

```
<pubDate>Wed, 16 Apr 2003 09:00:00 EST</pubDate>
```

rating

The `rating` element can advise others on sexual content and other possibly objectionable material in the RSS feed or the sites to which it links.

The element contains rating text from the Internet Content Rating Association, which supports the PICS rating system at the Web site `http://www.icra.org`.

An example:

```
<rating>'(pics-1.1 "http://www.icra.org/ratingsv02.html" comment
➥"ICRAonline v2.0" l gen true for "http://www.cadenhead.org/workbench"
➥r (nz 1 vz 1 lb 1 ob 1 cz 1) "http://www.rsac.org/ratingsv01.html" l gen
➥true for "http://www.cadenhead.org/workbench"  r (n 0 s 0 v 0 l 2))'</rating>
```

The preceding element indicates that my weblog might contain two kinds of possibly objectionable material—crude profanity and the promotion of alcohol use. Don't tell my mother.

skipDays

The `skipDays` element contains one to seven day elements that represent days when the RSS feed should not be checked for updates.

A day element contains one of the days of the week: Sunday, Monday, Tuesday, Wednesday, Thursday, Friday, or Saturday.

The following element indicates that an RSS feed never updates on the weekends:

```
<skipDays>
  <day>Saturday</day>
  <day>Sunday</day>
</skipDays>
```

Radio does not offer a way to set this up from the Prefs menu.

skipHours

The skipHours element contains 1 to 24 hour elements that represent hours in the day when the RSS feed should not be checked.

The hour specified in each hour element uses Greenwich Mean Time, which is either four or five hours ahead of Eastern time in the U.S., depending on whether Daylight Savings Time is in effect.

The following skipHours element indicates that the feed should be skipped at the following times in EST: midnight, 1 a.m., 4 p.m., 6 p.m., 7 p.m., 9 p.m., 10 p.m., and 11 p.m.

```
<skipHours>
  <hour>4</hour>
  <hour>2</hour>
  <hour>3</hour>
  <hour>6</hour>
  <hour>5</hour>
  <hour>21</hour>
  <hour>23</hour>
  <hour>0</hour>
</skipHours>
```

As the example demonstrates, the order of the hours does not matter. You can use Radio's RSS Configuration preferences page to choose the number of hours that should be skipped. Specific hours cannot be chosen—Radio picks the hours during which the feed is most likely to be inactive.

textInput

The textinput element associates the feed with a Web form that contains a text field. This element is both optional and almost completely ignored by news aggregators—even the RSS 2.0 specification states that its purpose is "something of a mystery."

If it is used, textinput must contain four elements: description, link, name, and title.

The description element contains a description that explains the purpose of the text field.

The link element specifies the URL of a CGI program that accepts input from the field.

The name element contains the name of the field.

The title element contains the text label to be displayed on the form's Submit button.

Here's an example:

```
<textinput>
  <description>Search the Workbench Weblog</description>
  <link>http://www.cadenhead.org/cgi-bin/search.cgi</link>
  <name>searchTerm</name>
  <title>Begin Search</title>
</textinput>
```

ttl
The ttl element indicates the number of minutes the RSS feed can be cached before it should be deleted. A news aggregator could rely on a cached copy of a feed until the expiration of the TTL, which stands for "time to live."

The following element causes a feed to be cached no longer than 15 minutes:

```
<ttl>15</ttl>
```

webMaster
The webMaster element identifies the email address of the person in charge of technical issues related to the feed. For example:

```
<managingEditor>webmaster@example.com</managingEditor>
```

Describing Feed Items

The rss element, the root element of RSS 2.0, can contain one item element for each item in the feed. Although most feeds appear to offer from 5-15 items, there's no restriction regarding the number of items a feed can contain.

All 10 elements contained within an item element are optional. However, it must contain either a title element or a description element.

The title element contains a headline for the item and description contains a one- or more-paragraph summary of the item. A third element, link, contains the URL of the item.

With these three elements, an RSS feed can adopt a news-style approach with a headline as the title, story link as the link, and a lead paragraph as the description.

Matt Croydon, the publisher of the Postneo weblog, takes this approach:

```
<item>
  <title>Weblogs for Software Developers</title>
  <link>http://postneo.com/2003/01/31.html#a1910</link>
  <description>Web logs (commonly known as &quot;blogs&quot;), message
➥boards and other online forums are becoming increasingly important vehicles
➥for developers to attract customers—and development talent—well before an
➥application even enters the beta stage.</description>
</item>
```

Most browser-based RSS clients handle this information in a similar fashion—the title becomes a hyperlink to the link and is displayed with the description. Some clients omit the description entirely or truncate it if the text exceeds a certain length.

The description element can contain HTML that has been encoded so that it can be used as XML character data, as in this revised Postneo example:

```
<description>&lt;A href=&quot;http://rss.com.com/2100-1001-
➥982854.html?type=pt&amp;amp;part=rss&amp;amp;tag=feed&amp;amp;subj=
➥news&quot;&gt;CNet&lt;/A&gt;Web logs (commonly known as &quot;blogs&
➥quot;), message boards and other online forums are becoming
➥increasingly important vehicles for developers to attract
➥customers—and development talent—well before an application even
➥enters the beta stage.</description>
```

This example makes use of four character entities: & for an ampersand (&), > for a greater-than sign (>); < for a less-than sign (<), and " for a quotation mark (").

Another way to place HTML in a description is to place the text within a CDATA tag, as in this rewritten example:

```
<description><![CDATA[<a href="http://rss.com.com/2100-1001-982854.
➥html">CNet</a>: Web logs (commonly known as &quot;blogs&quot;),
➥message boards and other online forums are becoming increasingly
➥important vehicles for developers to attract customers—and
➥development talent—well before an application even enters the
➥beta stage.]]></description>
```

Some weblogs don't use a title or link on any items, instead putting everything in the description element.

TIP

Matt Croydon's Postneo weblog is a fixture in my Radio news aggregator. He's a computer science student at Montgomery College in Rockville, Maryland, and his weblog's a great read on the technology he's working with at the moment—such as Radio UserLand, Java, Python, Linux, BSD, and MySQL. It's published at `http://postneo.com`.

Other Elements

Seven other optional elements can appear in an `item` element: `author`, `category`, `comments`, `enclosure`, `guid`, `pubDate`, and `source`.

author

The `author` element identifies the email address of the author of the item:

```
<author>joe@example.com</author>
```

The author of an item can mean different things—such as the person who wrote that RSS item or the person who wrote the item to which it links.

category

An `item` can contain one or more `category` elements that categorize the item. The element contains the name of the category and also can have a `domain` attribute that identifies the system of categorization in some way.

This element functions exactly like the `channel` element that shares the same name. Here's an example:

```
<item>
  <title>OPML Directories</title>
  <link>http://radio.weblogs.com/0104487/2002/12/17.html#a492</link>
  <category>activeRenderer</category>
  <category>groupware</category>
</item>
```

Marc Barrot's slam weblog uses this element to offer a dynamic category-based view of the entries on his site. Clicking an `activeRenderer` link on his site opens a page containing weblog entries belonging to that category.

The slam weblog is published at `http://radio.weblogs.com/0104487`.

NOTE

The category-based view described here is not a standard feature of Radio. It requires LiveTopics, a Radio add-on tool by Novissio Ltd.

For more information on the tool, visit the Web site `http://www.novissio.com`.

comments

The `comments` element contains the URL for a Web page or CGI program that displays comments posted in response to the item, as in this example:

```
<comments>http://www.pycs.net/system/com-
ments.py?u=0000001&amp;amp;
➥p=538&amp;amp;link=http%3A%2F%2Fwww.
```

➥cadenhead.org%2Fworkbench
➥%2F2003%2F02%2F01.html%23a538</comments>

At present, Radio weblogs hosted on the main Radio Community Server display comments using a CGI program on the domain `http://radiocomments.userland.com`.

enclosure

The `enclosure` element identifies files that can be downloaded from the provider of the feed. It's used most often to deliver audio and video files—Radio can be configured to download these files in the middle of the night so they're available the next day for immediate playback.

The element has no contents (in other words, it's an empty element). It has three attributes: `url`, the URL of the file; `length`, its size; and `type`, its MIME type.

Adam Curry, a broadcaster and entrepreneur best known for being an early MTV veejay and founding OnRamp, uses the `enclosure` element on his Radio weblog to publish an RSS-based broadcast called the Payload Channel.

Here's an example based on one of his offerings:

```
<item>
  <title>payload channel</title>
  <link>http://live.curry.com/2003/01/28.html#a2996</link>
  <description>A Windows Media File of my most recent Helicopter Flying
➥lessons.</description>
  <enclosure url="http://live.curry.com/mp3/Heli-Lesson.wmv"
➥length="15179579" type="text/plain"/>
</item>
```

Curry's site is available at `http://live.curry.com`.

guid

The `guid` element contains an identifier associated with the item—a text or numeric code that will never be used on another item from the same RSS feed.

The method of generating a unique identifier is up to the RSS feed's publisher. Radio handles this by using the item's permalink as its `guid`, as in this example:

```
<guid>http://www.cadenhead.org/workbench/2003/02/01.html#a538</guid>
```

A permalink is an URL that links directly and permanently to a specific weblog item.

The `guid` element can have an `isPermalink` attribute that has a Boolean value. The Boolean value is `true` if the identifier is a permalink and `false` otherwise.

pubDate

The pubDate element contains the publication date of the item, which takes the same format as the channel element named pubDate. An example follows:

```
<pubDate>Wed, 16 Apr 2003 09:00:00 EST</pubDate>
```

If the publication date is in the future, an RSS client might choose not to display it until that time.

source

The source element is used to give credit to a source that reported an item first. It contains the name of the item's source, such as a site, publication, or person.

The element also can have an url attribute with the URL of the source's RSS feed.

Here's an example:

```
<source url="http://mailbox.univie.ac.at/~prillih3/blog/
⮕rss.xml">The Aardvark Speaks</source>
```

To see a Radio weblog that makes use of this element, visit Joe Jenett's jenett.radio site at http://coolstop.com/radio.

Summary

Radio UserLand encourages the exploitation of RSS, an effective format for sharing content on the Internet.

RSS began as a simple XML dialect but has been expanded to support new features such as item categorization, multimedia downloads, and permalinks.

The RSS 2.0 files produced by Radio make a weblog's content available to several diverse audiences—search engines that support RSS, news aggregators, Web publishers, non-visual Web browsers, and any other software that can parse XML.

Radio's news aggregator reads each of the popular RSS formats—versions 0.9, 0.91, 0.92, 1.0, and 2.0—along with UserLand's original <scriptingNews> formats.

By becoming familiar with the rules of an RSS format such as version 2.0, a Radio developer might find new uses for the protocol.

OPML

The outliner in Radio UserLand serves a multiplicity of purposes—including specific tasks like database editing and programming, and general tasks like Web page and document creation.

Underneath Radio's outline view lives OPML (the Outline Processor Markup Language), a UserLand-created format for the representation of outlines.

This appendix describes the particulars of OPML, an XML-based format that is being implemented by other software developers for their own outliners and other list-based data.

Storing Outlines as OPML

If you poke around the main Radio folder on your system, you'll find several files with the file extension .opml.

These files are stored to the specifications of the Outline Processor Markup Language, an XML-based format created by UserLand Software.

UserLand has a long history with the representation of text as outlines, as described at length in Chapter 8, "Creating Outlines." Company founder Dave Winer created several popular commercial outliners in the '80s and has continued the work with his Internet publishing and development software.

One file you might find is mySubscriptions.opml, an outline containing a list of the RSS feeds to which you subscribe.

Listing B.1 contains an OPML file.

LISTING B.1   An Example OPML File

```
 1: <?xml version="1.0" encoding="ISO-8859-1"?>
 2: <!-- OPML generated by Radio UserLand v8.0.8 -->
 3: <opml version="1.1">
 4:   <head>
 5:     <title>Favorites</title>
 6:     <dateCreated>Thu, 16 Jan 2003 04:33:01 GMT</dateCreated>
 7:     <dateModified>Thu, 16 Jan 2003 04:35:09 GMT</dateModified>
 8:     <ownerName>Rogers Cadenhead</ownerName>
 9:     <ownerEmail>rogers@cadenhead.org</ownerEmail>
10:     <expansionState></expansionState>
11:     <vertScrollState>1</vertScrollState>
12:     <windowTop>53</windowTop>
13:     <windowLeft>0</windowLeft>
14:     <windowBottom>487</windowBottom>
15:     <windowRight>775</windowRight>
16:     <cloud domain="radio.xmlstoragesystem.com" port="80" path="/RPC2"
➥registerProcedure="xmlStorageSystem.rssPleaseNotify"
➥protocol="xml-rpc"/>
17:   </head>
18:   <body>
19:     <outline text="#flRender &quot;false&quot;"/>
20:     <outline text="A Whole Lotta Nothing" type="link"
➥url="http://a.wholelottanothing.org/"/>
21:     <outline text="Anil Dash" description="" type="link"
➥url="http://www.dashes.com/anil/"/>
22:     <outline text="Jake's Radio 'Blog" type="link"
➥url="http://jake.userland.com/"/>
23:   </body>
24: </opml>
```

OPML begins with a processing instruction that identifies it as XML data:

```
<?xml version="1.0" encoding="ISO-8859-1"?>
```

The version attribute must be 1.0. The encoding attribute, which indicates the character set used in the data, is optional.

The root element of OPML, opml, requires a version attribute to identify the OPML version in use—it's presently 1.1.

This element must contain two elements: head, which holds header information about the outline and how it should be presented, and body, which contains the outline items. Neither has an attribute, so all OPML 1.1 files take the following form:

```
<?xml version="1.0">
<opml version="1.1">
  <head>
    <!-- header elements here -->
  </head>
  <body>
    <!-- body elements here -->
  </body>
</opml>
```

head **Elements**

Each of the elements in the head is optional.

The title element contains the title of the outline, which can be its filename or something more descriptive.

The dateCreated and dateModified elements contain timestamps showing when the outline was first created and last edited. These follow the rules of RFC 822, an Internet standard for text messages—the basic form is *day abbreviation, day month abbreviation year hour:minute:second timezone*, as in my own personal creation date:

```
<dateCreated>Thu, 13 Apr 1967 08:30:00 CDT</dateCreated>
```

(Send presents in care of the publisher.)

The ownerName and ownerEmail elements identify the person, group, or entity responsible for the outline.

Four elements are used by Radio when displaying an outline: windowLeft, windowTop, windowRight, and windowBottom. Each contains a pixel value; Radio opens the outline window with each edge at the specified position. Other OPML clients that have a graphical user interface may support it as well.

Two head elements hold the state of the outline the last time it was edited: verticalState and horizontalState. Radio keeps track of expanded and collapsed subheads when an outline is saved, restoring that condition when it is loaded again. The software also displays the same portion of the outline that was visible as it was saved.

The expansionState element contains a comma-separated list numbering the expanded parents in the outline—such as 1, 5 or 1, 4, 7.

The numbers in the list represent the position, counting down from the top, of an expanded parent. This process begins with the entire outline in a collapsed state, traveling down the list and opening a parent when its number is present. The count starts over at the top after each expansion.

Figure B.1 contains three views of the same outline:

- Completely collapsed

- After the first parent is expanded

- After the fourth parent is expanded

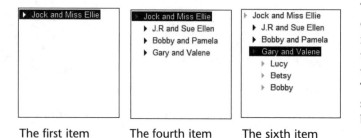

The first item   The fourth item   The sixth item

FIGURE B.1.   Restoring the outline state.

The vertScrollState element only contains one number: the outline item, numbering down from the top, that should be displayed as the top line of the outline window. This count assumes that the expansion state of the outline already has been restored.

If the rightmost outline in Figure B.1 was saved, it would have the following elements:

```
<expansionState>1, 4</expansionState>
<vertScrollState>1</vertScrollState>
```

The cloud element supports publish-subscribe notification, a technique employed by servers to notify OPML editors or viewers that an outline has changed.

If an OPML editor supports this kind of notification (as Radio does), outlines created with the software will contain a cloud element like this:

```
<cloud domain="radio.xmlstoragesystem.com" port="80" path="/RPC2"
➥registerProcedure="xmlStorageSystem.rssPleaseNotify" protocol="xml-rpc" />
```

The attributes of the cloud element identify an XML-RPC, SOAP, or HTTP Web service that supports notification.

UserLand Software calls this feature *instant outlining,* because it's comparable in some ways to instant messaging.

When a Radio user subscribes to an OPML file containing a cloud element like the preceding example, the pleaseNotify method of the XML-RPC server at port 80 of radio.xmlstoragesystem.com is called. This method tells the server that the user's copy of Radio should be notified whenever the outline changes.

When the outline changes, the server will contact each client that asked to be notified, using the XML-RPC or SOAP method requested when pleaseNotify was called.

When any subscribed outline changes, radio.xmlstoragesystem.com calls an XML-RPC method on your copy of Radio, causing the software to immediately request that file.

body **Elements**

The contents of an outline dwell within the body element, which has no attributes. It holds outline elements that represent items in the outline.

An outline element has four primary attributes:

- text, which holds the item's text

- isComment, a Boolean attribute which determines whether the item is a comment (true) or not (false)

- isBreakpoint, a Boolean attribute indicating the item is a debugging breakpoint (true) or not (false)

- type, a name indicating the type of information the outline represents

The isComment and isBreakpoint attributes are part of the Radio outliner's support for UserTalk programming. These attributes will not be present in an outline that isn't a script or program of some kind.

The type attribute contains a name, typically short, for the kind of information represented by an item. A normal outline, such as the ones shown in Figure B.1, would not have a type attribute.

Because an outline item also might contain other attributes to provide additional information, the type attribute identifies the purpose of an item. For example:

```
<outline text="Daring Fireball" description="Macintosh punditry and
➥curmudgeonry." htmlUrl="http://daringfireball.net/" language="unknown"
➥title="Daring Fireball" type="rss" version="RSS"
➥xmlUrl="http://daringfireball.net/index.xml"/>
```

This element, taken from a mySubscriptions.opml file, contains an outline item representing an RSS subscription—as established by the type attribute value "rss". The description, language, title, version, and xmlUrl attributes are all specific to this kind of outline item.

Another example:

```
<outline text="Graham Parker - Success" album="The Mona Lisa's Sister"
➥artist="Graham Parker" song="Success" type="remoteSong"
➥whenPlayed="Mon, 03 Feb 2003 23:41:45 GMT"/>
```

This element is from an outline created by the Music tool, a Radio UserLand playlist manager and organizer for audio files. Each item in the outline is an audio file (such as a song). The type attribute identifying these items is "remoteSong" and it contains several attributes about the file—artist, song, album, and text. There's also a whenPlayed attribute holding a timestamp.

The OPML specification does not limit the types that can be present, nor how they are to be interpreted by software that makes use of this data.

CAUTION

Some XML processing software and libraries might have trouble handling OPML files—its extension mechanism is unusual for an XML-based format. Implementors can add new attributes to an outline element simply by giving its type attribute a previously unused value that describes its purpose.

All of the outline elements shown thus far have been empty elements—they do not contain any other elements.

An outline also can contain one or more outline elements, wrapping them between an <outline> start tag and an </outline> end tag.

OPML represents the hierarchy of parents and subheads in an outline by placing one outline element (a subhead) within another (its parent).

Listing B.2 shows the body element, and its contents, for the outline shown in Figure B.1.

LISTING B.2   The Outline File sample.opml

```
 1: <?xml version="1.0" encoding="ISO-8859-1"?>
 2: <!-- OPML generated by Radio UserLand v8.0.8 -->
 3:
 4: <opml version="1.1">
 5:   <head>
 6:     <title>sample.opml</title>
 7:     <dateCreated>Tue, 04 Feb 2003 03:26:27 GMT</dateCreated>
 8:     <dateModified>Tue, 04 Feb 2003 03:27:51 GMT</dateModified>
 9:     <ownerName>Rogers Cadenhead</ownerName>
10:     <ownerEmail>rogers@cadenhead.org</ownerEmail>
11:     <expansionState>1, 4</expansionState>
12:     <vertScrollState>1</vertScrollState>
13:     <windowTop>179</windowTop>
14:     <windowLeft>202</windowLeft>
```

LISTING B.2 Continued

```
15:        <windowBottom>357</windowBottom>
16:        <windowRight>575</windowRight>
17:    </head>
18:    <body>
19:        <outline text="Jock and Ellie">
20:          <outline text="J.R. and Sue Ellen">
21:            <outline text="John Ross"/>
22:          </outline>
23:          <outline text="Bobby and Pamela">
24:            <outline text="Christopher"/>
25:          </outline>
26:          <outline text="Gary and Valene">
27:            <outline text="Lucy"/>
28:            <outline text="Betsy"/>
29:            <outline text="Bobby"/>
30:          </outline>
31:        </outline>
32:    </body>
33: </opml>
```

The hierarchy of outline items is established in lines 19[nd]31. The subheads of a parent are enclosed within its start and end tags. For example, the "Gary and Valene" item is a parent with three subheads: "Lucy", "Betsy", and "Bobby".

Serving OPML Files

An OPML file can be delivered by a Web server using the MIME types text/xml or text/x-opml. Some browsers, such as Internet Explorer and Mozilla, display the XML data with all of its tags visible, indented to show each level of the document.

> **CAUTION**
>
> Radio's outliner uses indentation to establish a hierarchy of items, so it might appear that an OPML file is doing the same thing. This isn't the case. Indentation is irrelevant in XML; only the placement of one element inside another establishes a relationship between the two.

To support the widest audience of Web browsers, UserLand's servers for Radio weblogs examine the Accept header of an HTTP request to determine whether a browser handles text/x-opml. If so, the OPML file is sent back as XML. If not, the OPML is rendered in HTML using list tags.

Summary

Outline Processor Markup Language (OPML) represents an outline's display state and its contents, structuring the hierarchy of items into a hierarchy of XML elements.

As XML-based formats go, OPML is a quick read because of the limited number of official tags and attributes. However, because of the `outline` element's capacity to hold unknown new attributes, the practical implementation of OPML requires an understanding of the ways it is being used.

Radio UserLand employs outlines to represent databases, scripts, RSS subscriptions, audio playlists, and many other types of content.

XML

Radio UserLand supports XML, a popular and versatile standard for data representation that is used heavily in Web services, Internet publishing, and many other kinds of computing.

This support is manifested in several ways: XML documents can be edited in Radio's outliner, the UserTalk scripting language has more than a dozen verbs for reading and writing XML, and Radio employs the XML dialects RSS, SOAP, and XML-RPC.

This appendix is an XML primer for Radio users who are new to the subject.

Reading and Writing XML

Data portability has become an important part of today's computing landscape. There are a large variety of operating systems and software being used to create data, and to the eternal shame of the programming community, much of this data can be read only by the software that created it.

Spurred in part by the popularity of the Internet, a new data standard was introduced in 1996: the Extensible Markup Language (XML).

XML enables data to be completely portable, read and written by software on different operating systems without compatibility problems.

XML is a format for storing and organizing data that is independent of any software program that works with the data. The data can serve as a file format, networking protocol, and database format. Software that can read XML data is called an *XML parser*.

Creating XML data is simple because it's structured as text—any software that outputs text can be used to produce XML, even a text editor.

Data that is compliant with XML is easier to reuse for several reasons:

- XML data is structured in a standard way, making it possible for software programs to read and write the data as long as they support XML. There are XML editors and parsing software libraries for every common programming language.

- This use of a common format frees data from the software used to create it. An XML file that contains a company's employee database can be parsed by Radio and many other XML tools. This is true no matter what kind of information the database contains. If it holds only the employee's name, ID number, and current salary, XML parsers can read it. If it also contains birthday, blood type, hair color, and incriminating photographs, parsers can read that too.

- XML also encourages reuse because the language is designed to be self-documenting, making it easy for people to understand the purpose of a document just by looking at it in a text editor. Anyone who opens an XML document, such as an employee database, should be able to figure out the general structure and content of the file.

Listing C.1 contains a sample XML file.

LISTING C.1   An XML File Named `collection.librml`

```
 1: <?xml version="1.0"?>
 2: <!DOCTYPE Library SYSTEM "librml.dtd">
 3: <Library>
 4:    <Book>
 5:       <Author>Taro Gomi</Author>
 6:       <Title>Everyone Poops</Title>
 7:       <PublicationDate edition="Hardcover" isbn="0916291456">
 8:          03/1993
 9:       </PublicationDate>
10:       <Publisher>Kane/Miller Book Publishing</Publisher>
11:       <Subject>Fiction</Subject>
12:       <Review>gomi-everyonepoops.html</Review>
13:    </Book>
14:    <Book>
15:       <Author>Matt Neuburg</Author>
16:       <Title>Frontier: The Definitive Guide</Title>
17:       <PublicationDate edition="Paperback" isbn="1565923839">
18:          03/1998
19:       </PublicationDate>
```

LISTING C.1   Continued

```
20:      <Publisher>O'Reilly & Associates</Publisher>
21:      <Subject>Fiction</Subject>
22:      <OutOfPrint/>
23:    </Book>
24: </Library>
```

Even if you've never seen XML data before, the contents of Listing C.1 ought to make sense, aside perhaps from the ?xml and !DOCTYPE lines at the top. As you can see, it's a book database of some kind.

XML data consists of processing instructions, tags, elements, attributes, comments, and character data.

The ?xml processing instruction indicates the data is formatted as XML version 1.0. All XML data must begin with a processing instruction of this kind.

Tags in XML are comparable to HTML tags. There are start tags that take the form <tagNameHere>, end tags that take the form </tagNameHere>, and stand-alone tags that take the form <tagNameHere/>.

Start tags begin with a < character followed by the name of the tag and a > character, such as <Book>.

End tags begin with the </ characters followed by a name and a > character, such as </Book>. A start tag, end tag, and the contents in between form an XML element.

Stand-alone tags begin with a < character followed by the name of the tag and the /> characters, such as <OutOfPrint/>. These tags form an empty element.

Elements can be nested within other elements, creating a hierarchy of XML data that establishes relationships within that data. In Listing C.1, everything in lines 15–22 is related; each tag defines something about the same book.

When elements contain character data rather than another element, that data is the value of that element. In Listing C.1, the Author element in Line 15 has the value Matt Neuburg. All of the characters within the element's start and end tags have meaning in XML—even whitespace and new lines.

Tags can include attributes, data that provides additional information about the element. Attributes are defined within a start tag or stand-alone tag, taking the form <tagNameHere attributeName="attributeValue">.

The name of an attribute is followed by an equals sign and text within quotation marks. In Lines 7–9 of Listing C.1, the PublicationDate element includes two attributes: edition, which has a value of "Hardcover", and isbn, which has a value of "0916291456".

Comments can be placed in XML data within <!-- and -->, as in this example:

```
<!-- Created on 5/29/03; 9:13:22 PM -->
```

Creating Well-Formed XML

XML encourages the creation of data that's understandable and usable even by someone who doesn't have the program that created it and cannot find any documentation that describes it.

To ensure that XML data can be read by a parser, it must be structured correctly according to a few basic rules.

First, the data must begin with a ?xml processing instruction.

Second, the data must have a single root element with start and end tags that enclose all of its other elements. In Listing C.1, the root element is Library.

Third, the character data in an element must not contain the < and > characters because they are used by XML to demarcate the beginning and end of tags. Special character entities can be used in their place: < for < and > for >.

Finally, the start and end tags that enclose an element must be nested correctly. If a start tag is contained within an element, its end tag also must be enclosed within that element. The following fragment of an XML document breaks this rule:

```
<?xml version="1.0"?>
<Library>
    <Book>
</Library>
    </Book>
```

The ending </Book> tag cannot be outside of the Library element.

Data that follows all of these rules is said to be *well-formed*, a term that means it is structured correctly. By insisting upon well-formedness, XML simplifies the task of writing programs that work with the data. XML parsers will reject data that is not well formed rather than attempting to guess what the correct structure should be.

Radio produces well-formed XML and will reject XML data that is not well formed. For instance, if you attempt to subscribe to an RSS news feed that is not well formed, Radio will refuse the request and display an error message such as the following: `"Poorly formed XML text, we were expecting a tag. (At character #509.)"`

Checking for Valid XML

Although XML is described as a language and compared with HTML, it's actually much larger in scope. XML is a markup language that defines how to define a markup language.

Although that concept might sound confusingly circular, it's important to understand because it explains how XML can be used to define data as varied as news headlines, health care claims, genealogical records, and molecules.

The "X" in XML stands for Extensible, and it refers to organizing data for a specific purpose. Data that's organized using the rules of XML can represent an infinite variety of things:

- A programmer at a telemarketing company can use XML to store data on each outgoing call, saving the time of the call, the number, the operator who made the call, and the result.

- A hobbyist can use XML to keep track of the annoying telemarketing calls she receives, noting the time of the call, the company, and the product being peddled.

- A programmer at a government agency can use XML to track complaints about telemarketers, saving the name of the marketing firm and the number of complaints.

Each of these examples uses XML to define a new language that suits a specific purpose. Although they could be called XML languages, they're more commonly described as XML dialects or XML document types.

Radio works with several XML dialects —RSS, SOAP, and XML-RPC—and one XML-based format, OPML.

When a new XML dialect is created, the formal way to define it is to create a document type definition (DTD). This determines the rules that the data must follow to be considered valid in that dialect.

Listing C.2 contains a DTD for the book database.

LISTING C.2   The Document Type Definition File `librml.dtd`

```
 1: <!ELEMENT Library (Book?)+ >
 2: <!ELEMENT Book (Author?, Title, PublicationDate?, Publisher?,
➥Subject?, Review?)* >
 3: <!ELEMENT Author (#PCDATA)>
 4: <!ELEMENT Title (#PCDATA)>
 5: <!ELEMENT PublicationDate (#PCDATA)>
 6: <!ATTLIST PublicationDate edition CDATA "" isbn CDATA "">
 7: <!ELEMENT Publisher (#PCDATA)>
 8: <!ELEMENT Subject (#PCDATA)>
 9: <!ELEMENT Review (#PCDATA)>
10: <!ELEMENT OutOfPrint EMPTY>
```

In Listing C.1, the XML file contained the following line:

```
<!DOCTYPE Library SYSTEM "librml.dtd">
```

The !DOCTYPE processing instruction identifies the DTD that applies to the data. When a DTD is present, many XML tools can read XML created for that DTD and determine whether the data follows all the rules. If it doesn't, it will be rejected with a reference to the line that caused the error. This process is called *validating the XML*.

Often, data will be structured as XML but not defined using a DTD. Presuming it's well formed, this data can be parsed to extract its contents, but it cannot be checked for validity according to the rules of its dialect.

DTDs aren't quite as self-documenting as XML data—the particulars of the format are beyond the scope of this primer. Where Radio is concerned, there's no need to learn how to create a DTD because the software does not make use of one in any way.

The only thing Radio insists upon in the production and consumption of XML is well-formedness.

NOTE

UserLand Software has not created official DTDs for OPML or any of the XML dialects that it created, although unofficial ones have been offered by other developers.

Validity addresses one of the motivations behind the development of XML: the inconsistency of HTML. Although it remains a wildly popular way to organize data for presentation to users, Web browsers have always been designed to allow for inconsistent and even incorrect use of HTML tags.

Web page designers can break numerous rules of valid HTML, as it's defined by the World Wide Web Consortium, and their work still loads normally into Mozilla, Internet Explorer, and other browsers. Millions of people are putting content on the Web without paying heed to valid HTML. They test their content to make sure it's viewable in Web browsers, but don't worry whether it's structured according to the rules of HTML.

By publishing data as XML, Web publishers make it available in a form that's fit for consumption by computers.

> **NOTE**
>
> The World Wide Web Consortium, founded by Web inventor Tim Berners-Lee, maintains the standard versions of HTML and XML. You can find out more from the consortium Web site at `http://www.w3.org`. If you want to validate a Web page to see whether it follows all the rules of standard HTML, visit `http://validator.w3.org`.

Using XML

There's strong demand on the Internet for software that collects data over the network. Some programmers accomplish this by reading a Web page's HTML markup and parsing it to find the relevant data, which can be highly error-prone because of the inconsistency in how HTML can be used to organize Web content. Software that puzzles through the markup tags of a page to extract information can be broken by changes to the site's design, errors in markup, and other problems.

To exchange data more reliably, some Internet sites are making content available as *Web services*—standard interfaces to data on their servers that can be used over a network by client software.

Most Web services make use of two XML-based protocols that are supported by Radio: XML-RPC and SOAP. Some offer data as XML that can be requested using a URL.

The e-commerce site Amazon.Com offers a Web service that can be used to see its 15 top-selling products for any search term. This data is provided as XML using the company's own dialect.

To see an example of this data, load the following URL with a current version of Mozilla, Internet Explorer, or another browser that supports XML:

```
http://rcm.amazon.com/e/cm?t=naviseek&l=st1&search=Kick%20Start&
➥mode=books&p=102&o=1&f=xml
```

This URL request will produce an XML document containing the top 15 books with "Kick Start" in their titles (in the URL, %20 represents a space). The XML data can be stored in Radio's database, converted into RSS for use in the news aggregator, or dynamically published in a weblog.

The World Wide Web Consortium offers the full XML specification and a guide to XML resources at `http://www.w3.org/XML/`.

> **NOTE**
>
> Amazon's XML service is available only to members of its Associates program, which pays referral fees to sites that send customers to them through links. The "naviseek" portion of the URL refers to my own Associate account and should be replaced with your membership code if you sign up. For more information on the program and its XML interface, visit `http://associates.amazon.com/`.

Summary

This appendix introduced Extensible Markup Language, better known as XML, and showed how to employ some of its dialects in Radio UserLand.

XML can be used in several ways in Radio, which supports its OPML and RSS formats and the SOAP and XML-RPC protocols. You can use the UserTalk scripting language and Radio outliner to read and write XML.

As a standard for structuring data, XML is a versatile way to produce and consume information, especially in areas such as Internet publishing, content management, and Web services.

XML-RPC

One of the things that distinguishes Radio UserLand from other Web publishing platforms is its connectivity to other software. It offers considerable support for scripting and networking.

One of the ways to stay connected with Radio is through its support for XML-RPC, a remote procedure call protocol that delivers XML data over HTTP, the protocol used to deliver World Wide Web content.

Radio is an XML-RPC client and server, enabling it to call procedures in other software and handle calls of its own. This appendix documents the XML-RPC protocol.

Using XML-RPC

There have been numerous attempts to create a standard protocol for remote procedure calls (RPC), a way for one application to call a procedure in another application over the Internet or another network.

XML-RPC was released in 1998 as a draft specification by Dave Winer of UserLand Software, and first implemented in Frontier, the company's content management and Web hosting software that preceded Radio.

The XML-RPC draft took on a life of its own, appearing in software from RedHat, Microsoft, and many other developers in the commercial and open source worlds.

XML-RPC, which was designed to be simple to learn and implement, exchanges information using a combination of HTTP and XML. The protocol's full specification can be read on the Web at http://www.xmlrpc.com/spec.

The protocol supports these data types:

- base64: Binary data in Base64 format

- boolean: 1 (true) or 0 (false)

- dateTime.iso8601: A string containing the date and time in ISO8601 format (for example, 20030713T08:45:05 is 8:45:05 p.m. on July 13, 2003)

- double: Eight-byte signed floating-point numbers

- int (also called i4): Signed integers ranging in value from -2,147,483,648 to 2,147,483,647

- string: Text

- struct: Name-value pairs of associated data where the name is a string and the value can be any of the other data types

XML-RPC also supports the array data type, which holds any other kind of data, including arrays.

Using the protocol, clients and servers transmit data using HTTP for transport and XML for encoding. Data is exchanged through client requests and server responses.

An XML-RPC request is XML data that is sent to a server as part of an HTTP POST request. POST requests normally are used to transmit data from Web browser to Web server—programs such as Common Gateway Interface scripts, Java servlets, and Frontier take the request, act on the data, and send HTML back in response. XML-RPC, by comparison, uses HTTP as a convenient protocol for communicating with a server and receiving a response back.

The request consists of two parts: the HTTP headers required for a POST transmission and the XML-RPC request encoded using XML. An example is shown in Listing D.1.

LISTING D.1 An XML-RPC Request

```
 1: POST /XMLRPC HTTP/1.0
 2: Host: www.advogato.org
 3: Connection: Close
 4: Content-Type: text/xml
 5: Content-Length: 151
 6: User-Agent: OSE/XML-RPC
 7:
 8: <?xml version="1.0"?>
 9: <methodCall>
10:     <methodName>test.square</methodName>
11:     <params>
12:         <param>
```

LISTING D.1   Continued

```
13:            <value>
14:                <int>13</int>
15:            </value>
16:        </param>
17:    </params>
18: </methodCall>
```

This request contains two sections: HTTP headers and XML data. The XML-RPC server is at `http://www.advogato.org/XMLRPC`, the remote procedure being called is `test.square`, and the procedure is being called with one argument, the integer 13.

Procedure names in an XML-RPC request do not include parentheses. They may consist of either a program identifier followed by a procedure name or just a procedure name, depending on the configuration of a particular XML-RPC server. The identifier can be the name of a program or some other addressing scheme—this varies depending on the server implementation, which is permitted in the XML-RPC specification.

An XML-RPC request can contain more than one argument of the supported data types, enclosing each in its own `param` element.

An XML-RPC response is XML data sent back from a server using HTTP. The response also consists of HTTP headers and an XML response, as shown in Listing D.2.

LISTING D.2   An XML-RPC Response

```
 1: HTTP/1.0 200 OK
 2: Date: Wed, 05 Feb 2003 23:47:09 GMT
 3: Server: Apache/1.3.26 (Unix) Debian GNU/Linux mod_virgule/1.40 PHP/4.1.2
 4: ETag: "PbT9cnw52OqREFNAAMgXsX=="
 5: Content-MD5: PbT9cnw52OqREFNAAMgXsX==
 6: Content-Length: 157
 7: Connection: close
 8: Content-Type: text/xml
 9:
10: <?xml version="1.0"?>
11: <methodResponse>
12:    <params>
13:        <param>
14:            <value>
15:                <int>169</int>
16:            </value>
17:        </param>
18:    </params>
19: </methodResponse>
```

TIP

To see more examples, Dumpleton Software publishes a free XML-RPC debugger that can be used to call remote procedures and see the XML data representing the request and response. It's on the Web at `http://www.dscpl.com.au/xmlrpc-debugger.php`. One XML-RPC server you can try this with is on my Web site. The server is available at the URL `http://cadenhead.org:4413` and supports the procedure `dmoz.getRandomSite` with no parameters.

This response is similar to the request, except that a `methodResponse` element encloses the data instead of a `methodCall` element. The response is 157 bytes in size, uses the `text/xml` mime type, and returns one value: the integer 169.

An XML-RPC response must contain one return value, even if the remote method does not need to return anything. The value can be any of the supported data types.

These XML-RPC examples are based on the Advogato XML-RPC interface, which is documented on the Web at `http://www.advogato.org/xmlrpc.html`.

Sending an XML-RPC Request

The data representing an XML-RPC request is structured as XML, beginning with a processing instruction declaring this fact:

```
<?xml version="1.0">
```

The root element, `methodCall`, has no attributes and contains the remaining elements in the request: a `methodName` element to identify the remote procedure to call and a `params` element holding the parameters with which it will be called (if any).

The `methodName` element contains the name of the procedure. The only permitted characters in this element are the alphanumeric characters and the colon (:), forward slash (/), period (.), and underscore (_).

This element can simply be a procedure name (such as `getRandomSite`) or a program identifier followed by a procedure name (`dmoz.getRandomSite`). This is dictated by the XML-RPC server handling the request—nothing in the protocol dictates how programs and procedures are to be named.

The `params` element can be absent if the method is to be called without any parameters. Otherwise, it should contain one `param` element for each parameter, as in Listing D.3.

LISTING D.3 Another XML-RPC Request

```
 1: <?xml version="1.0"?>
 2: <methodCall>
 3:   <methodName>metaWeblog.getPost</methodName>
 4:   <params>
 5:     <param>
 6:       <value><i4>544</i4></value>
 7:     </param>
 8:     <param>
 9:       <value><string>rcade</string></value>
10:     </param>
11:     <param>
12:       <value><string>swordfish</string></value>
13:     </param>
14:   </params>
15: </methodCall>
```

Each param contains one value element. This element contains one of the elements representing a data type supported by XML-RPC: the simple types base64, boolean, dateTime.iso8601, double, int, string or two more complex types, array and struct.

For each of the simple types, the parameter's value is contained within the element. For example:

```
<param>
  <value><boolean>1</boolean></value>
</param>
```

The string element is the only one that does not need to be wrapped in an identifying tag of that name. It can be omitted, as in this example:

```
<param>
  <value>rcade</value>
</param>
```

A struct element holds one or more name-value pairs, each enclosed within a member element, as in this example:

```
<param>
  <value>
    <struct>
      <member>
        <name>fileMask</name>
```

```
      <value><string>*.html</string></value>
    </member>
    <member>
      <name>folder</name>
      <value><string>/home/rcade/</string></value>
    </member>
  </struct>
</param>
```

An array element holds a data element with one or more value elements:

```
<param>
  <value>
    <array>
      <data>
        <value><string>cnn</string></value>
        <value><i4>50</i4></value>
        <value><string>any</string></value>
      </data>
    </array>
  </value>
</param>
```

As the example illustrates, the values within an array do not need to be the same type.

The values within an array or struct can hold their own array or struct. This recursive capability makes it possible to send complex data in a request.

Receiving an XML-RPC Response

An XML-RPC response begins with an XML processing instruction and has the root element methodResponse.

This element will contain a params element if the procedure call was successful and a fault element if it wasn't. The params element contains one param element, which contains one value element. This value can contain any of the basic and complex data types sent in a request. Listing D.4 contains a response that would follow the request in Listing D.3.

LISTING D.4 A Successful XML-RPC Response

```
 1: <?xml version="1.0"?>
 2: <methodResponse>
 3:   <params>
 4:     <param>
 5:       <value>
 6:         <struct>
 7:           <member>
 8:             <name>dateCreated</name>
 9:             <value>
10:               <dateTime.iso8601>20020314T08:29:24</dateTime.iso8601>
11:             </value>
12:           </member>
13:           <member>
14:             <name>description</name>                      '
15:             <value>The inventor of the term blog is giving up his
➥verb. "I've gotta do something else with this site," says Peter Merholz,
➥who began one of the first 25 weblogs in May 1998. "More essays. No
➥blogging."</value>
16:           </member>
17:           <member>
18:             <name>postid</name>
19:             <value><i4>544</i4></value>
20:           </member>
21:           <member>
22:           <member>
23:             <name>title</name>
24:             <value>No blogging</value>
25:           </member>
26:           <member>
27:             <name>link</name>
28:             <value>http://peterme.com/archives/00000364.html</value>
29:           </member>
30:         </struct>
31:       </value>
32:     </param>
33:   </params>
34: </methodResponse>
```

When the procedure is not called successfully, the methodResponse element contains one fault element representing an error message.

The `fault` element contains a `value` element that holds a `struct`. It has two name-value pairs: `faultCode`, an integer representing the error's numeric code, and `faultString`, the error message. For a full error response, see Listing D.5.

LISTING D.5   An Unsuccessful XML-RPC Response

```
 1: <?xml version="1.0"?>
 2: <methodResponse>
 3:   <fault>
 4:     <value>
 5:       <struct>
 6:         <member>
 7:           <name>faultCode</name>
 8:           <value><int>4</int></value>
 9:         </member>
10:         <member>
11:           <name>faultString</name>
12:           <value><string>Can't evaluate the expression because the
➥name "10" hasn't been defined.</string></value>
13:         </member>
14:       </struct>
15:     </value>
16:   </fault>
17: </methodResponse>
```

The values used with a `faultCode` are not established by the XML-RPC specification, so they're likely to vary from server to server.

UserLand Software maintains a directory of XML-RPC implementations for Java, C++, PHP, and other languages at http://www.xmlrpc.com.

Summary

XML-RPC was designed to be the lowest common denominator of remote procedure call protocols, exchanging information with any software that supports HTTP and XML parsing.

The protocol is part of Web services implemented by many software developers on Windows, Macintosh, Linux, and Unix systems.

Radio UserLand can be used as both an XML-RPC client and server, establishing connections to programs regardless of their implementation language or operating system.

Index

SYMBOLS

A

How can we make this index more useful? Email us at indexes@samspublishing.com

E

How can we make this index more useful? Email us at indexes@samspublishing.com

G - H

How can we make this index more useful? Email us at indexes@samspublishing.com

How can we make this index more useful? Email us at indexes@samspublishing.com

How can we make this index more useful? Email us at indexes@samspublishing.com

How can we make this index more useful? Email us at indexes@samspublishing.com

KICK START

< QUICK >
< CONCISE >
< PRACTICAL >